The Poetry of
Relationship

The Poetry of Relationship:

The Wordsworths and Coleridge, 1797–1800

Richard E. Matlak

College of the Holy Cross

MACMILLAN

First published by
MACMILLAN PRESS LTD
Houndmills, Basingstoke, Hampshire RG21 6XS
and London
Companies and representatives
throughout the world

ISBN 0-333-62089-5

A catalogue record for this book is available
from the British Library.

10   9   8   7   6   5   4   3   2   1
06 05 04 03 02 01 00 99 98 97

Printed in the United States of America by
R.R. Donnelley & Sons
Harrisonburg, VA

To Jo
with love

Contents

Abbreviations

ASP, SP   *The Salisbury Plain Poems of William Wordsworth:* Salisbury
               Plain, *or* A Night on Salisbury Plain; Adventures on Salis-
               bury Plain *(including* The Female Vagrant); Guilt and Sor-
               row; or Incidents upon Salisbury Plain. Ed. Stephen Gill.
               Ithaca, NY: Cornell University Press, 1975.
BL   *Biographia Literaria: Or, Biographical Sketches of My Literary Life
               and Opinions.* Eds. James Engell and W. Jackson Bate. Vol. 7
               in *The Collected Works of Samuel Taylor Coleridge.* Princeton, NJ:
               Princeton University Press, 1983.
Borderers   *The Borderers,* by William Wordsworth. Ed. Robert Osborn.
               Ithaca, NY: Cornell University Press, 1982.
Brett and Jones *Wordsworth and Coleridge, Lyrical Ballads.* 2nd ed. Eds. R. L.
               Brett and A. R. Jones. New York: Routledge, 1991.
CEY   Mark L. Reed. *Wordsworth: The Chronology of the Early Years,
               1770-1799.* Cambridge, MA: Harvard University Press,
               1967.
CPW   *Coleridge: Poetical Works.* Ed. Ernest Hartley Coleridge. New
               York: Oxford University Press, 1912.
De Selincourt *William Wordsworth: The Prelude, or Growth of a Poet's Mind.* Ed.
               Ernest De Selincourt. 2nd ed. rev. Helen Darbishire. Ox-
               ford: Clarendon, 1959.
DS   *"Descriptive Sketches" by William Wordsworth.* Ed. Eric Birdsall.
               Ithaca, NY: Cornell University Press, 1984.
DWJ   *Journals of Dorothy Wordsworth: The Alfoxden Journal 1798, The
               Grasmere Journals 1800-1803.* 2nd ed. Ed. Mary Moorman.
               New York: Oxford University Press, 1971.
EW   *"An Evening Walk" by William Wordsworth.* Ed. James Averill.
               Ithaca, NY: Cornell University Press, 1984.
EY   *The Letters of William and Dorothy Wordsworth: The Early Years,*
               1787-1805. Ed. Ernest de Selincourt. 2nd ed. rev. Chester
               L. Shaver. Oxford: Clarendon, 1967.
Gill   *The Oxford Authors: William Wordsworth.* Ed. Stephen Gill.
               New York: Oxford University Press, 1984.

Hayden   *William Wordsworth: The Poems,* 2 vols. Ed. John O. Hayden. New Haven: Yale University Press, 1977.

H at G   *Home at Grasmere: Part First, Book First, of "The Recluse" by William Wordsworth.* Ed. Beth Darlington. Ithaca, NY: Cornell University Press, 1977.

LB   Lyrical Ballads, *and Other Poems, 1797-1800.* Eds. James Butler and Karen Green. Ithaca, NY: Cornell University Press, 1992.

Moorman   Mary Moorman. *William Wordsworth: A Biography.* 2 vols. Oxford: Clarendon, 1957.

Prelude   The Prelude *1799, 1805, 1850: Authoritative Texts, Context and Reception, Recent Critical Essays.* Eds. Jonathan Wordsworth, M. H. Abrams, and Stephen Gill. New York: Norton, 1979.

Prose   *The Prose Works of William Wordsworth.* Ed. W. J. B. Owen and Jane Worthington Smyser. 3 vols. Oxford: Clarendon, 1974.

RC   *"The Ruined Cottage" and "The Pedlar" by William Wordsworth.* Ed. James Butler. Ithaca: Cornell University Press, 1979.

STCL   *Collected Letters of Samuel Taylor Coleridge.* Ed. Earl Leslie Griggs. 6 vols. Oxford: Clarendon, 1956-71.

STCNB   *The Notebooks of Samuel Taylor Coleridge.* Ed. Kathleen Coburn. Princeton, NJ: Princeton University Press, 1957- .

Woof   *Dorothy Wordsworth: The Grasmere Journals.* Ed. Pamela Woof. New York: Oxford University Press, 1993.

WPW   *The Poetical Works of William Wordsworth.* Eds. Ernest de Selincourt and Helen Darbishire. 5 vols. Oxford: Clarendon, 1940-49; rev. 1952-59.

1799   The Prelude, *1798-1799 by William Wordsworth.* Ed. Stephen Parrish. Ithaca, NY: Cornell University Press, 1977.

Introduction

I. The Micro-context

This study of the literary and biographical relations of William and Dorothy Wordsworth with Samuel Taylor Coleridge follows an impressive body of scholarship engendered by Thomas McFarland's "The Symbiosis of Coleridge and Wordsworth" (1972): Lucy Newlyn's *Coleridge, Wordsworth, and the Language of Allusion* (1986), Paul Magnuson's *Coleridge and Wordsworth: A Lyrical Dialogue* (1988), and Gene W. Ruoff's *Wordsworth and Coleridge: The Making of the Major Lyrics, 1802-1804* (1989).[1]

The unfolding of my argument will reveal its indebtedness to McFarland and Magnuson especially; to the former for his convincing application of psychobiography to poetic relationship, and to the latter for a lesson in formal, intertextual analysis. However, my attention to Dorothy Wordsworth's biographical and textual influence on her brother's early poetry leads to interpretations that challenge the sufficiency of these accounts. My emphasis upon the rhetoric of the intertextual relationship between Wordsworth and Coleridge as being primarily and formally forensic rather than dialogic, as Magnuson maintains, or meditative, as M. H. Abrams has argued, also introduces an historical context to intertextuality that locates the origin of the greater Romantic lyric in the heated political debates of the 1790s rather than in the meditations of the seventeenth century.[2]

As far as the heart of the matter goes, the poetic exchange of William Wordsworth and Coleridge has always gotten the serious critical scrutiny it deserves. Reservations about the persuasiveness of specific works in intertextual relationship remain, but the weighty critical, textual, and biographical apparatus now available for genetic and biographical studies have supported increasingly sounder arguments, as we find fully displayed in Magnuson's *Lyrical Dialogue*. Taking full advantage of the Cornell Wordsworth and Princeton Coleridge editions for their earliest and variant texts,[3]

Lyrical Dialogue posits a combined "canon based upon a chronology of writing and publication" generated through dialogue. Magnuson reads the resulting corpus as *"one work,"* to quote Coleridge, "as an Ode is one work" (*STCL,* Vol. I, p. 412), meaning that fugitive lyric turns, abrupt transitions, and freely associative sequencing between works as between stanzas are intrinsic; that each part of the dialogue, be it a whole poem, a canceled draft, a fragment, an early draft, or a later revision, is part of an evolving, always open-ended, undetermined text; but that, finally, the relationship between parts, as between stanzas, is completed, now fully published (as far as we know), and thus interpretable. Contemporary readers who ignore the intertextualities of lyrical dialogue, Magnuson says, are "listening to one half a telephone conversation."[4]

The exclusion of Dorothy Wordsworth from the "telephone conversation" could make one defensive about arguing for the relevance of her texts. However, it would be better to keep an open ear on the issue. Mikhail Bakhtin's insight on "hidden dialogicality" leaves as much opportunity for Dorothy's voice to be heard as her brother's, or Coleridge's, although we may have to detect and decode its influence differently:

> Imagine a dialogue of two persons in which the statements of the second speaker are omitted, but in such a way that the general sense is not at all violated. The second speaker is present invisibly, his words are not there, but deep traces left by these words have a determining influence on all the present visible words of the first speaker.[5]

We might also expect that what is anticipated, but left unstated within an evolving dialogue might also count dramatically as a response to an absence of expected traces. In a phrase, the powerfully unstated might be called "silent" as opposed to "hidden" dialogicality.

There have been attempts to make a place for Dorothy's influence as an independent writer, or a writer whose importance is independent of William, most notably by Anne K. Mellor in *Romanticism and Gender* (1993),[6] but Dorothy Wordsworth's function in the creative exchange between Coleridge and her brother is still uncertain. The primary reason for ignoring the question of her influence is clear: she wrote informal prose, mainly letters and journals. She will receive her due for emotional influence, but is credited for little more than occasional textual influence. And then it is difficult—some would say irrelevant—to argue for the significance of emotional influence on literary texts.

Elizabeth A. Fay develops a unique argument for Dorothy's influence upon her brother's poetry and vocation that perceives the paucity of her canon as but the tip of a mountain that ignores the "collaboratively engendered" mass below the mist. Just as Magnuson finds the generative condition of the poetry of W. Wordsworth and Coleridge to be dialogue, Fay posits a "compelling imagination" behind the poet "'Wordsworth'... as opposed to the man" that makes William Wordsworth "at once a performance of himself and two enacting selves: William and Dorothy Wordsworth combined." Thus, we cannot discuss Dorothy's work as in dialogue with her brother's poetry, because "[n]ecessary to the collaborative production of poetry is the bond of twinship, D. Wordsworth's version of romantic fusion."[7] I will return to Fay's concept of "Wordsworth" and its usefulness for literary interpretation when I argue for the responsive nature of Dorothy's Journals to her brother's poetry and the resulting tension they provoke in his verse. For now, let me say of Fay's intriguing thesis that it takes the opinion of the Wordsworths about the perfection of their relationship too seriously in arguing for an amicable creative twinship. The stress that Dorothy's oppositional ideas provided her brother's poetry, the confusion that his commitment to her made for his early moral life, and his emotional desires for her that he finally wrote into a state of sublimation all fed the incendiary power of his genius as remarkably, but differently, as the creative breeze, the oppositional winds, of Coleridge's ideas and verse.

Therefore, although Dorothy wrote relatively little—letters of biographical interest; about 170 printed pages of journals of natural description and daily life; an occasional poem; and a few children's stories—what she wrote that was out of accord with his sympathies and beliefs mattered intensely to her brother's poetry. The potential for Dorothy's combined biographical and textual influence is even more significant and traceable psychologically and intertextually.

II. The Macro-context

Though this study primarily approaches texts from the micro-perspectives of biography and psychobiography, a review of the macropolitical scene of the 1790s is necessary for understanding the forensic nature of the poetic exchange. A moment's reflection on very familiar works makes it obvious that the defining poems of British Romanticism are argumentative. Divided or antagonized perception becomes the principal motif of single works, such as Wordsworth's "Elegiac Stanzas," Joanna Baillie's *Count Basil*, Percy Shelley's *Julian and Maddalo*, and John Keats's "Ode to a Nightingale." Poets represent irresolvable contraries in their juxtaposition of works, such as William Blake's *Songs of Innocence* and *Songs of Experience*, Percy Shelley's *Hymn to Intellectual Beauty* and *Mont Blanc*, Felicia Hemans's "The Homes of England" and "The Graves of a Household." In cases of close relationship among authors, radical positions provide the energy for poetic debate, as found in the dialogue of Wordsworth's *Intimations Ode* with Coleridge's *Dejection: An Ode*, and Lord Byron's *Manfred* with Mary Shelley's *Frankenstein*. Authors may avoid taking sides by representing all sides of the argument, as Keats does in developing the aesthetic position of open-endedness he termed "Negative Capability," best represented in his epical *Hyperion* poems, the "Vale of Soul-making" letter, and his great odes. Additional permutations on a rhetoric of ironic polarity are found in the 1817 version of Coleridge's *Rime of the Ancient Mariner*, which fails to reconcile the "opposite or discordant qualities"[8] of text and gloss. Finally, I will argue here that the genre of poems commencing with Coleridge's "Eolian Harp" is structured upon the rhetorical pattern of classical debate. As another intellectual outgrowth of heated political times, the poetic dialogue of the Wordsworths and Coleridge found its rhetorical and formal foundation in time-tested modes of argument and persuasion.

But all of these major literary statements reflect the tensions and uncertainties of powerfully contested world views and value systems. Edmund Burke's *Reflections on the Revolution in France* (1791) figures centrally in the forensic climate of British Romanticism, because it crystallized the ideological debate over the imminent cultural perils of modernity. A brief description of the background of its impact might be useful here, especially because Wordsworth and Coleridge spent their formative political years in its wake. The French Revolution was the focus of the debate, but observers, alerted by Burke, understood that more than a form of government was involved.

Despite disappointment with the leadership of France and the progress of its revolution by 1795 or so, intellectuals, idealists, and liberal politicians felt the moral imperative to advance human and political rights take hold. The 1790s established an agenda of liberalization and a debate over power, values, and aspirations on the classic issues of early modernity: the human rights issues of equal opportunity for women and a growing working class inspired by the "Rights of Man" but believed to be unprepared for democracy; the uncertain economic implications of abolishing slavery; the booms-and-busts of a war-fed capitalist economy; the squalor and crime brought on by rapid urbanization; the new cash relationship between labor and capital; a growing concern for overpopulation; and the spiritual impoverishment Dr. Thomas Arnold later described as a utilitarian "national society, formed for no higher than physical ends; to enable men to eat, drink, and live luxuriously." Although there was impatience with synthesis or compromise on these issues, it was difficult to be entirely confident of one's own position. Blake attempted to make a good of evil in *The Marriage of Heaven and Hell* (1793) by asserting that "Opposition is true friendship," but the historical context for doubt, skepticism, and irony was ideal.

We also have come to appreciate an irony contrary to the radical "Spirit of the Age" as defined by William Hazlitt and persuasively advanced by M. H. Abrams in his seminal essay of the same title.[9] For the central values of literary romanticism are found nowhere as compactly and eloquently combined as in Burke's conservative *Reflections*. Burke's arguments in defense of tradition shaped a host of topical concerns of first-generation poets and essayists: a constant emphasis upon experience and tradition as a test of value; skepticism towards novelty, rationalism, and theory; a faith in the heart and instinct over the light of reason; a demand to follow nature in arriving at a standard for human behavior and action; a defense of the romance of chivalry and medieval values over modern utilitarianism; a devotion to individual changes of heart over revolutionary political action; a pride in nationalism and tradition; a perception of the organic unity of society as a reflection of nature; and a trust in spontaneity over method in the development of deeply felt arguments in prose or poetry.

"Indulging myself in the freedom of epistolary intercourse," Burke says near the opening of his *Reflections*, subtitled *Letter Intended to Have Been Sent to a Gentleman in Paris*, "I beg leave to throw out my thoughts, and express my feelings, just as they arise in my mind, with very little attention to formal method."[10] Certainly a bold and yet formally appropriate rhetorical pose to assume against a revolution caused, as Burke goes on to argue, by the misapplication of Reason and rational argument. In impassioned, florid prose, Burke ironizes the heady idealism of rationalism in support of reactionary values and sentiments. Burke's unabashedly confrontational defense of tradition inspired deeply felt public, but equally often internalized, rhetorical discourses that affected the literature of the times, as the poems listed above reveal.

III. The Structure of Poetic Argument

Coleridge's "The Eolian Harp" breathes[11] the forensic air of its time. Bio-graphically, the poem represents Coleridge's intellectual pugnacity, for he was an habitually argumentative young man. Formally, the poem ingeniously appropriates the traditional structure of classical argumentation for rational poetic discourse. Coleridge admitted that "Eolian Harp" was his favorite personal poem. As we will see, Wordsworth found it a powerful and convenient text to argue against in the greatest poem of his early career, *Lines Written A Few Miles Above Tintern Abbey* (1798).

Though Coleridge had composed blank verse prior to "Eolian Harp," or "Effusion XXXV," as it was first titled in *Poems on Various Subjects* (1796), it is his first poem to use the five-part classical form for argumentation, though in a nascent state that suggests a serendipitous synapsis. The first published form of the poem contains three verse paragraphs containing sections equivalent to an *exordium*, a *narratio*, a *propositio* (derived from the *narratio*), and a *peroratio*. By 1803 a proposition is more clearly stated, and by 1817, the paragraphing conforms to the five parts of classical discourse. The textual development of this single poem suggests that one out of thirty-six bursts of poetry in *Poems* (1796) made a connection with Coleridge's prose and the structural pattern of his thought, because of topical similarity, the necessity of recognizing divine revelation as the one spiritual light.

Succeeding revisions and future poems of argumentative intent be-come more definitively shaped either out of habit or because at some point Coleridge self-consciously promoted this development. In fact, the line of poems beginning with "Eolian Harp" through "Frost at Midnight" evolves structurally in relation to rhetorically active periods in Coleridge's life. "Eolian Harp" was an outgrowth of the personal and religious concerns from summer 1795 to spring 1796, when Coleridge was delivering thirteen lectures on politics and religion and assisting poet-friend and future brother-in-law Robert Southey in composing another dozen. The poem reflects Coleridge's enthusiasm for public oration and the shape of the rhetorical pattern habitually employed. The second phase of the form's development occurred from January 9 to February 13, 1796, as Coleridge lectured and engaged in impromptu debates in the course of soliciting subscribers for his periodical *The Watchman*. "Reflections on Having Left a Place of Retirement," composed in 1796, represents a biographical culmination of this period of forensic activity and more firmly employs the form of classical argument in poetry. The final period of development occurs during the *annus mirabilis*. "Frost at Midnight," composed in February 1798, follows Coleridge's preaching to secure a dissenting ministry in Shrewsbury in January 1798. It was then a short formal step from "Frost at Midnight" to Wordsworth's *Tintern Abbey*, the greatest of these argument poems. Coleridge thus provided a concise point of departure for engaging metaphysical and psychological issues in a compellingly appropriate argumentative structure. Wordsworth used the poem as a cognitive map for exploring a visionary opposition.

IV. Overview of the Present Study

Part One, "Family Biography and *The Borderers*," follows the growing influence of Dorothy Wordsworth on her brother's poetic and emotional maturation from his juvenilia to his first and only play, *The Borderers*, which was being written and revised when Coleridge entered their lives. After a ten-year separation from William and her brothers, Dorothy is rediscovered by William as a surrogate for "all that heaven has claim'd"—mother, father, loving home life, and family pride. More perplexingly to William, Dorothy becomes the source of guilt-inspired commitments and troubling fixations that work on the imagination that works on the poetry in its quest for relief from a troubled family biography. The evolving psychodrama reaches denouement in the text and psychobiographical context of William's *The Borderers*, a failed play of successful repression of incestuous desires and romantic jealousy.

Part Two, "'This Dialogue of One,'" explores the creative antagonism Wordsworth enjoyed with Coleridge, now allied with Dorothy against her brother, in William's reaching advantage as a visionary poet. Reading Wordsworth's *Ruined Cottage* and Coleridge's *Rime of the Ancyent Marinere*[12] as an initial encounter over the challenge of poetic and moral responsibility towards an auditor (i.e., the audience), we find the origins of Wordsworth's genius in mastering countertexts against his exalted visionary claims. This process of oppositional inspiration concludes with Wordsworth allying himself with the human face of Erasmus Darwin's scientific treatise *Zoonomia* (1794-96) in marshaling arguments to support natural supernaturalism against the combined skepticism of Dorothy's journals and Coleridge's conversation poems. Deeper faults in life-narrative more troublingly affect the triumphant synthesis of *Lines Written A Few Miles Above Tintern Abbey*.

Part Three, "A Winter's Tale," follows the Wordsworths from their seclusion first at Goslar, Germany, and then at Grasmere, England, where William and Dorothy painfully rid themselves of dependency on Coleridge to explore the self-sufficiency of their relationship. *Home at Grasmere* relates a return to the domestic paradise of youth as an epic challenge to the fatalism of the Fall in John Milton's *Paradise Lost.* Coleridge eventually returns to the Wordsworths from Germany and London in his own attempt to recover the past, in his case, the glory and promise of the *annus mirabilis* spent with the Wordsworths, but the purpose of the return is never achieved. Coleridge's developmental spiral is regressive rather than progressive, and biographical redundancies, or the patterns of his personal history, ruin his attempt to break free of the past.

Finally, "Second Selves," the Coda to this study, will argue that *Michael* represents Wordsworth's final recognition that even the nearest to one and most dear cannot be expected to share, to understand, to feel a responsibility for, nor, perhaps, even to sympathize with the values that one cherishes. For, it is not just that Luke disappoints his father. Michael's wife Isabel is the fault line that the traditional cottage values are built upon. Knowing of the incipient antagonism between the aspirations and values of men and women from his own experience with his sister, William Wordsworth transfers the hopes he had placed in his sister in *Tintern Abbey* to the "youthful Poets, who among these Hills / Will be my second Self when I am gone."[13] As a confirmation of this reading of *Michael,* the Coda concludes with a brief examination of two poems of Wordsworth's American "second Self," Robert Frost, who makes of Wordsworth's crack in the relationship between married cottagers a canyon in two poems from his great early volume, *North of Boston* (1914), "The Death of the Hired Hand" and especially "Home Burial."

The many scholarly influences on this study are buried in the endnotes and sometimes mentioned in the text. Personal and intellectual influence has been another, and far more fugitive, matter. Certainly those who have read this manuscript in whole or part have given unselfishly of that most valued commodity of time and generously of their critical acumen. I thank my colleague Christopher Merrill for reading this work in its entirety from the point of view of a practicing poet, fine essayist, and student of Romantic poetry. A second colleague and poet, Robert Cording, has cared enough to argue with me over some of my readings during the course of our career together. Anne K. Mellor has broadened my understanding of the Romantic context and has thereby enriched—and updated—my readings. I have benefited from the criticisms of Thomas McFarland, Nicholas Roe, Jonathan Wordsworth, Duncan Wu, Peter Manning, Paul Magnuson, Paul Sheats, Theresa Kelley, William Galperin, Timothy Morton, and others who have responded to related papers delivered over the years before the Wordsworth Summer Conferences in Grasmere, at sessions of MLA, over the course of an NEH Summer Seminar in Romanticism directed by Anne Mellor while she was at Stanford, and before the UCLA Romanticism Study Group. The most important intellectual and professional debt I owe is to Kenneth R. Johnston, whose critical touch, superb scholarship and writing, and professional support have been mine to enjoy and to benefit from since my graduate years at Indiana University. The time to work out most of this manuscript was provided generously by the College of the Holy Cross through leaves and sabbaticals. Lastly, this book is dedicated to my wife, Jo, who has taught me how to live with the realities of difference and thereby I have learned to recognize and to understand the Poetry of Relationship.

Parts of this book have appeared as articles in various journals: "Wordsworth's Lucy Poems in Psychobiographical Context," *PMLA*, 93 (January 1978), 46-65, and "The Men in Wordsworth's Life," *The Wordsworth Circle*, 9 (Autumn 1978), 391-97, have been revised and expanded for Part Three; "Classical Argument and Romantic Persuasion in *Tintern Abbey*," *Studies in Romanticism*, 25 (Spring 1986), 97-129, and "Wordsworth's Reading of *Zoonomia* in Early Spring," *The Wordsworth Circle*, 21 (Spring 1990), 76-81, are included, although developed differently, for Part Two. I wish to thank the editors of these very respected journals for their permission to "recycle" these earlier publications. I also owe an immense debt of gratitude to the librarians of Dinand Library of the College of the Holy Cross, of the Widener Library of Harvard University, of the O'Neill Library of Boston College, and of the English Faculty and Bodleian libraries of Oxford University. The final gratitude I will pay is to my first point of contact with St. Martin's Press, acquisitions editor Laura Heymann, whose enthusiasm for this project and then patience provided the appropriate conditions for its completion.

Although it may be understood, I must acknowledge that the faults and inadequacies of this book are solely mine.

Part One

Family Biography and The Borderers

William Wordsworth's compulsive fidelity towards his younger sister Dorothy was the controlling emotional force of his early life, despite the fact that until they settled at Racedown in 1795, most of their lives were spent apart. And, then, one could not represent their separation—at any time—as John Donne's "two soules . . . which are one" as "gold to ayrey thinnesse beate," but rather more appropriately with the figure from Oliver Goldsmith's *Traveller* selected by Dorothy herself to represent the dogged tenacity of their mutual commitment: "We drag at each remove a length-ening chain."[1] The thematic and formal difficulties that readers have encountered in Wordsworth's early narratives, especially the Salisbury Plain poems through his one and only drama, *The Borderers*, are the aesthetic consequences of related biographical dilemmas.

The relevant biography begins with the death of their mother Ann Wordsworth and the subsequent dissolution of the family by their father John Wordsworth in 1778. It is doubtful that William as a child of eight years would feel an immediate responsibility for his younger siblings, Dorothy and younger brothers, John and Christopher. However, over time and mainly through his poetry, the pieces of an inchoate narrative emerge to reveal that William was troubled by guilt over the part his wishes and fantasies may have played in ruining their lives. Transforming the psychological episodes from the poetic record into imaginative story, we find that the motivation for the action of the poet's psychobiography is perhaps too familiar as far as Oedipal narratives go, but its arrangement of incidents, its plot—the soul of tragedy, as Aristotle says in his *Poetics*[2]—is certainly unique.

The story reconstructed goes something like this: John Wordsworth was responsible for his wife's death, but by what means and wherefore are murkier than anything else; he then dissolved his household to separate Dorothy from William, a surmise corroborated by their decade spent apart, since Dorothy was sent in one direction, William (and their brothers) in another; William's death wishes against their father were later fulfilled, making things even worse, especially for Dorothy; and when Dorothy and William finally renewed their relationship in late adolescence, the poet and his poetry began to reveal the influence of two sources of guilt: his ultimate culpability for the suffering of his sister and brothers because he had successfully wished their father dead and an awareness that his newly discovered love for Dorothy was not entirely fraternal. The misfortunes and psychological complications of William's later love affair with Annette Vallon, the French woman who bore his first child, cannot be explained apart from this story. Wordsworth left Annette, I will argue, in order to avoid risking another separation from his sister. The outcome of abandoning his French lover had poetic consequences that we are tired of hearing about because the leap from biography to biographical reading explains everything and nothing about the abandoned-woman theme of Wordsworth's poetry. However, I would like to risk coming at some standard cruxes of Wordsworth's poems not by leaping, but by plotting on, as it were, in reconstructing a tale that attends to the function of irrationality and dreams in weaving a tale of relationship between art and life.

Part One will move through early life and works to prepare for a biographical reading of *The Borderers* that reveals the poet—on behalf of self, sister, and brothers—dramatizing vengeance against a wandering father-figure prior to punishing his hero-surrogate, Mortimer, for acting upon primitive desires of patricide and incest. The biographical correlative of this action is the poet's ambivalence towards his father for dissolving family life and abandoning his daughter Dorothy. This projection of an essentially Oedipal dilemma upon a group experience makes *The Borderers* a modern fable of tribal vengeance and remorse that Freud hypothesized to be the psycho-origin of democracy in *Totem and Taboo* (1913). Freud's constellation of individual, fraternal, and group behaviors uncannily illuminates the darker recesses of the action, characterization, imagery, and politics of Wordsworth's play, and sheds light upon both the psychology of the poet's relationship with his sister and the political ramifications of his experiences with love.

1. "that was the beginning of my love"[3]

Despite Wordsworth's musings in "The Sparrow's Nest" (1802) about a shared childhood,[4] the real relationship of William and Dorothy began in 1787, when they and their brothers, Christopher and John, met as virtual strangers at their maternal grandparents' home at Penrith during the summer holidays. The boys had not seen Dorothy since their father had broken up housekeeping at Cockermouth in 1778, following his wife's death. Wordsworth's latest biographer, Stephen Gill, rightly states: "At such a crisis another family might have drawn closer together. This one split apart."[5]

Scattered like sheep across the Lake Country and midlands, the children suffered deeply from this long rent in their family life. Dorothy voiced their common lament: "How we are squandered abroad" (*EY*, p. 16). At the time of separation, Dorothy was seven years old; William, eight; Christopher, four; and John, six. They were now sixteen, seventeen, thirteen, and fifteen, respectively, and orphaned since their father's death from an illness brought on by exposure to a winter storm in 1784. The reunion became the occasion for a long-suppressed experience of family mourning. Dorothy wrote to Jane Pollard, the lasting friend of her first foster home in Halifax, Yorkshire: "Many a time have Wm, J, C, and myself shed tears together, tears of the bitterest sorrow, we all of us, each day, feel more sensibly the loss we sustained when we were deprived of our parents, and each day do we receive fresh insults, . . ." (*EY*, p. 3).[6] Dorothy suffered most acutely from the indignity of domestic help being permitted to insult the children, because relatives felt the children "have nothing to be proud of" (*EY*, p. 4). She reports that their uncle's neglecting to send horses for the boys at Hawkshead was typical. The brothers waited for a week after school's closing, while Dorothy sat in a state of anxiety over their delay, because in a letter to their uncle they failed to mention they would need horses for the trip. Finally, thinking "some one must be ill" (*EY*, p. 4), William took the initiative to rent a horse on his own. Unsurprisingly, the brothers and sister "always finish [their] conversations," which generally take a melancholy turn, Dorothy writes, "with wishing we had a father and a home" (*EY*, p. 5). After her brothers returned to school, Dorothy continued to live with constant reminders of being unwanted and felt her loss of father, home, and family even more acutely:

> Oh! Jane my dear, dear Friend. . . . [I]f I had a father, in his house you would have been received with a joy nothing could exceed! but it is in vain to wish! wishes will not recal him to life. Never, till I came to Penrith, did I feel the loss I sustained when I was deprived of a Father. (*EY*, p. 9)

Though there is no evidence that Dorothy ever blamed her father for insensitivity or neglect—or that anyone else in the family openly described it that way—the fact is that she could hardly avoid feeling that she was unwanted. For example, the presumption that her father would have made her the mistress of his hospitable home is contradicted by Dorothy's exclusion from family gatherings after his wife's death. There is no evidence in the letters that John Wordsworth even visited with his daughter. There is also no evidence of correspondence between Dorothy and her brothers. But the unkindest cut of all from Dorothy's point of view would have been missing the Christmas reunions John Wordsworth spent with his sons because Christmas was also Dorothy's birthday. Perhaps Dorothy denied that she was the victim of rejection with pragmatic arguments about winter travel. Perhaps she was uneasy about how much responsibility she should assume for her plight, as a child will often feel remorseful, rather than victimized, due to an implicit trust in the motivation of loving adults.[7] However, William, the brother closest to her in age and childhood experience, became sensitive to the poignancy of Dorothy's situation immediately after their first summer reunion.

Passages William wrote for *The Vale of Esthwaite* (1787-88) are inspired by such commiseration. The memory of an earlier wait for ponies becomes associated with his recent experience of waiting for horses because his father's death as fact or memory succeeds both:

> One Evening when the wintry blast
> Through the sharp Hawthorn whistling passed
> And the poor flocks, all pinched with cold
> Sad-drooping sought the mountain fold
> Long, long, upon yon naked rock
> Alone, I bore the bitter shock;
> Long, long, my swimming eyes did roam
> For little Horse to bear me home,
> To bear me—what avails my tear?
> To sorrow o'er a Father's bier.
> Flow on, in vain thou hast not flowed,
> But eased me of a heavy load;
> For much it gives my heart relief
> To pay the mighty debt of grief,
> With sighs repeated o'er and o'er,
> I mourn because I mourned no more.
> For ah! the storm was soon at rest,
> Soon broke [   ] upon my breast
> Nor did my little heart foresee

> She lost a home in losing thee.
> Nor did it know, of thee bereft,
> That little more than Heaven was left.[8]

Though this passage recounts a grievous loss, the impact of that loss has only been lately felt. Curiously, it seems that an undefined positive feeling rather than sorrow almost immediately followed the father's death. The lines, "For ah! the storm was soon at rest, / Soon broke [   ] upon my breast," require that a positive term be inferred for the bracketed omission in order to sensibly complete the meteorological metaphor of a sudden storm followed by—what else but?—sun or sunshine. Apparently, the permanent loss of a home that the Wordsworth children experienced only came to mean something in the compositional present, and, by association, figures in the poet's new experience of mourning. Thus, the belated mourning as repayment of a "mighty debt" requires an explanation.

The wait for the ponies is one of the original "spots of time" from the earliest manuscripts (1798-1799) of *The Prelude* where the mature poet introduces the complication of guilt to his memory of his father's death:

> The event,
> With all the sorrow which it brought appeared
> A chastisement, and when I called to mind
> That day so lately passed when from the crag
> I looked in such anxiety of hope,
> With trite reflections of morality
> Yet with the deepest passion I bowed low
> To God, who thus corrected my desires; . . .[9]

If Wordsworth felt responsible for "The event" of his father's death, he would feel responsible for "all the sorrow which it brought," including his sister's suffering. Thereby, a formative implication is made. He now owed her a home and recompense for the nurturant experience she had missed: relationship with her brothers, paternal love and protection, and childhood joy. *Vale of Esthwaite* also summons a "mighty debt" owed the deceased father, which is an oddly motivated obligation to grieve. The understandable "debt," however, is owed his sister, which the young poet has only lately discovered upon learning of Dorothy's lamentable years.

Vale of Esthwaite also introduces the poet's emotional and physical attraction to his sister:

> Sister, for whom I feel a love
> What warms a Brother far above,
> On you, as sad she marks the scene,
> Why does the heart so fondly lean?
> Why but because in you is given
> All, all, my soul would wish from Heaven?
> Why but because I fondly view
> All, all that Heaven has claimed in you?
>   (Hayden, p. 65, ll. 539-46)

"All" suggests that Dorothy bore recognizable similarities to their parents. Yet the rhetoric of this assertion is perplexing. The poet answers his question ("Why does the heart so foundly lean?") with questions that sound like answers ("Why but because in you is given . . . ?"). Perhaps this particular rhetorical anomaly may serve the function of permitting some wariness about expecting too much of this new relationship with his sister. The second question and response, however, is more curious:

> What from the social chain can tear
> This bosom link'd for ever there,
> Which feels, whene'er the hand of pain
> Touches this heaven connected chain,
> Feels quick as thought the electric thrill
> Feels it ah me—and shudders still?
>   (Hayden, p. 65, ll. 547-52)

Because the next four lines of the passage address the poet's boyhood friend, Richard Fleming, Duncan Wu has read the electric metaphor of the passage to mean that Fleming as an "incarnation of the poet, an allegorical figure, and a link in the divine chain . . . conducts the electric charge that will connect Wordsworth with heaven":[10]

> While bounteous Heaven shall Fleming leave
> Of Friendship what can me bereave?
> Till then shall live the holy flame,
> Friendship and Fleming are the same.
>   (Hayden, p. 65, ll. 553-56)

While Wu argues sensibly that the poet imagines his death to be imminent ("A still Voice whispers to my breast / I soon shall be with them that rest" [ll. 455-56]) and that, like Orpheus, his guilt will soon be assuaged by joining the dead (Wu, p. 12), it seems more plausible in the passage at hand to understand that the young poet is grasping for hope against suicidal inclinations.

In fact, the poet's question is rhetorical, as if there were really no reason to ask, "What from the social chain can tear / This bosom link'd forever there . . . ?" for the question continues with an implied response: the opposing vector of this vertical "social chain," which links the poet's bosom and heart to society (Dorothy and Fleming) below, is its "heav'n connected[ness]" which he reaches for when he longs to be connected with those above, such as his parents, perhaps when the pain of lost parental love is intense. His bosom then feels the potency of the "electric thrill," or the shocking desire to join his parents, to the point of leaving him "shudder[ing]" at his yearnings.[11] Could his sister offer a loving, alternative force to fend off such moments? The tension between form and content again leaves the matter unresolved, but not unresolvable.[12]

In summary: Dorothy's assistance in helping William to release his feelings of suppressed emotion; the concomitant guilt and sympathy provoked by her presence, along with the obligation to her that he now began to feel; and the palpable sense of both parents she aroused with, one supposes, an implied hope for recreating a domicile of recovered family love and security, all became the links of a new brother-sister relationship. And there was also context for a quasi-romantic awakening. The fact that William and Dorothy had not seen or even written to one another for a decade of their young lives made them virtual strangers, and yet the presumption of sibling love guaranteed a trustful atmosphere for relationship. Always shy in the presence of men, Dorothy was beguiled by the opportunity to know a young man intimately, but with welcome restrictions on romantic involvement that would prevent anxiety.[13] William treated his sister very dearly, and several years later had a sexual relationship in France with Annette Vallon, who seems to have been a woman very much like Dorothy.

2. "links of adamant"[14]

Wordsworth's relationship with Annette Vallon became an extension of his relationship with Dorothy. The comparable emotional tone of letters exchanged between Annette and Dorothy, the attraction the women seem to have shared for each other and for William, and William's behavior towards them suggest that Annette was in some ways enough like Dorothy for us to

consider her an eroticized surrogate. The best evidence of this association
between the women and its erotic component is William's behavior and
poetry after learning of Annette's pregnancy. Poems written and revised in
France reveal that Wordsworth was preparing to leave Annette as early as
the first trimester of her pregnancy, probably because their relationship
threatened his commitment to Dorothy.

The first poem to suggest a break with Annette is the melancholy
sonnet of May 1792, "Sweet was the walk along the narrow lane," which
reads as a disguised appeasement to Dorothy. William confesses to dwelling
in darkness to muse upon dreams shared with Dorothy until "a curious star"
and the "clouded Moon" interrupt. Here is the relevant version of the poem
proudly quoted by Dorothy in a letter to Jane Pollard. The poem was never
published during Wordsworth's lifetime:

> . . . on Melancholy's idol dreams
> Musing, the lone Spot with my Soul agrees,
> Quiet and dark; for [through] the thick wove Trees
> Scarce peeps the curious Star till solemn gleams
> The clouded Moon, and calls me forth to stray
> Thro' tall, green, silent woods and Ruins gray.
> (EY, p. 74)

The beckoning of the moon "call[ing]" the poet "forth to stray" suggests a
first poetic association with Dorothy that will be more fully explored in the
Lucy poems. Wordsworth's ongoing revision of Evening Walk[15] while in
France offers a passage and its revisions that may identify the cause of his
distraction in "Sweet was the walk." In Evening Walk Wordsworth gives wishes
full rein to develop the fantasy of establishing a sunny home in England
while he endures the palpably threatening darkness of the surrounding
French landscape. Hope must "throw . . . / On darling spots remote her
tempting smile," for she is unable to "chear / The weary hills, impervious,
black'ning near" (EW, ll. 409-12). Hope thus "decks" for the poet

> a distant scene,
> (For dark and broad the gulph of time between)
> Gilding that cottage with her fondest ray,
> (Sole bourn, sole wish, sole object of my way;
> How fair it's lawn and silvery woods appear!
> How sweet it's streamlet murmurs in mine ear!)
> Where we, my friend, to golden days shall rise,

Till our small share of hardly-paining sighs
(For sighs will ever trouble human breath)
Creep hush'd into the tranquil breast of Death.
(*EW*, ll. 413-22)

The manuscript variant of the line "Sole bourn, etc." reveals more strongly
the intensity of Wordsworth's uncompromising commitment to his sister:
"Sole borne Sole [?vow,] sole [ob]ject of my way" (*EW*, p. 119).

Wordsworth's concurrent revisions of *Descriptive Sketches* and *Evening
Walk* develop equally telling contrasts among love, politics, and landscape
that define the cultural differences between England and the continent, and
between their corresponding love relationships. *Evening Walk* is British,
familial, monarchical, and picturesque; *Descriptive Sketches* is European, erotic,
revolutionary, and sublime. The females of *Descriptive Sketches* are flirtatiously
alluring; the images of love in *Evening Walk* are companionable and maternal.
The human lovers of *Descriptive Sketches* are furtive, while animal counterparts
in *Evening Walk* reveal an open and natural sexual pride.

A "descriptive sketch" near Lake Como finds the poet entranced by
music, dance, and "fair dark-eye'd maids,"

Binding the charmed soul in powerless trance,
Lip-dewing Song and ringlet-tossing Dance,
Where sparkling eyes and breaking smiles illume
The bosom'd cabin's lyre-enliven'd gloom
(*DS*, ll. 93-96)

He presents a second erotic scene outside the "bosom'd" cabin, where the
delicious languor of repressed desire spreads like a contagion from female
to male, until the satisfaction of musical sublimation wanes and frustrated
passion turns to "woo[ing] / The thicket":

Slow glides the sail along th' illumin'd shore,
And steals into the shade the lazy oar.
Soft bosoms breathe around contagious sighs,
And amourous music on the water dies.
Heedless how Pliny, musing here, survey'd
Old Roman boats and figures thro' the shade,
Pale Passion, overpower'd, retires and woos
The thicket, where th' unlisten'd stock-dove coos.
(*DS*, ll. 112-19)

Spousal swans in *Evening Walk* counter the titillation of these bosom-afflicted lovers with a natural, animal dignity. The male swan

> swells his lifted chest, and backward flings
> His bridling neck between his tow'ring wings;
> Stately, and burning in his pride, divides
> And glorying looks around, the silent tides:
> On as he floats, the silver'd waters glow,
> Proud of the varying arch and moveless form of snow.
> . . . .
> The female with a meeker charm succeeds,
> And her brown little ones around her leads,
> Nibbling the water lilies as they pass,
> Or playing wanton with the floating grass:
> She in a mother's care, her beauty's pride
> Forgets, unweary'd watching every side,
> She calls them near, and with affection sweet
> Alternately relieves their weary feet;
> Alternately they mount her back, and rest
> Close by her mantling wings' embraces prest.
>   (*EW*, ll. 195-200, 209-18)

Male pride and female obsequiousness are displayed by a rooster and hen-house: "Sweetly ferocious round his native walks, / Gaz'd by his sister-wives, the monarch stalks" (*EW*, ll. 129-30). (Would it were as possible for a young man with a lover, a sister, and perhaps a sister's friend to unashamedly dwell with an idolatrous brood!) The phrase "sister-wives," of course, suggests a natural precedent, so to speak, for a human sister-wife. Looking ahead to where such thinly disguised allegory will lead, William first compares his relationship with Dorothy in *Home at Grasmere* (1801) to Adam and Eve, the primal siblings, and then to a pair of missing swans from Grasmere Lake, whom, he fears, were destroyed by a dalesman hunter. Putting the Miltonic and natural allusions together with biography, we will develop a psycho-narrative of an adult brother and sister returning to the home/paradise from which they were expelled as children for preferring their mutual love to their father's, and hence feeling anxiety over the remnants of his power.

Wordsworth wrote to a friend in May 1792, the same month Dorothy received her sonnet: "It is at present my intention to take orders in the approaching winter or spring. My Uncle the Clergyman will furnish me with a title." He closes: "I shall return to England in the autumn or the beginning

of Winter" (*EY*, pp. 76, 78). In September Wordsworth wrote his brother
Richard for £20, which he soon received (*EY*, p. 80, n. 2), and requested that
Richard find him lodgings in London, for he planned to be "in Town during
the course of the month of October" (*EY*, p. 81). Wordsworth probably
intended to leave some or most of the money with Annette, yet two more
weeks in France to see Annette through the birth and to see his first child
could not have made any difference financially. By early December, several
weeks before the birth of his daughter Anne-Caroline, Wordsworth was on
British soil.

The troublesome biographical issues consequently raised are Wordsworth's departure from France prior to the birth of his child and his failure
to marry. He explains in *The Prelude* (1805), "Reluctantly to England I
returned / Compelled by nothing else than absolute want / Of funds for
my support" (*Prelude*, Book IX, ll. 190-92), and his biographers generally
have been sympathetic to his claim.[16] Though the quest for financial
support would seem as critical an undertaking as Wordsworth had ever
attempted, the latest version of *The Prelude* (1850) acknowledges that the
search for funds was a fortuitous rationale:

> Dragged by a chain of harsh necessity,
> So seemed it,—now I thankfully acknowledge,
> Forced by the gracious providence of Heaven,—
> To England I returned, else . . .
> . . . .
> Doubtless, I should have then made common cause
> With some who perished; haply, perished too,
> A poor mistaken and bewildered offering,—[17]

Wordsworth's use of the chain metaphor suggests a wider, more inclusive
sense of perishing than may be intended. Dorothy as the parental link of a
social chain in *The Vale of Esthwaite;* guilt aroused by the father's death related
to an obligation to provide for his sister; nostalgia for his sister's companionship in "Sweet was the walk" when one might have expected the foremost
consideration for Annette; the composition of the domestic dream passage
for *Evening Walk* in France; bewitching foreign romance contrasted with
English love; his departure from France so close to the birth date of his child;
and his failure to marry Annette when he had months to formally accept his
legal and moral responsibility—all lead us to the conclusion that Wordsworth felt compelled to escape marriage and return to England for Dorothy's
sake. His return did not preclude future marriage, but does provide evidence
of immediate priorities.

While in London, Wordsworth corresponded regularly with Dorothy, and her correspondence with Jane Pollard reflects a revival of old themes: loving her brothers and dreaming of residence with William and Jane. She acknowledges the bittersweet compulsion of her relationship with William and her brothers:

> kind as are my Uncle and Aunt, much as I love my sweet Cousins, I cannot help heaving many a Sigh at the Reflection that I have passed one and twenty years of my Life, and that the first six years only of this Time was spent in the Enjoyment of the same Pleasures that were enjoyed by my Brothers, and that I was then too young to be sensible of the Blessing. We have been endeared to each other by early misfortune. We in the same moment lost a father, a mother, a home, we have been equally deprived of our patrimony by the cruel Hand of lordly Tyranny. These afflictions have all contributed to unite us closer by the Bonds of affection notwithstanding we have been compelled to spend our youth far asunder. "We drag at each remove a lengthening Chain" this Idea often strikes me very forcibly. Neither absence nor Distance nor Time can ever break the Chain that links me to my Brothers.
> (*EY*, p. 88)

The quoted line derives from the opening of Goldsmith's *The Traveller*:

> Where'er I roam, whatever realms to see,
> My heart untravell'd fondly turns to thee;
> Still to my brother turns, with ceaseless pain,
> And drags at each remove a lengthening chain.
> (ll. 7-10)

Goldsmith's dedication to *The Traveller*, which is a subtext of this letter to Jane, indicates that Dorothy was prepared to sacrifice her comforts for independence with William. Goldsmith writes admiringly of his brother who, "despising Fame and Fortune, has retired early to Happiness and Obscurity, with an income of forty pounds a year" (p. 245).

This letter also contains Dorothy's criticism of William's poetry, especially *An Evening Walk*, though (or perhaps because) it was dedicated to her as *An Epistle in Verse Addressed to A Young Lady From the Lakes of the North of England*. The poem seems to have two important purposes: it is partly William's retribution to Dorothy for the past they might have shared, which it achieves by recreating the special moments she missed; and it is

partly a claim for poetic promise, which they might fulfill through a mutual
vocation:

> When school-boys stretch'd their length upon the green,
> And round the humming elm, a glimmering scene!
> . . . .
> —Then Quiet led me up the huddling rill,
> Bright'ning with water-breaks the sombrous gill;
> To where, while thick above the branches close,
> In dark-brown bason its wild waves repose,
> Inverted shrubs, and moss of darkest green,
> Cling from the rocks, with pale wood-weeds between;
> Save that, atop, the subtle sunbeams shine,
> On wither'd briars that o'er the craggs recline;
> Sole light admitted here, a small cascade,
> Illumes with sparkling foam the twilight shade.
> Beyond, along the visto of the brook,
> Where antique roots its bustling path o'erlook,
> The eye reposes on a secret bridge
> Half grey, half shagg'd with ivy to its ridge.
> —Sweet rill, farewel!
>
> (*EW*, ll. 61-62, 71-85)

Dorothy's criticism of this early offering of William's poetry suggests that
she intended to take an active interest in her brother's vocation. She all but
says that if William had sought her advice, it would have been a better poem:
"By this Time," she wrote to Jane of both *Descriptive Sketches* and *An Evening
Walk*, which were published in January 1793,

> you have doubtless seen my Brother Williams Poems and they have
> already suffered the Lash of your Criticisms. I should be very glad if
> you would give me your opinion of them with the same Frankness with
> which I am going to give you mine. The Scenes which he describes
> have been viewed with a Poet's eye and are pourtrayed with a Poet's
> pencil; and the Poems contain many passages exquisitely beautiful, but
> they also contain many Faults, the chief of which are Obscurity, and a
> too frequent use of some particular expressions and uncommon words
> for instance *moveless*, which he applies in a sense if not new, at least
> different from its ordinary one; . . . I regret exceedingly that he did not
> submit the works to the Inspection of some Friend before their Publi-

cation, and he also joins with me in this Regret. Their Faults are such
as a young Poet was most likely to fall into and least likely to discover,
and what the Suggestions of a Friend would easily have made him see
and at once correct. It is however an Error he will never fall into again,
as he is well aware that he would have gained considerably more credit
if the Blemishes of which I speak had been corrected. My Brother Kitt
and I, while he was at Forncett, amused ourselves by analysing every
Line and prepared a very bulky Criticism, which he was to transmit to
William as soon as he would have [ad]ded to it the [remarks] of his
Cambridge Friends.

(EY, pp. 88-89)

Of the same poems, Coleridge exclaimed that "seldom, if ever, was the
emergence of an original poetic genius above the literary horizon more
evidently announced."[18] Coleridge's impression is not entirely hyperbolical.
Christopher Wordsworth also mentions a "literary society" at Cambridge
discussing William's works along with those of the eminent contemporary
authors, Erasmus Darwin, Anna Seward, and William Lisle Bowles.[19]

3. "that woman was to have been my wife"[20]

Dorothy Wordsworth's vocational development has become a case study
for feminist scholarship on Romanticism. Margaret Homans in particular
writes authoritatively on Dorothy's vocational frustrations in *Women Writers
and Poetic Identity* (1980). Homans argues that the masculine poetic tradition
embodied in the verse of John Milton and heard in her brother's poetic
voice combined to inhibit Dorothy as a poet. The "identification of the
speaking subject as male," especially in *Paradise Lost,* had the effect of
empowering male poets to sing of anything human or divine.[21] The
counterargument that Dorothy lacked the talent to be a great poet is not
unreasonable, but the artfulness of Dorothy's early journals—their precise
attention to objects of natural observation, their rhythm that some have
parsed as incipient *vers libre,* and their simple yet elegant diction—must be
valued for preceding the theoretical audacity of William's later Preface to
Lyrical Ballads (1800):

> I do not know how without being culpably particular I can give my
> Reader a more exact notion of the style in which I wished these poems
> to be written than by informing him that I have at all times endeavoured

> to look steadily at my subject, consequently I hope it will be found that
> there is in these Poems little falsehood of description, . . . Is there then,
> it will be asked, no essential difference between the language of prose
> and metrical composition? I answer that there neither is nor can be any
> essential difference.
>
> (Brett and Jones, pp. 251, 253)

This passage, indeed, could as easily read as a gloss on Dorothy's journals. But while Dorothy's prose excels in diction, tone, and poise, it is undeniable that poetic form was the Achilles heel of her verse. Susan M. Levin's judgement, I think, is definitive: "Uneven in quality, Dorothy's poetry sometimes has the effect of making us more appreciative of her talents as a prose writer."[22] Dorothy tried but failed to ventriloquize the masculine voice her brother embodied whenever language was to be visibly, conventionally framed. Whether Dorothy's prose would later exert an "anxiety of influence" upon William's poetry is worthy of speculation, but for the present it was Dorothy's life and frustrated vocation that provided fruitful complexities for her brother's early verse.

In reflecting on the stifled vocational desires of her youth, Dorothy claims in "Irregular Verses" to have "reverenced the Poet's skill, / And might have nursed a mounting will / To imitate the tender Lays / Of them who sang in Nature's praise," but self-conflict, timidity, mistrust, and pride prevented her from following the path her brother was now beginning. Dorothy then provides what Susan J. Wolfson cleverly identifies as "a countertext to the growth of a poet's mind":[23]

> Bashfulness, a struggling shame
> A fear that elder heads might blame
> —Or something worse—a lurking pride
> Whispering my playmates would deride
> Stifled ambition, checked the aim
> If e'er by chance "the numbers came."
> —Nay even the mild maternal smile,
> That oft-times would repress, beguile
> The over-confidence of youth,
> Even that dear smile, to own the truth,
> Was dreaded by a fond self-love;
> "Twill glance on one—and to reprove
> Or," (sorest wrong in childhood's school)
> "Will *point* the sting of ridicule."[24]

This painful apology for suppressed talent largely indicts the women of Dorothy's early life for crippling her emotional and intellectual esteem. But yet as Elizabeth Fay makes clear, Dorothy's hypersensitivity rendered the "maternal smile" its destructive potency.[25] In private with Jane Pollard, Dorothy felt safe from the "sting of ridicule." As children, they hid away to indulge Dorothy's fantasies; as a young woman, Dorothy recreates their trysts in correspondence.

William's letters now gave Dorothy hope that he would provide them an intellectual and emotional sanctuary for female friendship to flourish. She writes to Jane:

> When I think of Winter I hasten to furnish our little Parlour, I close the Shutters, set out the Tea-table, brighten the Fire. When our Refreshment is ended I produce our Work, and William brings his book to our Table and contributes at once to our Instruction and amusement, and at Intervals we lay aside the Book and each hazard our observations upon what has been read without the fear of Ridicule or Censure. We talk over past days, we do not sigh for any pleasures beyond our humble Habitation "The central point of all our joys."
>
> (EY, p. 88)

The memory of her brother's past attention is romanticized as well. In May 1791, Dorothy blandly described their Forncett walks:

> You may recollect that at that time the weather was uncommonly mild; we used to walk every morning about two hours, and every evening we went into the garden at four or half past four and used to pace backwards and forwards 'till six. Unless you have accustomed yourself to this kind of walking you will have no idea that it can be pleasant, . . .
>
> (EY, p. 47)

Now, fully two years later, and not having seen William for nearly three years, Dorothy charges the memory of their walks with the passion of an active courtship:

> Oh Jane the last time we were together he won my Affect[ion] to a Degree which I cannot describe; his Attentions to me were su[ch] as the most insensible of mortals must have been touched with, there was no Pleasure that he would not have given up with joy for half an Hour's Conversation with me. It was in Winter (at Christmas) that he was last

> at Forncet and every Day as soon as we rose from Dinner we used to
> pace the gravel walk in the Garden *til six o'clock* when we received a
> Summons (which was always unwelcome) to Tea.
>
> (*EY*, pp. 95-96)

Since that time of extraordinary attentiveness, Dorothy says, "I have paced
that walk in the garden which will always be dear to me from the Remembrance of those long, long conversations I have had upon it supported by
my Brother's arm. Ah Jane!" Dorothy sighs, "I never thought of the cold when
he was with me" (*EY*, p. 96).

While writing to Jane of the future she imagined for them, Dorothy
was also speculating with Annette of another future. In Annette's confiscated
letter to William of March 20, 1793, Annette explicitly refers to a comparable domestic arrangement and thanks Dorothy for her compassion: "Your
last letter gives me a sense of your presence. With every line, I saw the
sensibility of your soul and I am moved by the interest you take in my
difficulties. They are large, my dear sister."[26] Dorothy's tears for Annette
were generous, but there is little doubt that Dorothy's domestic preference
was to live with Jane.

As Dorothy anticipates her coming reunion with William and Jane,
her passions break through in a rush of infatuation for both. Of William she
writes:

> I must be blind, he cannot be so pleasing as my fondness makes him. I
> am willing to allow that half the virtues with which I fancy him endowed
> are the creation of my Love, but surely I may be excused! he was never
> tired of comforting his sister, he never left her in anger, he always met
> her with joy, he preferred her society to every other pleasure, . . . he
> had no pleasure when we were compelled to be divided.
>
> (*EY*, p. 98)

Dorothy proudly quotes from his letters: "How much do I wish that each
emotion of pleasure and pain that visits your heart should excite a similar
pleasure or a similar pain within me, by that sympathy which will almost
identify us when we have stolen to our little cottage!" In another letter he
wrote: "Oh my dear, dear sister with what transport shall I again meet you,
with what rapture shall I again wear out the day in your sight. I assure you
so eager is my desire to see you that all obstacles vanish. I see you in a
moment running or rather flying to my arms" (*EY*, pp. 101-02). William's
desire for Dorothy does not suggest a need or wish for the company of

others, but his ardor has the effect of arousing Dorothy's hope for a similar experience with Jane:

> I entreat you my love to think of me perpetually, to think of what will be our felicity when we are again united if we meet with health and strength equal to our vivacity and youthful ardour of mind, think of our moonlight walks attended by my own dear William, think of our morning rambles when we shall—after having passed the night together and talked over the pleasure of the preceding evening, steal from our lodging-room, perhaps before William rises, and walk alone enjoying all the sweets of female friendship. Think of our mornings, we will work, William shall read to us. Oh my dear friend how happy we shall be!
>
> (*EY*, pp. 102-03)

As the date of their reunion nears after this six-year separation, Dorothy indulges in jubilant anticipation:

> Oh count, count the Days, my Love till Christmas how slowly does each day move! and yet three months and Christmas will not be here. Three months!—long, long months I measure them with a Lover's scale; three months of Expectation are three Ages!
>
> (*EY*, p. 108)

On Christmas Day, Dorothy would turn twenty-two.

William was now painfully divided over meeting his obligations to Annette and their child and living up to the dreams he had spun with his sister. He was spending a month on the Isle of Wight with William Calvert, where the British navy was massing before entering the war against France, which had been declared in February 1793. Possibly, as David V. Erdman has suggested, Wordsworth sought to make arrangements for passage into France, but nothing came of it.[27] Continuing the tour, the friends experienced an accident in Calvert's coach and Calvert continued on horseback, leaving Wordsworth to venture on foot. Wordsworth traveled north through Salisbury Plain, the Wye Valley, and then into Wales, where he met up with his friend from Cambridge University, Robert Jones. The poems deriving from memories and experiences of this period—the Salisbury Plain poems, "We Are Seven," *Tintern Abbey*, and a brief, visionary segment of *The Prelude*—represent the common plight of the poet as well as his poems' victims, forlorn women separated from their men by war or death and, as we shall later discuss, new insights on sibling relationship. In *Tintern Abbey*,

Wordsworth describes his emotional condition on this lonely walking tour as "more like [that of] a man / Flying from something that he dreads, than one / Who sought the thing he loves" (ll. 71-73), suggesting the ambivalence he was feeling over his French experience and his responsibilities.

An impressive line of biographical scholars and critics—Ernest de Selincourt, David V. Erdman, James R. MacGillivray, Mark L. Reed, Paul D. Sheats, George McLean Harper, Herbert Read, Kenneth R. Johnston, Stephen Gill, and Nicholas Roe—believes that Wordsworth made a daring trip to France sometime between mid-September and early October 1793. The evidence for a return trip is principally Thomas Carlyle's comment that Wordsworth told him he was in Paris for the execution of the French journalist Gorsas, which occurred on October 7, 1793. Carlyle paraphrases and quotes from his discussion with Wordsworth:

> He had been in France in the earlier or secondary stage of the Revolu-
> tion; had witnessed the struggle of Girondins and Mountain, in partic-
> ular the execution of Gorsas, "the first deputy sent to the scaffold"; and
> testified strongly to the ominous feeling which that event produced in
> everybody, and of which he himself seemed to retain something:
> "Where will it end, when you have set an example in this kind?"[28]

George McLean Harper also includes a comment made by Alaric Watts that a man identified only as Bailey told Wordsworth that he was in danger and Wordsworth "decamped with great precipitation."[29] Gill finds it entirely plausible that "a courageous but desperate 23-year-old might have disregard-ed" common sense in an audacious undertaking, though he fails to infer any consequential results.[30] Mary Moorman prefers not to endorse the return trip, but admits "in spite of all the difficulties, the conversation of Carlyle is hard to reject outright."[31] Though insensitive to the emotional need for such a bold venture, Moorman asks the important question:

> A motive for so difficult and risky an undertaking is not very easy to
> find. Some will have it that it was a desperate attempt to reach and
> marry Annette. But, if so, why did he go to Paris? On the whole, he is
> more likely to have gone for political reasons.
>
> (Moorman, Vol. I, p. 239)

While one cannot weigh the proportion of political to personal motivation in Wordsworth's return to Paris, neither type of motivation can be discount-ed. If Wordsworth did delay in Paris out of political curiosity and/or indecisiveness over what he ought to do next, when the alert went out that Englishmen were in danger of arrest, he probably "decamped with great precipitation," not to save his skin, as Bailey's comment implies, but to visit with Annette before departing for England.[32] But what was to be achieved? Having returned at great risk, would he marry Annette to assume legal responsibility for his child and to offer her an opportunity for social respectability?[33]

There is really only one text to consult in seeking enlightenment on these issues, the Tale of Vaudracour and Julia composed for the 1805 *Prelude*. Although there has lately been a thoughtful reaction against the "ubiquitous biographical reading[s]" of the Tale in order to emphasize the poet's political intentions,[34] it would be better to argue for an inclusive reading. Our discussion of *Evening Walk* and *Descriptive Sketches* revealed that the twenty-three-year-old poet aligned styles of loving with national culture and politics. Regardless of one's preference for biographical or historical readings, Wordsworth describes lovemaking in a revolutionary setting as a political act during the compositional period of his earlier poems in 1792-93 as well as during his composition of the Tale of Vaudracour and Julia in 1804. It is a corroborating and fascinating coincidence of literary history on the issue of politics and love that Mary Wollstonecraft was sharing an equally consequential romance in France at the same time as Wordsworth. Her relationship with the American Gilbert Imlay commenced in France, December 1792, just as Wordsworth was leaving Annette, and continued between Paris and Le Havre until April 1795, when she returned to London a broken, unmarried, and abandoned woman, with her child by Imlay. In her great depression over Imlay's perfidy, she later repeatedly attempted suicide. Certainly revolutionary Paris was an experimental community of free love for English men and women of age, and in this sense, then, illicit lovemaking became sanctioned in and by political context.[35]

The Tale of Vaudracour and Julia can be presumed reliable on the issue of character motivation, because Wordsworth intended an authentic account for his autobiography of what still seemed an important event, and not only to him. Both his sister and Mary Hutchinson Wordsworth, his wife of two years, would have expected him to acknowledge the existence and significance of his mistress and their child. It goes without saying that they would be interested in William's considered explanation for his falling in love so quickly, for having sex so readily, and for failing to wed, especially if he had returned to France in 1793 to achieve some closure. If Erdman is correct in suggesting that Wordsworth constructed the tale to provide essential factual and emotional truth,[36] then we have a great deal to learn from Wordsworth's tale—maybe most from its failures. Reading the tale closely with its probable model in hand—Helen Maria Williams's wildly heroic, but apparently true incident of Monsieur and Madame du Fosse—will offer pointed contrasts on issues needing clarification:[37] the nature of Wordsworth's relationship to Annette, including its political overtones; his resulting reluctance to marry; and the psychological outcome of discovering that he had been using Annette as a political and sororal surrogate. The contrasts with Williams's tale provide an implicit foil for the poet's vacillating hero.

The tale begins with a description of the lovers' relationship as childhood companions: "From their cradles up, / . . . / Friends, Playmates, Twins in Pleasure, . . . / . . . / Nor ever happy if they were apart" (*Prelude,* Book IX, ll. 569-75). The sharing of early experience is recognized as a prerequisite for lasting love—"A basis this for deep and solid love, / And endless constancy, and placid truth" (*Prelude,* Book IX, ll. 576-77)—which introduces the first significant contrast with Williams's tale and with Wordsworth's experience with Annette, because du Fosse was not raised with his wife, Monique; he met her when she served as governess for his younger siblings. His love for her derives from esteem of her disposition and character (Williams, p. 128). It is not difficult to surmise an intention. The tale begins by overlaying a sibling relationship on the lovers' childhood, because the poet wishes to acknowledge that ideal love must have a foundation in early life, which herein implies a predisposition to fall in love with someone like his sister.

In Wordsworth's tale, companionate love becomes erotic love as the children mature. Vaudracour "beheld / A vision, and he lov'd the thing he saw" (*Prelude,* Book IX, ll. 581-82). The common world now swarming with enchantment, spirits "overblessed for life" (*Prelude,* Book IX, l. 594), the lovers follow nature's course, though Wordsworth suggests an honorable intention and yet some political ploy on Vaudracour's part. Perhaps it was "through effect / Of some delirious hour" that self-control was abandoned to sexual passion, but Wordsworth plants a significant doubt to motivate his surrogate. His royalist father had rejected Julia for her plebeian background; thus, it could also be that Vaudracour grew "inwardly prepared to turn aside / From law and custom" to force a marriage with her pregnancy (*Prelude,* Book IX, ll. 596-603). The strategy of Vaudracour's lovemaking fails, however, as his father's commitment to his aristocratic line overrides a "natural" commitment to blood.

The political implications of Vaudracour's love are clear. He is a normal young man who gives his passions free play with a woman he madly

loves, but he has used love to test the political will of his father, a represen-
tative of the Second Estate. Poetically and biographically this is either Scylla
and/or Charybdis: either Vaudracour loved Julia as a sister and/or he loved
her as a vehicle for political rebellion; either Wordsworth loved Annette as
a replacement for Dorothy and/or as a political presence to use against his
lover's Royalist family.

The failure of Wordsworth's lovers to elope is the second significant
contrast with Williams's tale. Baron du Fosse is similarly opposed to his son's
choice of spouse, but his son goes through the marriage ceremony not once,
but three times!—the first time in France in a secret service, and then,
inexplicably, twice in England after they leave the country to avoid the
Baron's warrant for his son's arrest.[38] Writing against this irrational emphasis
on marriage may have been part of the tale's attraction for Wordsworth.
Wordsworth had given Vaudracour the singular motivation of impregnating
Julia to take on the obligation of marrying her, so how could Wordsworth
now parallel his biographical experience in having Vaudracour excusably
avoid marriage?

Adverting to the biographical reality of Wordsworth's relationship
with Annette suggests how strongly the issue of marriage would stand forth
for resolution. Wordsworth would have known the great importance of
marriage to Annette as much for social respectability as for a reasonable
assurance of his commitment. She wrote:

> I would like to tell you . . . that I am happy, but I would be deceiving
> you. You could not believe it; but at least I can in truth assure you that
> were it possible for my friend to come to give me the glorious title of
> his spouse, in spite of the cruel necessity which would oblige him to as
> soon leave his wife and child I would tolerate more easily an absence
> which would be in truth painful. But I could at the same time find in his
> daughter a compensation which is forbidden to me now.[39]

When Wordsworth returned to France to see Annette, there seemed to be
little he could or should do to avoid marriage, but he delayed in Paris, as in
an approach-avoidance conflict, until delay was no longer possible.

A neglected section of the Tale of Vaudracour and Julia suggests
the emotional confusion of Wordsworth's return to Annette and its
definitive, practical outcome. The scene is Vaudracour's reaction to the
decision of Julia's parents that, because the lovers cannot be honorably
wed, they will have to part. Vaudracour's response to the decision
indicates that he valued his powerlessness. Though Wordsworth's com-

parable experience might have occurred in 1792, or before his first departure, the presence of the child in the tale more strongly suggests that the related event occurred during his return in 1793. When Julia hears that she must give up her child and be immured in a convent as an unwed mother, her response is natural indignation: "Julia was thunderstricken" by the words of her mother and she insists "on a Mother's rights / To take her child along with her" (*Prelude*, Book IX, ll. 840-43). Upon hearing of the mother's decision, friends and domestics are "overwhelm'd with grief," uncertain of how they should bear the news to Vaudracour, for fear of his response:

> but great
> Was their astonishment when they beheld him
> Receive the news in calm despondency,
> Composed and silent, without outward sign
> Of even the least emotion.
> (*Prelude*, Book IX, ll. 849-53)

Julia is baffled, and outraged. She chides him, and Vaudracour responds with a symbolic act:

> When Julia scattered some upbraiding words
> Upon his slackness, he thereto return'd
> No answer, only took the mother's hand
> (Who loved him scarcely less than her own child)
> And kissed it, without seeming to be pressed
> By any pain that 'twas the hand of one
> Whose errand was to part him from his love
> For ever.
> (*Prelude*, Book IX, ll. 854-61)

The sudden and startling roundness Vaudracour's character receives with this kiss is the culmination of the Tale's undercurrent of ambivalence. Earlier, Vaudracour had tried to use his murder of his father's henchman as a reason for breaking with Julia,[40] yet seeing the infant caused him to reconsider. Later, as Erdman has emphasized, Vaudracour achieves a definitive insight on the great cost of his physical attraction to Julia: "'Julia, how much thine eyes / Have cost me!'" (*Prelude*, Book IX, ll. 818-19).[41] In an unpublished revision, Wordsworth deplores the inadequacy of language to render his understanding of Vaudracour's anguish:

> He started greeting the blank air with words
> Forc'd from him partly by his own sad thoughts
> Partly by heavenly sight of her dear eyes
> Words which I know and could by living voice
> Repeat the same, but have not heart to trust
> Their tender meaning to this lifeless pen.[42]

The poet's poignant admission of "know[ing]" Vaudracour's thoughts and words when summoning the "heavenly sight of her dear eyes," and yet refusing to trust their intimacy to the medium of his art, provides a rare compositional moment. Earlier in this autobiographical text the poet stood strong in rendering the mimesis of transcendent consciousness, especially the apocalypse of imagination in the 1805 redaction of the Simplon Pass episode—"Imagination!—lifting up itself / Before the eye and progress of my song / Like an unfathered vapour, etc." (Prelude, Book VI, ll. 525-48)—but now he falters in composition before an old wound of human love. When Julia's mother renders her decision, Vaudracour spontaneously expresses the depth of his ambivalence. He shows empathy for the mother's agony, and feels relief that marriage has been prevented.

Vaudracour's psychological fate becomes defined by guilt. In a compensatory reaction, he seeks the responsibility of rearing his child. Wordsworth must have intuited that the more self-sacrificial the behavior, the more effectively guilt can be dissipated.[43] Though France is resounding with the "voice of Freedom" as the early stages of the revolution progress, Vaudracour retreats to a cottage with his child and a nurse. Eventually through an act of negligence the child dies to end the narrative, and Vaudracour is reduced to madness: "in those solitary shades / His days he wasted, an imbecile mind" (Prelude, Book IX, ll. 934-35). Wordsworth concludes by absolving himself of the tale's determinacy: "The Tale I follow to its last recess / Of suffering or of peace, I know not which— / Theirs be the blame who caused the woe, not mine" (Prelude, Book IX, ll. 909-11). There is a starkly contrasting authorial intrusion in Williams, in which she compliments the tale's fact and her narration for being just as the reader would wish—"Does not the old Baron die exactly in the right place; at the very page one would choose?" (Williams, p. 193). Words-worth's identification with his hero, which here means empathy for his past self, prevents not only aesthetic detachment but also aesthetic control over his tale, as if he is re-experiencing the fatalism.

If this biographical-textual reconstruction is generally sound, it would be inaccurate to find Wordsworth an embittered man upon his return from France in October 1793, for only because of his powerlessness did he succeed in failing to achieve a marital solution. To borrow a phrase from Kenneth R. Johnston, it was a biographical "triumph of failure."[44] The sonnet "There is a little unpretending rill" recalls the impotence and resulting joy. Written prior to his return to France in 1802 to inform Annette of his intended marriage to Mary Hutchinson, the sonnet commemorates William's 1794 reunion with Dorothy as if to assure her of his continued love. The rill offers an emblem of the vacillation and impotence associated with Wordsworth-Vaudracour: the "unpretending Rill / Of limpid water . . . / . . . quivers down the hill, / Furrowing its shallow way with dubious will" as it images the uncertainty but personal freedom of the Wordsworths after William's return from France in lines that never appeared in the published poem, for he was happier than he had a right to be:

> For on that day, now seven years back when first
> Two glad Foot-Travellers through sun and shower,
> My love and I came hither, while thanks burst
> Out of our hearts to God for that good hour
> Eating a traveller's meal in shady Bower
> We from that blessed water slaked our thirst[45]

This recollection indirectly assures Dorothy that the pending marital commitment, elided with past and present obligations to Annette, will be equally unthreatening to their relationship.

4. "sunk into despair"[46]

From early April to mid-May 1794, the Wordsworths experimented at living together in Keswick at Windy Brow, a rental home owned by the Calverts. Wordsworth revised *Evening Walk* and Dorothy prepared a fair copy of *Salisbury Plain*. This expanded, but never published, text of *Evening Walk* reveals several developments of psychology, imagery, and theme for Wordsworth's future work: his feeling of childhood immortality (*EW*, ll. 29-51); the experience of altered states of consciousness in the presence of natural scenery (ll. 83-94); an awareness of nature's pantheistic potential (ll. 119-32); the transformation of landscape by natural light (ll. 155-90); an association with the swans of Grasmere (ll. 414-67); and an early poetic association with Milton (ll. 686-88).[47]

Though the experiment in cohabitation thus seemed auspicious, its brevity was planned. The Wordsworths intended to remain until William found employment (*EY*, p. 115), but they could not impose indefinitely on the family living in Calvert's cottage. By the latter part of May, they were with relatives in Whitehaven. At this point, Wordsworth's letters to his college friend William Mathews begin to speculate in detail about a journal that Mathews could edit out of London and Wordsworth could contribute to from any less expensive residence, while continuing to work on his poetry. It would be a journal of political and literary consequence, devoted to the progressive, nonrevolutionary improvement of society and to the correction of government with a body of first principles. The plan had much in common with Coleridge's coming *Watchman*, and with many like-minded journals inspired by William Godwin's enormously influential *Enquiry Concerning Political Justice*, published a year earlier (1793).

For the moment, Wordsworth could not afford his plans, and begged off coming to London to travel with Raisley Calvert, the brother of William Calvert, who intended to support Wordsworth out of his independent income (*EY*, pp. 126-27). Shortly, Raisley Calvert's health began to fail and his desire to help mankind through Wordsworth's talent was translated into a legacy. By January 1795, after sitting at Calvert's side throughout a four-month tubercular decline, Calvert had died, and Wordsworth was free. Though there were some restrictions on his use of the final legacy of £900, they were sensible, and mainly established so that Wordsworth's relations would not collect what he owed them for his education, which would nullify Calvert's intent.

Biographers generally follow Wordsworth's lead from *The Prelude* in acknowledging the vocational significance of the Calvert legacy, but Marjorie Levinson is correct to call attention to a "certain defensiveness, betrayed by the excessive formality and lofty indirection of Wordsworth's style":[48]

>   A Youth—he bore
>   The name of Calvert; it shall live, if words
>   Of mine can give it life—without respect
>   To prejudice or custom, having hope
>   That I had some endowments by which good
>   Might be promoted, in his last decay
>   From his own Family withdrawing part
>   Of no redundant patrimony, did
>   By a Bequest sufficient for my needs

> Enable me to pause for choice, and walk
> At large and unrestrained, nor damped too soon
> By mortal cares. Himself no Poet, yet
> Far less a common spirit of the world,
> He deemed that my pursuits and labors lay
> Apart from all that leads to wealth, or even
> Perhaps to necessary maintenance,
> Without some hazard to the finer sense,
> He cleared a passage for me, and the stream
> Flowed in the bent of Nature.
> > (*Prelude*, Book XIII, ll. 349-67)

Wordsworth's earlier sonnet, "To the Memory of Raisley Calvert," speaks as thankfully of Calvert's dying concern, but its depiction of the poet's appropriate reward for the sacrifice of the deceased raises an important question:

> This care was thine when sickness did condemn
> Thy youth to hopeless wasting, root and stem—
> That I, if frugal and severe, might stray
> Where'er I liked; and finally array
> My temples with the Muse's diadem.
> > (Hayden, Vol. I, p. 569, ll. 4-8)

It may be true that Raisley Calvert was so selfless that his final pleasure came in musing upon Wordsworth "stray[ing] / Where'er [he] liked" and "array[ing] / [His] temples" in glory while Raisley himself wasted away, "root and stem." But it was probably not so. Raisley's principal aspiration was that Wordsworth should prove useful to mankind. Why does Wordsworth misrepresent Calvert's dying intention?

Wordsworth's tending of the consumptive Calvert was not really an act of altruism or friendship. Wordsworth referred to Raisley Calvert in a letter of 1805 as "a young man with whom, though I call him Friend, I had had but little connection." Wordsworth also identifies Calvert's legacy as an act of philanthropy, rather than friendship: "the act was done entirely from a confidence on his part that I had powers and attainments which might be of use to mankind" (*EY*, p. 546). Let us grant that Wordsworth's exchange of care and companionship for money was honorably and feelingly discharged, but he did wish that it would end sooner rather than later. From October 1794 to January 1795, Wordsworth wrote a series of letters that

reflect directly or in passing on the melancholy languor and mental distraction of a profoundly depressing experience.

It seems there was little hope for Raisley even at the outset of his
decline. Wordsworth wrote to William, Raisley's older brother, that he
would accompany Raisley to Lisbon, where he wished to retreat for his
health, if William could finance the trip: "I . . . would accompany him thither,
and stay with him till his health is re-established. . . . Would it not exalt you
in your own esteem to retrench [financially] a little for so excellent a
purpose?" (EY, p. 129). Yet, the fact that Raisley had recently promised
Wordsworth a legacy of £600, which Wordsworth admitted forthrightly—
"hav[ing] no doubt but that you [William Calvert] will do both him and
myself the justice to hear this mark of his approbation of me without your
good opinion of either of us being at all diminished by it" (EY, p. 130)—
leads one to believe that all of their thoughts were on final things. Within
a week or so, Raisley was too ill to travel and thus Wordsworth undertook
to nurse him in Keswick.

Wordsworth informs his older brother Richard of the responsibility
he has undertaken and begins to lose composure over the risk of losing
Raisley's legacy unless they can find some way of preventing relatives from
pouncing on his good fortune to repay £460 advanced for his education. In
a rambling, nervous letter of October 10, 1794, Wordsworth repeats the
case to Richard three times that 1) Raisley wants to help him to benefit
society, and thus 2) relatives must be warded off, by 3) Richard agreeing to
take on immediate responsibility for the educational debt. "I have said
nothing at all on the hardship of my case," William continues, "if I should
be deprived of this legacy, merely from the circumstance of my not having
inherited a farthing of my fathers property, which will be the case, if you
will not engage to secure me from this debt to my aunt as far as relates to
this six hundred pound. . . . Pray write immediately as no time is to be lost.
. . . I have used much repetition in this letter from a wish [to] be perspicuous
and from writing in a hurry" (EY, pp. 131-32).

Richard complied, but with justifiable annoyance: "There is one Circumstance which I will mention to you at this time. I might have retired into the
Country and I had almost said enjoyed the sweets of retirement and Domestick
life if I had only considered my own Interest." Because he had not, his business
has prospered through hard work and thus he can be of assistance. He hopes
all of their industry will lead to independence (EY, p. 132). William let this rest
in his next letter, for now he was requesting Richard to come to Keswick to
assist in making out a will. Raisley was being "dilatory," using as excuses that
he had not seen the bond insuring the legacy's protection and, furthermore,

did not like the local attorney. Raisley had increased the promised legacy to £900, which intensified Wordsworth's self-interest (*EY*, pp. 133-34).

After the will's preparation, William focused more on Raisley's physical decline and on his desire to get on with his life: "he worsens daily," William wrote to Mathews, "I have a most melancholy office of it" (*EY*, p. 137). The letter was set aside for two weeks, after which Wordsworth continues: "I have lately undergone much uneasiness of mind. . . . I am now at Penrith, where I have been some time, my poor friend is barely alive. I shall not stay here any longer than to see him interred," and then moves on to other matters of concern—politics, his poetry, a journal he and Mathews might edit, etc. (*EY*, pp. 138-39).

On January 12, Raisley Calvert died. Given time to reflect on what Calvert had done on his behalf, Wordsworth would regret his self-interest, much as he harbored guilt for his father's demise.[49] The consequences of this muddle of self-interest, money, and death bear significantly on the murder for gain in *Adventures on Salisbury Plain*, as Calvert's decline and death became yet another source of turbulence for Wordsworth's imagination.

Wordsworth now moved to London to work as a political journalist— he said he wanted to get away from "cataracts and mountains," which would not suffice as "constant companions" (*EY*, p. 136); but he was also a man supported by a dying bequest to help humanity, and how could he do so except by writing and speaking on significant political and social issues? It is thus an attractive and probable speculation that he worked with a circle of political radicals to publish *The Philanthropist* as he and Mathews had planned.[50] Doubtless, for the primary purpose of political discussion, he began meeting regularly with William Godwin,[51] who was at the height of his influence for the *Enquiry*. But Godwin's philosophy would have been important to Wordsworth for more systematically thinking through the suffusion of political ideology into even intimate relationships. The book "Of Property" in *Enquiry* also could offer soothing reasoning to a young man confused and conscience-stricken over personal (and paternal) responsibilities.[52] As Wordsworth was to observe of mental distress due to guilt, or "when we have been unworthily employed":

> then it is that we repair to systems of morality for arguments in defence
> of ourselves; & sure enough are we to find them. . . . [L]ifeless words,
> & abstract propositions, will not be destitute of power to lay asleep the
> spirit of self-accusation & exclude the uneasiness of repentance.[53]

To put it bluntly, Godwin's position on cohabitation, romance, marriage, and parenthood offered an attractive blend of common sense and rationalization to excuse Wordsworth's behavior towards Annette, although their child complicated things a great deal. Conversely, if there had been any discomfort in living with Dorothy as the reason for his leaving Annette, Godwin also could justify the preference with his extolling of friendship over romance and blood relationship.

Here is Godwin on romance:

> The method is for a thoughtless and romantic youth of each sex to come together, to see each other, for a few times and under circumstances full of delusion, and then to vow to each other eternal attachment. What is the consequence of this? In almost every instance they find themselves deceived.[54]

On the political and moral ramifications of resulting marriage:

> the institution of marriage is made a system of fraud; and men who carefully mislead their judgments in the daily affair of their life must be expected to have a crippled judgment in every other concern. Add to this that marriage is a monopoly, and the worst of monopolies. . . . So long as two human beings are forbidden, by positive institution, to follow the dictates of their mind, prejudice will be alive and vigorous.
>
> (*Enquiry*, p. 762)

On permanent marital cohabitation:

> it is absurd to expect the inclinations and wishes of two human beings to coincide, through any long period of time. To oblige them to act and to live together is to subject them to some inevitable portion of thwarting, bickering and unhappiness. This cannot be otherwise.
>
> (*Enquiry*, p. 761)

Finally, and perhaps most importantly, Godwin favored friendship in opposition to romance, which would justify Wordsworth's commitment to his friend and sister, and Godwin also offered a brilliant rationalization for solacing a wandering father. When sexual intercourse becomes as demystified as eating and drinking for maintaining a healthful existence, rather than as a stimulus—or worse, obligation—to marry, the resulting offspring will be raised communally. Indeed, in an enlightened community of open love and sexual relationships, it will not be possible to know the father of "each individual child." But, "such knowledge will be of no importance," for no human being ought to be preferred because of blood relationship. The mother may be the principal nourisher and guardian of the child, but not necessarily. If she found "her share of the burthen unequal . . . then it would be amicably and willingly participated by others" (*Enquiry*, p. 765). Transcending blood and emotion was the ideal of friendship: "if by friendship we understand that affection for an individual which is measured singly by what we know of his worth, [it] is one of the most exquisite gratifications, perhaps one of the most improving exercises, of a rational mind" (*Enquiry*, p. 763).[55]

Such reasoning on marriage, friendship, and child-rearing determine Wordsworth's next move. By late summer 1795 Wordsworth was preparing to leave London. Possibly, as Johnston has argued, Wordsworth was fleeing the London scene because *The Philanthropist* recently had taken a dangerous radical turn that he could not support politically or personally.[56] Or to take Nicholas Roe's account, Wordsworth may have been suffering from a self-division, a psychomachy, over his status as a failed, even timorous, revolutionary, when compared with the French patriots he had known and who had died for their beliefs:

> Wordsworth's frustrated history as radical journalist and French revolutionary was bound-up with his later career as a poet. His inability to fulfil his revolutionary calling underlined his welcome for the unity. . . being achieved by his settlement with Dorothy at Racedown, and his deepening commitment to poetry. Thereafter, the coherence of his identity as poet depended on the suppression of his passionately inconsistent radical selves.[57]

For such reasons it is likely that Wordsworth would welcome an excuse to leave London for Dorothy now that he had made some attempt to carry out the responsibility of Calvert's legacy as an activist.

Wordsworth also came upon a curious way to earn some £50 per annum. He agreed to care for the three-year-old son of Basil Montagu, a woeful and dissolute widower he had befriended in London. As Montagu describes it, Wordsworth "unremittingly, and to me imperceptibly, endeavoured to eradicate my faults, and to encourage my good dispositions. . . . After some time he proceeded to take my child from my Chambers in London in [to] Dorsetshire, where he was about to settle with his Sister" (*EY*, pp. 146-47, note 4). The child, Basil Caroline Montagu, born December 27, 1792, was twelve days older than Wordsworth's daughter, Anne-Caroline, and worth noting for a touch of irony that supports the surrogate paternity of Wordsworth's endeavor is the fact that the children shared middle names.

From another friend of these London days, Aza Pinney, Wordsworth ex-tracted the promise of a rent-free residence in Dorset, Racedown Lodge. With Calvert's legacy, Montagu's child, Pinney's house, and Godwin's philosophy, Wordsworth left an active, political life to live in relative isolation with Dorothy, his friend and sister.

Dorothy's fantasy of living with Jane now ended as well because Jane had engaged to marry. The young women "parted, sorrowful; by duty led," as Dorothy was to recall in her "Irregular Verses," after their long-anticipated reunion in the summer of 1795. Dorothy's anticlimactic image for the end was parting with a handshake "at the end of the lane" (*EY*, p. 146).[58] In Dorothy's letter congratulating Jane on her new home and life, she explains the benefits of the life she and William are commencing at Racedown, with little Basil in tow:

> One of the first and greatest is that it may put William into a way of getting a more permanent establishment, and on my account that it will greatly contribute to my happiness and place me in such a situation that I shall be *doing something*, it is a painful idea that ones existence is of very little use which *I* really have always been obliged to feel; above all it is painful when one is living upon the bounty of one's friends, a resource of which misfortune may deprive one and then how irksome and difficult it is to find out other means of support, the mind is then unfitted, perhaps, for any new exertions, and continues always in a state of dependence, perhaps attended with poverty.
>
> (*EY*, p. 150)

Providing vocational assistance to her brother would allow for shared achievement. Setting up a household with Dorothy and Basil seems an efficient psychological strategy on William's part to fulfill obligations, though Godwinian principles of social responsibility and personal relation-ship provided mirrors and smoke for self-deception.

Within a month of their moving to Racedown, William received a letter from France. Annette mentioned sending half a dozen, none of which reached the Wordsworths (*EY*, p. 161). Emblematic of the bio-graphical confusion, the letter he received does not survive, but some of the ones he did not receive do, for they had been confiscated by a French post office. Perhaps in the received letter(s), Annette also wove her anti-Godwinian narration of obsessive longing, after which Wordsworth would soon model Margaret, his passionately passive heroine of *The Ruined Cottage*:

I cannot be happy without him, I desire him every day, but I shall have plenty of reasons for submitting to the lot which I must undergo. I often call to my aid that reason which too often is weak and powerless beside my feelings for him; . . . he will never picture justly the need I have of him to make me happy; mastered by a feeling which causes all my unhappiness, I cherish always his dominion over me, and the influence of his dear love on my heart which is always concerned with him. His image follows me everywhere; often when I am alone in my room with his letters I think he has entered. . . . Ah my dear sister this is my continual state; emerging from my mistake as from a dream I see him not, the father of my child; he is very far from me. This scene is often repeated and throws me into extreme melancholy.[59]

Life at Racedown was melancholy for William as well, permitting too much time for self-reflection. While Dorothy felt purposefully employed with the raising of Basil and domestic cares, William was troubled and listless. Dorothy wrote to Jane: "We are now surrounded by winter prospects without doors, and within have only winter occupations, books, solitude, and the fire-side, yet I may safely say we are never dull" (*EY*, p. 160). Wordsworth wrote sarcastically to Mathews:

Our present life is utterly barren of such events as merit even the shortlived chronicle of an accidental letter. We plant cabbages, and if retirement, in its full perfection, be as powerful in working transformations as one of Ovid's Gods, you may perhaps suspect that into cabbages we shall be transformed. Indeed I learn that such has been the prophecy of one of our London friends. . . . As to writing it is out of the question. Not however entirely to forget the world, I season my recollection of some of its objects with a little ill-nature, I attempt to write satires! and in all satires whatever the authors may say there will be found a spice of malignity.

(*EY*, p. 169)

The opening lines of the imitation of Juvenal he was now working on reveal that the malignity was at least partly self-directed:

But whence this gall this lengthened face of woe
We were no saints at twenty,—be it so
Yet happy they who in lifes later scene
Need only blush for what they once have been

Who pushed by thoughtless youth to deeds of shame
Mid such bad daring sought a cowards name
I grant that not in parents hearts alone
A striplings years may for his faults atone . . .
                    (*EY*, p. 172)

This seems to be saying that he was no saint in 1790-91, at the age of twenty, when he dismayed his family with touring rather than reading for his exams and then with returning to France to explore the extremes of irresponsibility in a love affair. Consequently, unlike others who were too cowardly to test the limits of social convention, he indeed must do more than blush: "Yet happy they who . . . [when] pushed [coerced?] by thoughtless youth [comrades?] to deeds of shame / Mid such bad daring sought a cowards name," that is, there were those who preferred to be called cowards rather than to commit bad deeds.

The Prelude depicts this period of Wordsworth's life as a time of inward suffering and relentless self-analysis that now found no relief in Godwinian rationalizing. Between two women, two children, two possible futures—no matter how remote one might seem—Wordsworth analyzed the forces that pulled him in opposition—passion, duty, love, and especially the chains of early and late responsibilities: to the dream of a dying youth; to the hopes of a lonely, unwed mother; to his daughter carrying the name of his mother Ann Wordsworth; and to his sister:

                    Thus I fared,
        Dragging all passions, notions, shapes of faith,
        Like culprits to the bar, suspiciously
        Calling the mind to establish in plain day
        Her titles and her honours, now believing,
        Now disbelieving, endlessly perplexed
        With impulse, motive, right and wrong, the ground
        Of moral obligation, . . .
                    (*Prelude*, Book X, ll. 888-95)

Personal and political motivations considered independently would have been baffling enough, but intertwined, they left the poet, "Sick, wearied out with contrarieties, / Yield[ing] up moral questions in despair" (*Prelude*, Book X, ll. 899-900). The spring of 1796 was the nadir, when Wordsworth was "dead / To deeper hope" (*Prelude*, Book XI, ll. 24-25).

Wordsworth's fulfilling his commitment to his sister thus appears to be the catalyst of his melancholia during the period from 1793 to the spring of 1796. When they finally had the home they desired, the home he had fancied for her in *Evening Walk,* the depression reached its lowest point, deepened by the letter(s) of Annette. It was indeed guilt that caused the depression, as Herbert Read once argued, rather than the inadequacies of Godwinism, as Ernest de Selincourt and Emile Legouis have claimed, or moral questions in the abstract as Mark Reed maintains, or the failure of the French Revolution, as Paul Sheats has suggested.[60] Read, however, did not get the framework of the depression correct. He imagines a young man who falls in love in a foreign land, returns home, and never quite forgets the excitement of his affair.[61] The model suggested here is of a man who leaves a trusting woman behind, has an affair abroad, with a woman much like his domestic love, and inevitably discovers that his first loyalty remains at home. That commitment to his home love having been fulfilled, his reward is guilt and growing ambivalence over the morality of his compulsive fidelity. Added to this was the possibility that he would do nothing to truly merit Calvert's legacy. Dorothy had drawn him away from critical obligations. It is hardly surprising that Wordsworth's poetic themes now focused on guilt, ambivalence, and abandonment, all of which would have to be resolved before he could begin afresh.

5. "Wherefore this repetition?"[62]

Wordsworth's experience with his sister begins to provide narrative direction and motivation for the revision of *Salisbury Plain* (*SP*), which Wordsworth undertook from September to November 1795 (*CEY,* p. 171), to make the new poem, *Adventures on Salisbury Plain* (*ASP*). Indeed, the differences between the Salisbury Plain poems derive from fairly specific biographical occurrences between the periods of their composition: diminishing the political context of *SP* to emphasize personal responsibility; attributing a murder for gain in *ASP* to the male protagonist; giving the male a wife he seeks to return to while drifting amicably with a Female Vagrant in the latter poem; idealizing the sibling relationship between brother and sister, also in *ASP*; and making the Female Vagrant the happier of the two, while the male is inconsolable for the murder.

The political context of *ASP* is minimized by the deletion of the frame of *SP*—the opening six stanzas and the concluding eleven—which had mounted a harangue against tyrants, superstition, monarchy, and other enemies of Reason. The Female Vagrant is still victimized by the American war, but the male traveler, now the discharged Sailor, is a fugitive from justice for robbery and unprovoked murder. The military's denial of his claim for compensation at the time of his discharge led to his robbing and killing; however, his victim was an innocent traveler, rather than one who might be guilty by some stretch of moral imagination. While Wordsworth wishes his reader to understand that brutality, mistreatment, and injustice provide a pretext for murder, he is not suggesting that war had inured the soldier to killing, for the soldier feels his guilt heavily, fainting three times when the memory of his deed is sparked either by the narration of the Female Vagrant or by events. As we will see more starkly presented in *The Borderers*, Wordsworth is precluding the use of mitigating circumstances to justify immoral and criminal behavior. The poet needs the soldier sympathetically judged to serve the purpose of relieving his own guilt, rather than excused.[63]

In *Salisbury Plain*, the Female Vagrant reveals the inadequacy of natural solace after she reaches the deep sorrow of the tale's conclusion. Following her soldier spouse to America, she lost children, husband, and sanity in the wake of war:

> "The pains and plagues that on our heads came down,
> Disease and Famine, Agony and Fear,
> In wood or wilderness, in camp or town,
> It would they brain unsettle even to hear.
> All perished, all in one remorseless year,
> Husband and children one by one, by sword
> And scourge of fiery fever; every tear
> Dried up, despairing, desolate, on board
> A British ship I waked as from a trance restored."
> (*SP*, ll. 316-24)

Returning to England, "Remote from man and storms of mortal care" (*SP*, l. 357), she experiences a sea-change that preserves her sanity: "Some mighty gulf of separation passed / I seemed transported to another world" (*SP*, ll. 370-71), her only desire now to rest and weep on the water, free of hopes for life. The vessel dashes her reverie when it reaches shore, and for three years she wanders with her eye fixed on the sun setting "Down to the land where hope to me was lost" (*SP*, l. 390). Her justifiable despair trivializes the sentimental absorption in nature's beauty the male earlier offered when glancing at the morning sun, for now "human sufferings and that tale of woe / Had dimmed the traveller's eye with Pity's tear" (*SP*, ll. 399-400).

Though the doleful events and conditions of the Female Vagrant's life are not revised away in *Adventures on Salisbury Plain,* she now becomes a consolation to the guilt-obsessed Sailor. Of course the later poem need not explain these important character changes, but evidence from the poems and from the biographical information adduced to this point make possible a reasonable explanation. One indicative change in the Female Vagrant's latter-narrative is using sibling relationship as the prototype for ideal conjugality. In *Salisbury Plain* not much is made of foundations for love; we learn only of immediate joy:

> "There was a youth whose tender voice and eye
> Might add fresh happiness to happiest days.
> At uprise of the sun when he was by
> The birds prolonged with joy their choicest lays,
> The soft pipe warbled out a wilder maze,
> The silent moon of evening, hung above,
> Showered through the waving lime-trees mellower rays;
> Warm was the breath of night: his voice of love
> Charmed the rude winds to sleep by river, field, or grove.
>   (*SP*, ll. 271-79)

In *Adventures on Salisbury Plain,* a sister's childhood love for a brother establishes her ideal for marital relationship:

> "There was a youth whom I had loved so long,
> That when I loved him not I cannot say.
> 'Mid the green mountains many and many a song
> We two had sung, like little birds in May.
> When we began to tire of childish play
> We seemed still more and more to prize each other:
> We talked of marriage and our marriage day;
> And I in truth did love him like a brother,
> For never could I hope to meet with such another.
>   (*ASP*, ll. 325-33)

It seems likely that Wordsworth is seeing his Female Vagrant through the prism of Dorothy's experience first at Windy Brow and now at Racedown, which is to say that Dorothy's life and feelings provide a model for the

Female Vagrant and her narrative. William's experience offers a similar model for the Sailor of *Adventures on Salisbury Plain*. The disconsolate nature of the earlier Female Vagrant and the plot of her life corresponds with Dorothy's early life: the Female Vagrant's loss of family and home represents Dorothy's loss of mother, father, brothers and home life; the Female's drifting afterwards is akin to Dorothy's drifting between relatives' homes; the Female's relationship with the male traveler is like William's return to Dorothy, including their fleeting time together at Windy Brow, where they roamed the landscape while the first Salisbury Plain poem was being composed;[64] the Female's dissatisfaction with natural solace reflected Dorothy's dissatisfaction that their lives were then still unsettled. Now, in *Adventures on Salisbury Plain*, the problems of the Female Vagrant remain the same, but they are diminished by her attitude; circumstances in Dorothy's life had improved at Racedown. The meaningful addition of the Sailor's guilt becomes the primary concern of the later narrative.

In *Adventures on Salisbury Plain*, it is the Female Vagrant who suggests the turn to nature after telling her tale, while the sailor remains disconsolate:

> "But come," she cried, "come after weary night
> Of such rough storm the breaking day to view."
> So forth he came and eastward look'd: the sight
> Into his heart a [   ] anguish threw;
> His wither'd cheek was ting'd with ashy hue.
> He stood and trembled both with grief and fear,
> But she felt new delight and solace new,
> And, from the opening east, a pensive chear
> Came to her weary thoughts while the lark warbled near.
> (*ASP*, ll. 568-576)

The Sailor's remorse is intense, and mingled with the obscurity of his crime. When he sees his house, anger at not being able to live out his fantasy of pouring money into his wife's apron causes him to murder a stranger. His domestic love and long-denied passion are forgotten in the moment. Here is the description of his fervid desire to return and the impulsive act that prevents it:

> For years the work of carnage did not cease,
> And Death's worst aspect daily he survey'd
> Death's minister: then came his glad release,
> And Hope returned and pleasure fondly made

Her dwelling in his dreams. By thought betray'd,
He seems to feel his wife around him throw
Her arms and she, this bloody prize of victory laid
In her full lap, forgets her years of woe
In the long joy and comfort from that wealth to flow.

He urged his claim; the slaves of Office spurn'd
The unfriended claimant; at their door he stood
In vain, and now towards his home return'd,
Bearing to those he loved nor warmth nor food,
In sight of his own house, in such a mood
That from his view his children might have run.
He met a traveller, robb'd him, shed his blood;
And when the miserable work was done
He fled, a vagrant since, the murderer's fate to shun.
                    (*ASP*, ll. 82-99)

Either the Sailor fails in character to remember to get the money to his wife, or the poet forgets that he should have, as the Sailor runs off to avoid execution. Later, when he meets the strife-torn family of a battered child, he identifies himself with the abusive father, and the child with the man he murdered:

[He] stroked the child, outstretch'd
His face to earth, and as the boy turn'd round
His batter'd head, a groan the Sailor fetch'd.
The head with streaming blood had dy'd the ground,
Flow'd from the spot where he that deadly wound
Had fix'd on him he murder'd. Through his brain
At once the griding iron passage found;
Deluge of tender thoughts then rush'd amain
Nor could his aged eyes from very tears abstain.
                    (*ASP*, ll. 640-648)

The Sailor's principal moment of relief comes when he admonishes the father for battering his child: "'Tis a bad world, and hard is the world's law; / Each prowls to strip his brother of his fleece" (*ASP*, ll. 658-59). He then offers a retrospect on the need to cherish family bonds: "Much need have ye that time more closely draw / The bond of nature, all unkindness cease, / And that among so few there still be peace / . . . / While his pale lips these homely truths disclose, / A correspondent calm stole gently on his woes"

(*ASP*, ll. 660-666). The Sailor is reunited with his wife on her deathbed. She recognizes his voice, he admits his guilt to cottagers, and is soon executed: "Blest be for once the stroke which ends, tho' late, / The pangs which from thy halls of terror came, / Thou who of Justice bear'st the violated name!" (*ASP*, ll. 817-19).

As in *Salisbury Plain*, Wordsworth selects narrative events for *Adventures on Salisbury Plain* that allow him to explore the sense of biographical experience. The Sailor's life now bears the same relationship to William as the Female Vagrant's life bears to Dorothy. The Sailor experiences separation from his wife due to war, Wordsworth experiences separation from Annette due to war; the Sailor is cheated of the money he wishes to present to his wife by his military superiors, Wordsworth is denied money for supporting Annette by his family; the Sailor develops a relationship with the drifting Female Vagrant on the way home to his wife, Wordsworth spends time with Dorothy, the true distraction from Annette; the Sailor robs and murders an innocent man on Salisbury Plain, which recalls the line, "Each prowls to strip his brother of his fleece," Wordsworth begins a journey-for-gain on Salisbury Plain with William Calvert and, later, impatiently awaits Raisley Calvert's early death to collect the promised legacy; the Sailor endangers his life to reach home, apparently without money, to part from his dying wife, just as Wordsworth endangers his life to return to Annette in France to permanently part. Finally, the poet accepts an imagined retribution through the execution of the Sailor.

It is difficult to be confident of the poet's consciousness of these general relationships between biography and narrative; if intended, *Adventures on Salisbury Plain* is a confessional allegory, similar to the later tale of Vaudracour and Julia. However, their emblematic imprecision and chronological disorder suggest that at least some of the narrative events are unconscious biographical correlatives serving psychological ends more effectively than aesthetic. For example, the narrative context of the Sailor's act of murder is ill-conceived: Why does he not simply rob his victim? Or why don't we learn why he had to kill the wealthy traveler? If the Sailor's goal is to provide money for his wife and children, why doesn't he get the money to them, especially since he is so near their home? While Alan Liu's recovery of historical documents on the relationship between war and crime shows that economically motivated crimes rose during periods of peace due to the unemployment of veterans,[65] we are trying to account here for a crime that transcends the economic and political motivation of an essentially good, very sentimental, man. However, our considering the act of murder as emblematic of death wishes against Raisley Calvert reveals the function and appropriateness of this flawed narrative. Wordsworth could not receive the £900 legacy he desperately needed without Raisley dying, therefore, concretizing his guilt required a murder rather than a simple robbery. Also, Wordsworth probably had to confront his lack of desire for returning to Annette now that he had the financial support of the Calvert legacy. Thus, the Sailor does not get his ill-gotten gold to his family despite the fact that the monetary purpose of his crime was to do just that.

6. "permanent, obscure and dark"[66]

Finally we reach the point where these strains of biography and early poetry culminate in imaginative combination. *The Borderers,* begun later in 1796 and completed in its first form by the spring of 1797, continues the plundering of early family experience to satisfy the psychological function of Wordsworth's art. Examining *The Borderers* from the same perspective as *Salisbury Plain* and *Adventures on Salisbury Plain,* we note a linear development of several themes. The function of institutional government, once so prominent in affecting the lives of characters, is here virtually absent, as Rivers makes clear in his wickedly ironic lines on the hopefulness of the play's political milieu: "Happy are we / Who live in these disputed tracts that own / No law but what each man makes for himself. / Here justice has indeed a field of triumph!"[67] The play continues with the theme of murder by featuring two characters guilty of homicide. Finally, natural therapy now carries a philosophical claim. As I suggested at the outset of Part One, *The Borderers* receives illumination when read in the light of the social psychology of Freud's *Totem and Taboo,* which writes large the Oedipal dilemma as the cornerstone of societal and group neurosis. This association is a fertile one, because Wordsworth explores social stress and group politics in terms of family organization, power, and dynamics. We will first examine the biographical connections and then consider Wordsworth's leap from personal to group dynamics as an example of the primitive politics that Freud described. We will see that Freud's anthropological speculations on tribal politics elicit a quite complete and yet parsimonious interpretation when compared with previous biographical and more recent New Historical readings of *The Borderers.*

As a document of biographical significance, *The Borderers* is generally read as a purgation, for after its composition (and the arrival of Coleridge) Wordsworth revived from depression and his "Great Decade" commenced; therefore, the arguments go, writing the play was therapeutic, although what needed purged changes from reader to reader. Oscar James Campbell and Paul Meuschke provide the classic statement on Annette's dramatic influence:

We believe that this drama offers clear evidence that its initial aesthetic impulse was the remorse that his abandonment of Annette had aroused in him. We believe that he endeavored to cleanse his mind from the paralyzing emotion by adopting the rational doctrines of Godwin, in the hope that they would emancipate his will from the control of his feelings. These theories failed him completely. . . . He began to see, therefore, that the natural ties and fundamental relations from which he had attempted to escape were more fundamental than the Godwinian rationalism to which he fled. They, therefore, became the facts upon which his new aesthetic was built.[68]

R. F. Storch finds the play an expulsion of psychic energy that "beats to the very pulse of its times," because it "holds the intellectual cross-currents of the age in a solution of moral passion." Its achievement is a comprehensive, anthropological representation of its historical moment, including the motivational darkness underlying its politics. In this attempt to provide cultural catharsis for his generation, "Wordsworth's was the first poetic imagination to work through rebellion, guilt and despondency in order to reassert the possibility of hope and joy."[69] Erdman provides an extension of Storch's argument in focusing more exclusively on the politics of purgation, though his poet is in thoughtful control of his senses and emotions as he looks retrospectively on his (and France's) political aggressions:

> The Borderers, offered as a sacrifice on the altar of peace with France, did succeed as a purgation, for some years at least, of Wordsworth's warlike spirit. It dispelled the bad dreams of unjust tribunals that had succeeded to the sublime "senselessness of joy." There is no brandishing of swords in the Lyrical Ballads.[70]

Finally, Thomas McFarland continues to place the play in the broadest biocultural context, agreeing with Erdman that "The Borderers was written precisely to purge the moral perplexities engendered by the Revolution. . . . In simplest terms, The Borderers, as a vehicle for expelling the anti-humane philosophy of Rivers, almost had to be written if Wordsworth were to become a great poet."[71]

The argument I will advance is uncertain of the happy endings of purgative readings; to wit, that after purgation, genius flourished; or that there is a causal connection between the aesthetic failure that is The Borderers and the poems of the next decade. The issue of aesthetic failure or at least the cause of the oddities and improbabilities that blemish the characterization and action of the play is of importance in itself for understanding the complete bio-aesthetic moment of 1797-98. In the analysis that follows, I will build on the New Historical reading of Alan Liu because I think its interest in family relations and dynamics is correct. However, I will try to show that a clearer understanding of Wordsworth's biographical and psychological dilemmas provide a more satisfactory explanation for the play's strange turns and improbabilities than do Liu's broader historical determinants.

Liu's reading of *The Borderers* in *Wordsworth: The Sense of History* argues that "poetic criminality [in *The Borderers* is] in excess of [contemporary] criminal history" (Liu, p. 226), because "crime [becomes] a projection of the excess that is the family" (Liu, p. 220). Liu argues that Mortimer's overreaction to Herbert's alleged pandering in a pre-text or pre-plot the poet never got "right" (Liu, p. 235) is an unconscious response to threatened family and social values that had permitted Mortimer to distance himself from the behavior of the Other—the poor, the disenfranchised, the infanticidal population of paupers—to whom he felt himself superior. To put it another way, Mortimer is crushed by a threat to the structure of the idealized family in witnessing love becoming a commodity:

> the case of Herbert seems to show, "love" for one's daughter . . . becomes interchangeable with acquisition and profit, custodianship with attention to the bottom line. Love, in short, is cupidity. . . . Whether or not we conceive Clifford to be Matilda's actual father, the imputed wish of Herbert (as her stepfather) to sell her services to the voluptuary comes near to being sexual abuse in its own right. In the end, therefore . . . that exchange fascinates Mortimer so horribly because it is the economic imagination of a perversion equivalent in structural significance to incest (as Levi-Strauss conceives it): exchange makes the middle-class nuclear family, in a sinister inversion of caritas, love its brothers, sisters, sons, or daughters as it loves others. (Liu, p. 272)

Liu concludes: "What legitimacy of family identity can there be if—as the case of Matilda seems to prove—any middle-class family member can be shown at any time to have been changed (like one coin for another) with the uncanny other: the illegitimate poor?" (Liu, p. 274).

I cannot say that I object or disagree with Liu on the grounds that David Perkins introduces, to wit, that Liu's method is self-contradictory, because "the principle of contextual explanation is . . . applied to Wordsworth's texts but not to the texts by which Wordsworth is interpreted."[72] Rather, I find the real limitation of Liu's approach to be his choice of exchange theory to explain behavioral excess and his own dramatic misreading of Wordsworth's self-awareness. In arguing that Mortimer is overcome with surprise that family members can treat one another as a commodity or that the family as an institution of natural love is a fiction, Liu implies that the poet's artistic sense falters as he confronts the demystification he discovers in composition. However, Wordsworth and his contemporaries were no strangers to familial demystification.

As we have already seen, Godwin's rationalism provided a strong attack on the nuclear family and the traditional moral values associated with heterosexual relationships. There is no reason to believe that Wordsworth failed to understand this. He defended leaving his mistress and child in France to find financial support, thus, verily exchanging intimacy for gain. He had nursed Raisley Calvert for financial gain. Financial gain becomes a staple of family relationships explored in his poetry. Robert of *Ruined Cottage* will leave Margaret for an enlistment bonus and, as Michael H. Friedman observes, the shepherd of "Last of the Flock" associates the rise and fall of family love with the fate of his livestock:

> Sir! 'twas a precious flock to me,
> As dear as my own children be;
> For daily with my growing store
> I loved my children more and more.
> Alas! it was an evil time;
> God cursed my in my sore distress,
> I prayed, yet every day I thought
> I loved my children less. . . .[73]

Finally, *Michael* will explore the economic foundation of traditional family values most powerfully.

Dismissing, then, the speculation that some real or supposed shock disoriented Wordsworth's aesthetic sense, we will read *The Borderers* as an attempt to deal with the events, passions, fears, fantasies, disappointments, mysteries, and unspoken desires of the family psychodrama developed above. We will find it coherent to support character correspondences between Dorothy and the play's heroine, Matilda, rather than between Annette and Matilda; between Wordsworth and Mortimer/Rivers, rather than between Wordsworth and only one of the two; between Baron Herbert and John Wordsworth, the father; and then between a series of biographical events and narrative complications, such as Mortimer's vague responsibility for Herbert's dying of exposure, which is parallel to Wordsworth's guilt over his father's death.

Considering the play in light of biographical matters described to this point, we will find some logic and purpose in the following turns of plot and characterization:

1. That Mortimer should be attracted to Herbert as a father—in fact, textual evidence indicates that Mortimer imagines he may be Herbert's missing son, and thus Matilda's brother;

2. That Herbert gave Matilda to another to raise after the death of his wife;

3. That Mortimer should be vulnerable to Rivers's ruse that Herbert was now planning his daughter's abandonment though he had just reclaimed her as the solace of his old age;

4. That Mortimer in an act of retributive justice should abandon Herbert to die of exposure, but in a manner that leaves responsibility for and cause of death both doubtful;

5. That Mortimer should fail to display any semblance of a normal heterosexual relationship with Matilda, several times wishing that she were dead for putting him in the predicament of punishing Herbert on her behalf and for teasing him with the fantasy that she might be sexually involved with a more exciting lover.

Each of these will be addressed before we consider the larger, equally difficult, political issues suggested by *Totem and Taboo*.

The filial attraction Mortimer feels towards Herbert is dependent partly on Matilda's pride in her father's life and virtues, partly on the physical semblance between father and daughter, and partly on undefined attractions and needs. Prior to the play's action, Mortimer had never seen Herbert, and Matilda herself has only in the past six months been reunited with her father since early childhood. Because Herbert was struck blind in his successful attempt to save Matilda from their burning home during the siege of Antioch in 1098, it was necessary for him to pass her off to a stranger for rearing, for his wife had died in the siege as well. Now that Matilda is in her late teens or early twenties, the aged Herbert feeling the approach of death has taken Matilda from her foster mother to be his solace. Significant details of the domestic tragedy that separated them include, besides the death of his wife, the questionable fate of an infant brother, who was being held by the mother at her death:

> *Herb*: Thy mother too—scarce had I gained the door—
> I caught her voice, she threw herself upon me,
> I felt thy infant brother in her arms,
> She saw my blasted face—a tide of soldiers
> That instant rushed between us, and I heard
> Her last death-shriek, distinct among a thousand.
>   (*The Borderers*, Act, I, Scene i, ll. 150-55)

Wordsworth's curious omission of the fate of the infant brother, from the earliest to the latest texts, allows Mortimer to develop the fantasy that he may be the missing son. The text of the Late Version (1842) of the play reads identically with the Early Version,[74] leading one to believe that Wordsworth intended to allow for the psychological association.[75]

Apparently an orphan from an early age, Mortimer believes that his affection for Herbert derives from Matilda's stories and his imagining what a father would be like:

> *Mort*: Though I have never seen his face, methinks,
> There cannot be a time when I shall cease
> To love him.—I remember, when a Boy
> Of six years' growth or younger, by the thorn
> Which starts from the old church-yard wall of Lorton,
> It was my joy to sit and hear Matilda
> Repeat her father's terrible adventures
> Till all the band of play-mates wept together,
> And that was the beginning of my love.
> And afterwards, when we conversed together
> This old man's image still was present: chiefly
> When I had been most happy.
>   (Act I, Scene i, ll. 60-71)

How Mortimer could have an image of a man he had never seen is left unexplained. Later on the heath, when he is about to abandon Herbert to die, Mortimer says again that Herbert looks as he had always imagined a father would: "Even such a man my fancy bodied forth / From the first moment that I loved the maid" (Act III, Scene iii, ll. 64-65). Part of this Platonic paternal image thus seems derived from a transformation of Matilda's appearance. In this same speech, Mortimer says he hears "a vein of [Matilda's] voice that runs through [Herbert's]" (Act III, Scene iii, l. 63); earlier, Herbert's facial resemblance to Matilda had thwarted Mortimer's attempt to slay him sleeping in the cave: "There was something in his face the very counterpart of Matilda" (Act II, Scene iii, l. 272). Again:

> *Mort:* 'Twas dark, dark as hell—yet I saw him—I tell thee I saw him, his face towards me—the very looks of Matilda sent there by some fiend to baffle me.—It put me to my prayers—I cast my eyes upwards, and through a device in the roof I beheld a star twinkling over my head, and by the living God, I could not do it—
>
> (Act II, Scene iii, ll. 287-91).

Mortimer's displaced love for Matilda, with whom he had grown up, prevents the murder in this scene; however, the flash of Herbert's face in a cave of total darkness suggests an hallucinatory image. (Could it be a traumatic memory of the fire flashing in Herbert's face at the blaze of Antioch?) Mortimer's response also suggests a primal love for Herbert that cannot be explained or dismissed:

> *Mort:* Is not the depth
> Of this man's crimes beyond the reach of thought?
> And yet in plumbing the abyss of vengeance
> Something I strike upon which turns my thoughts
> Back upon myself—I think again—my breast
> Concenters all the terrors of the universe,
> I look at him and tremble like a child—
>
> (Act II, Scene iii, ll. 59-65)

The effect is much the same when the act of justice—or vengeance—is attempted: "Twice did I spring to grasp his withered throat, / When such a sudden weakness fell upon me / I could have dropped asleep upon his breast" (Act II, Scene iii, ll. 196-98). Wordsworth's borrowing from Shakespeare's *Macbeth* is much to the point here. Lady Macbeth uses the same excuse when she is unable to kill Duncan the King in his sleep: "Had he not resembled / My father as he slept, I had done't."[76] The childlike reactions that Herbert provokes in Mortimer—the trembling as a child, the protective sleep—suggest a filial love that finally becomes an observed fact. Robert, the cottager who spoke with Herbert on the heath just prior to his death, hears and senses in Mortimer's concern the love of a son:

Mort: Well, well, he lives.
Oh God! He lives! What said he?

Robt: He only spake to me of a dear daughter
Who, so he feared, would never see him more,
And of a stranger to him, one by whom
He had been sore misused.—But you are troubled:
Perhaps you are his son?
                              (Act V, Scene ii, ll. 34-40)

Mortimer responds, "Heaven knows / I did not think he had a living child" (Act V, Scene ii, ll. 41-42), meaning that Rivers's "proofs" convinced him that Herbert was not Matilda's father, yet his vagueness suggests something more. "I did not think he had a *living* child" calls to mind the missing son of Antioch, unmentioned and forgotten in the father's overriding concern for his daughter, and a mysterious boy-child that Herbert will later thoughtfully reject.[77]

Herbert's overt rejection of a male border-figure[78] inspires Mortimer to consider abandonment the ideal mode of execution in that the punishment is equivalent to the crime of abandoning his son. Recalling his condition upon learning of his usurped lands, Herbert describes an encounter with an angelic boy:

Herb: Like a Mendicant
Whom no one comes to meet, I stood alone.
I murmured, but remembering him who feeds
The pelican and ostrich of the Desert,
From my own threshold I looked up to heaven,
And did not want glimmerings of quiet hope;
So from the court I passed and down the brook,
Led by its murmur, to the ancient oak
I came, and when I felt its cooling shade,
I sat me down and cannot but believe—
While in my lap I held my little babe
And clasped her to my heart—my heart that ached
More with delight than grief—I heard a voice
Such as by Cherith of Elijah called;
It said, "I will be with thee." A little boy
A shepherd's lad, ere yet my trance was gone,
Hailed us, as if he had been sent from heaven,
And said with tears that he would be our guide;
I had a better guide—that innocent babe

Who to this hour hath saved me from all evil,
From cold, from death, from penury and hunger.
Therefore I bless her: when I think of man
I bless her with sad spirit; when of God,
I bless her in the fulness of my joy!

                    (Act III, Scene iii, ll. 92-115)

Mortimer responds with a complementary religious insight into his mission to provide Herbert's appropriate end:

Mort: It dawns on me—I see the end for which
An arm invisible hath led me hither.—
He heard a voice—a shepherd's lad came
And was his guide—if once—why not again?
And in this desert? If never, then is he damned
Beyond a madman's dream!—Here will I leave him,
Here where no foot of man is found, no ear
Can hear his cries—it is a fearful ordeal!
But God is everywhere.

                    (Act III, Scene iii, ll. 122-130)

The slaying of Herbert, which was to have been an act of frontier justice befitting a wretched panderer, here becomes laden with obscure associations and motivations that suggest as much about Mortimer as about Herbert. Mortimer's implicit message to Herbert is, "You deserve to be abandoned for the deafening silence about your son and for then rejecting the help of the child who should have reminded you of your son. I, who either am or wish to be your son, despise you for it and intend to be avenged."

The vengeance is passive and awkwardly planned. Mortimer abandons Herbert on the heath and somehow forgets to leave Herbert some food, which he will believe to be of great consequence when he changes heart. Later, in a scene of dramatic irony reminiscent of the angelic boy, Robert, a once-imprisoned cottager, leaves Herbert to die fearing that he might be blamed for murder if be brings home a dead man. Mortimer misses the irony, but he does associate Robert's functional existence with the boy's: "I believe that there are beings / For unknown ends permitted to put on / The shape of man, and thou art one of them" (Act V, Scene ii, ll. 51-53). Robert offers evidence on Mortimer's behalf—"The old man died of cold— / You are not master of the elements. It was a bitter night—I was half-frozen" (Act V, Scene iii, ll. 189-91)—but without avail:

Mort: I will go forth a wanderer on the earth,
A shadowy thing, and as I wander on
No human ear shall ever hear my voice,
No human dwelling ever give me food
Or sleep or rest, and all the uncertain way
Shall be as darkness to me, as a waste
Unnamed by man! and I will wander on
Living by mere intensity of thought,
A thing by pain and thought compelled to live,
Yet loathing life, till heaven in mercy strike me
With blank forgetfulness—that I may die.
                    (Act V, Scene iii, ll. 265-75)

Many biographical details of the Wordsworth family are associated with Herbert's life and death. The absence of a mother and wife is dramatically inert, though the killing of Herbert's wife, with their son in her arms, relates to the early death of Ann Wordsworth. On the other hand, the lacuna of reference to that missing son does have dramatic consequence. Herbert's giving of his beloved daughter to another for rearing, and his dismissal of his son from memory, suggests John Wordsworth's breaking up of household following his wife's death, sending Dorothy to live with relatives for a decade, and packing off his sons for school at Hawkshead. Herbert's unjust loss of property suggests Lord Lonsdale's refusal to pay John Wordsworth and later his estate money owed for legal services. Herbert's death from exposure on the heath has its counterpart in the death of John Wordsworth after a night's exposure to a winter storm on the fells. The unconscious guilt that Wordsworth felt for his father's death is reflected in Mortimer's vaguely established guilt for the death of Herbert. Recalling the freedom and mischief-making Wordsworth associates with his youth in *The Prelude* and being aware of his sources for the landscape of the play's action, we might identify the lawless heath of Mortimer and company with the valleys and fells of *Prelude*'s ministry of fear from Book I, which also concludes in its 1799 form with the "spot of time" on the death of John Wordsworth.[79]

But Herbert is primarily the first paternal border figure of Words-worth's imagination,[80] whose presence as a character bespeaks an imagined return of the father, as if the poet were provoked to ask, What would happen if father *now* returned? How would he act towards us? But the central question is ours, the reader's, rather than the poet's: Why would Wordsworth imagine his father's return at this time? As Michael H. Friedman argues, *The Borderers* is almost entirely a play about fatherhood: "not only is Herbert an emblem of paternity, but he is an emblem of the traditional moral and social order as well."[81] But what does this mean for the family romance? I think that the play suggests most strongly that the motivation of the father's return would be to prevent brother-sister incest, for Herbert's late paternal claim upon Matilda's love is the only effective hindrance to her marrying Mortimer.[82]

Yet the romance of Matilda and Mortimer is also frustrated for reasons that suggest something other than Oedipal complications. Wordsworth's ambivalence towards Dorothy for being, like Matilda, the unwitting cause of his irresponsible behavior towards others is vented in Mortimer's aggression towards Matilda, but the physical discomfort Mortimer feels towards Matilda is more perplexing. Of course, if Mortimer identifies himself as Matilda's brother, as he seems to in recounting their developing relationship from childhood, we can expect narrative complications to prevent incest. But Mortimer is also fearful of a competing lover:

> *Rivers*: Last night
> When I returned with water from the torrent
> I overheard the villains.—Every word
> Like red hot iron burnt into my heart.
> Said one "It is agreed on.—The blind man
> "Shall feign a sudden illness—and the girl
> "Who on her journey must proceed alone,
> "Under pretence of violence be seized—
> "She is"—continued the detested slave,
> "She is right willing—A fool if she were not:
> "They say Lord Clifford is a savage man,
> "But faith! to see him in his silken tunic
> "Fitting his low voice to the minstrel's harp,
> "There's *witchery* in't. I never knew a maid
> "That could withstand it. True," continued he,
> "When we arrang'd the affair she wept a little
> "(Not the less welcome to my Lord for that),
> "And said, `my Father, he will have it so.'"
> (Act III, Scene ii, ll. 39-56; my italics)

Sexual jealousy becomes the unfailing hook that Rivers uses on Mortimer when he drifts from vengeful desires to sympathy for Herbert. The progress of the sexual theme leads from fear for Matilda, whom Clifford would abuse and abandon as he had other women (Act I, Scene iii, ll. 5-22); to this suspicion that she may enjoy her sexual fate (Act III, Scene ii, ll. 39-56); to

Mortimer's conviction that she loves Clifford (Act III, Scene iii, ll. 12-14); and, in fact, has already succumbed to lust:

> *Mort*: She smell'd most sweet and she was fair—and now
> They have snapped her from the stem.—Poh! let her lie
> Besoil'd with the mire, and let the houseless snail
> Feed on her leaves—you knew her well—ay there,
> Old man! you were a very lynx, you knew
> The worm was in her—
> (Act III, Scene iii, ll. 52-57)

Yet, on his first exchange of words with Matilda, Mortimer becomes immediately convinced of her innocence (Act III, Scene v, ll. 140ff). Although she has done nothing to provoke his jealousy, Matilda inevitably receives the blame of an insecure man: "The fault's not mine," Mortimer says to himself, "If she had never lived I had not done it" (Act V, Scene iii, ll. 38-39). With Matilda in his arms, he says, "—Oh, would—that thou had'st perished in the flames—" (Act V, Scene iii, l. 84), of course, with their mother.

Although the dramatic point of the play's sexual rivalry is clear, we might well question the awkwardness of its execution as well as its biographical relevance to a thesis on the father's return to prevent the incest of his children. Indeed, the sexual theme seems to undermine the biographical equivalency between Dorothy and Matilda, for would we not expect that Mortimer/Wordsworth would fear his own inclination to incest more than the threat of another lover? Unless, of course, there were some reason for thinking that Dorothy had an extrafamilial romance or infatuation at Racedown that the play also was confronting.

The arrival of Coleridge during the play's composition comes to mind. Dorothy immediately was enamored of Coleridge's brilliance. She shared with Mary Hutchinson, her female confidant, her attraction to Coleridge's wildish physical presence. She also found in Coleridge the sensitivity that earlier made William so marvelous in her eyes ("I must be blind, he cannot be so pleasing as my fondness makes him"):

> You had a great loss in not seeing Coleridge. He is a wonderful man. His conversation teems with soul, mind, and spirit. Then he is so benevolent, so good tempered and cheerful, and, like William, interests himself so much about every little trifle. At first I thought him very plain, that is, for about three minutes: he is pale and thin, has a wide

mouth, thick lips, and not very good teeth, longish loose-growing half-curling rough black hair. But if you hear him speak for five minutes you think no more of them. His eye is large and full, not dark but grey; such an eye as would receive from a heavy soul the dullest expression; but it speaks every emotion of his animated mind; it has more of the 'poet's eye in a fine frenzy rolling' than I ever witnessed. He has fine dark eyebrows, and an overhanging forehead. (*EY*, pp. 188-89)

In terms of Theseus's speech that Dorothy quotes from *A Midsummer Night's Dream*, she is describing a lover (like William) and a frenzied poet: "The lunatic, the lover, and the poet / Are of imagination all compact" (*A Midsummer Night's Dream*, Act V, Scene i, ll. 7-8). Though Dorothy records that Coleridge read only *Osorio* in response to William's *Ruined Cottage* during his first visit to Racedown, it would not be difficult to imagine Dorothy's delight when Coleridge finally read his favorite poem, "The Eolian Harp." How joyful it would seem after William's bleak narratives of abandoned women and *Incipient Madness* to hear Coleridge romantically recite:

> And that simplest Lute,
> Placed length-ways in the clasping casement, hark!
> How by the desultory breeze caress'd,
> Like some coy maid half yielding to her lover,
> It pours such sweet upbraiding, as must needs
> Tempt to repeat the wrong! And now its strings
> Boldlier swept, the long sequacious notes
> Over delicious surges sink and rise,
> Such a soft floating *witchery* of sound
> As twilight Elfins make, when they at eve
> Voyage on gentle gales from Fairy-Land,
> Where Melodies round honey-dropping flowers,
> Footless and wild, like birds of Paradise,
> Nor pause, nor perch, hovering on untam'd wing!
> (*CPW*, pp. 100-101, 11. 13-25; my italics)

Surely Dorothy would have felt the "witchery in't," just as Rivers had alleged of Matilda. To judge from Mary (Perdita) Robinson's poetic reaction to Coleridge's reading of "Kubla Khan" in 1800, "witchery" was a term that attached to the young Coleridge's performance of his verse. Writing as his amorous, adoring Sappho, Robinson imagines traveling with Coleridge through the landscape of his "new Paradise extended":

And now, with lofty tones inviting,
Thy NYMPH, her dulcimer swift smiting,
Shall wake me in ecstatic measures!
Far, far remov'd from mortal pleasures!
    In cadence rich, in cadence strong,
Proving the wondrous witcheries of song!
    I hear her voice! thy *sunny dome,*
Thy *caves of ice,* loud repeat,
Vibrations, madd'ning sweet,
    Calling the visionary wand'rer home.
She sings of THEE, O favour'd child
Of *Minstrelsy,* SUBLIMELY WILD!
Of thee, whose soul can feel the tone
Which gives to airy dreams *a magic* ALL THY OWN!
        SAPPHO[83]

Besides falling for Coleridge's romantic dazzle, Dorothy Wordsworth undoubtedly felt a more substantial attraction to Coleridge for his appreciation
of her intellect, sensibility, and taste. "Wordsworth & his exquisite Sister are
with me," he wrote to his publisher Joseph Cottle soon after meeting the
Wordsworths:

> She is a woman indeed!—in mind, I mean, & heart—for her person is
> such, that if you expected to see a pretty woman, you would think her
> ordinary—if you expected to find an ordinary woman, you would think
> her pretty!—But her manners are simple, ardent, impressive—.
>
> > In every motion her most innocent soul
> > Outbeams so brightly, that who saw would say,
> > Guilt was a thing impossible in her.—
>
> Her information various—her eye watchful in minutest observation of
> nature—and her taste a perfect electrometer—it bends, protrudes, and
> draws in, at subtlest beauties & most recondite faults. (*STCL,* Vol, I, pp.
> 330-31)

Such adulation for Dorothy's taste and critical sensibility is matchless.
Judging from Dorothy's lament over the stifled talent of her youth and from
her earlier criticism of William for not appreciating her critical faculties on
compositional matters, there is good reason to believe that Dorothy would

have been nigh overwhelmed by the extraordinary appreciation and attention of this brilliant, exciting man and poet.

The compositional history of *The Borderers* allows for the conjecture
that Clifford may have been Coleridge's shadow, for Rivers's sexual
temptation of Mortimer seems to have been written after June 1797, the
month of Coleridge's first visit to the Wordsworths and Dorothy's letter.[84]
Of course, the speculation that Matilda was untrue is as unfounded, and
finally as silly, as male sexual jealousy can make it. Mortimer implicitly
acknowledges the nonsense of it the moment he sees Matilda. However,
the irrationality of male insecurity does not discount its functional value
in art, as *Othello* and *The Winter's Tale* reveal even more radically than *The
Borderers*, nor any less in life. In other words, it is not unlikely that
Wordsworth would feel both jealous and annoyed over Dorothy's attraction to Coleridge after he had sacrificed so much on her behalf. It is
interesting that his hero-surrogate would so readily believe that Matilda's
father would prefer Clifford's lechery to the well-intentioned romancing
of a noble young man, but here the subtext of incest finally helps to make
sense of Mortimer's nonsense. Of course, the Lord Clifford ruse belongs
to Rivers, an alter ego who tempts Mortimer successfully because he shares
his victim's weaknesses, which leads us to the final and most troublesome
question of *The Borderers*: What is the psychological relationship of Mortimer to Rivers?

It is commonly observed that the characters of Rivers and Mortimer
reflect biographical and/or historical reality.[85] Certainly, Wordsworth's
psychological analysis of Rivers in his prefatory essay to the play seems, as
Mary Moorman has stated, at last a partial self-reflection of young Wordsworth:

> Let us suppose a young Man of great intellectual powers, yet without
> any solid principles of genuine benevolence. His master passions are
> pride and the love of distinction. He has deeply imbibed a spirit of
> enterprize in a tumultuous age. He goes into the world and is betrayed
> into a great crime.
>
>   That influence on which all his happiness is built immediately
> deserts him. His talents are robbed of their weight; his exertions are
> unavailing, and he quits the world in disgust, with strong misanthropic
> feelings. In his retirement, he is impelled to examine the reasonableness
> of established opinions and the force of his mind exhausts itself in
> constant efforts to separate the elements of virtue and vice. . . . While
> the general exertion of his intellect seduces him from the remembrance

of his own crime, the particular conclusions to which he is led have a tendency to reconcile him to himself. His feelings are interested in making him a moral sceptic and as his scepticism increases he is raised in his own esteem.

(The Borderers, pp. 62-63)

Corroboration for Wordsworth experiencing a similar state of mind is found in The Prelude, as we have noted above.[86] There is also Godwin's contention that, in 1795, he converted Wordsworth "from the doctrine of self-love to that of benevolence" (CEY, p. 164).[87] Wordsworth openly identified with Mortimer's sentiments by first publishing "The Convict" in The Morning Post under the pseudonym of Mortimer. At the time, December 1797, he was in London seeking to have his play staged.[88] When Mortimer unknowingly reenacts Rivers's crime through his abandonment of Herbert on the heath, the identities of the young men converge in a vortex of fatal biographical and dramatic redundancies.

Mortimer's confrontation of Rivers following his abandonment of Herbert reads as a fascinating piece of self-analysis and absolution, as if Mortimer/Wordsworth were talking to a past self with understanding and love, and Rivers/Wordsworth were speaking his lonely heart for the first time to the only being he had ever befriended. The following speech of Rivers recalls the solitariness Wordsworth sought in the Evening Walk of his youth:

Rivers: Oft I left the camp
When all that multitude of hearts was still
And followed on through woods of gloomy cedar
Into deep chasms troubled by roaring streams,
Or from the top of Lebanon surveyed
The moonlight desart and the moonlight sea;
In these my lonely wanderings I perceived
What mighty objects do impress their forms
To build up this our intellectual being,
And felt if aught on earth deserved a curse,
'Twas that worst principle of ill that dooms
A thing so great to perish self-consumed.
—So much for my remorse.

Mort: Oh, my poor friend!
By all that thou hast suffered doubly dear—

Rivers: When from these forms I turned to contemplate
The opinions and the uses of the world,
I seemed a being who had passed alone
Beyond the visible barriers of the world
And travelled into things to come.

Mort: Poor wretch!
My heart aches for thee.

Rivers: . . . I now perceived
That we are praised by men because they see in us
The image of themselves; that a great mind
Outruns its age and is pursued with obliquy
Because its movements are not understood.
I felt that to be truly the world's friend,
We must become the object of its hate.

Mort: I can forgive you.
(Act IV, Scene ii, ll. 127-158)

Besides forgiving, Mortimer later says he loves Rivers, and welcomes taking
on the suffering of both. It is in this rare moment of intimacy, when Rivers's
malign machinations are at rest, that we feel the true bond of sympathy
between the antagonist and protagonist. They do indeed come together in
unwitting weakness, as Alan Richardson argues in his Hegelian reading of
their relationship,[89] but for a moment each character transcends the irony
of the play's plot with care and sincerity.

It is here that I would like to introduce Freud's reflections from *Totem
and Taboo*, particularly those on the unholy alliance of brothers in collusion
against their father for his hegemony over the women of the primitive
tribe.[90]

Freud argues that totemism is the source of the deepest laws of
civilization against patricide and incest. His historical speculation on the
origin of totemism argues that brothers of the tribe banded against the
tyranny of the father over tribal women. After killing the patriarch, they
exulted in their successful vengeance and simultaneously expressed their
desire to be like the father by either literally or figuratively incorporating
him, but then guilt, remorse, ambivalence and good sense caused them to
do two things: refuse to install another as a father figure and refuse to take
the father's women. Thus fraternal rule prevailed as a primitive democracy

and religious ceremony came to center upon commemorative sacrifice of the totem, communion, rigid laws against incest and patricide, and pervasive, controlling guilt:

> They hated their father, who presented such a formidable obstacle to their craving for power and their sexual desires; but they loved and admired him too. After they had got rid of him, had satisfied their hatred and had put into effect their wish to identify themselves with him, the affection which had all this time been pushed under was bound to make itself felt. It did so in the forms of remorse. A sense of guilt made its appearance, which in this instance coincided with the remorse felt by the whole group. The dead father became stronger than the living one had been. . . . They revoked their deed by forbidding the killing of the totem, the substitute for their father; and they renounced its fruits by resigning their claim to the women who had now been set free. They thus created out of their filial sense of guilt the two fundamental taboos of totemism, which for that very reason inevitably corresponded to the two repressed wishes of the Oedipus complex.

Out of the ashes of murder and sacrifice, the psychology of primal democracy was born:

> Though the brothers had banded together in order to overcome their father, they were all one another's rivals in regard to the women. Each of them would have wished, like his father, to have all the women to himself. The new organization would have collapsed in a struggle of all against all, for none of them was of such over-mastering strength as to be able to take on his father's part with success. Thus the brothers had no alternative, if they were to live together, but . . . to institute the law against incest, by which they all alike renounced the women whom they desired and who had been their chief motive for dispatching their father.[91]

Prior to the play's dramatic action, Rivers assaulted and abandoned his sea-captain on a deserted island after being provoked by the crew to do it, thereby functioning as the vengeful hand of the primal horde in executing a father-figure. Rivers then renounced his right to the father's daughter, with whom he had a loving relationship (Act IV, Scene ii, ll. 80-91). As the ceremonial and symbolic extension of Freud's psychology anticipates, Rivers now seeks an outlet for his guilt and suppressed remorse in a sacrifice that must represent repetition of his patricide down to the nicest commemorative detail. Rivers's victim starved to death on a deserted island; thus, Mortimer recalls the action of Rivers by forgetting to leave Herbert a bag of food on a deserted heath. Mortimer's oversight is not improbable, but it is practically meaningless and morally preposterous, for no one would starve to death overnight, and even if Herbert had a small bag of food, how long would it last?[92] Inasmuch as the pathetic Herbert, as a blind father on the heath, recalls the blinded and even more pathetic Gloucester on the heath, Wordsworth the poet surely would not make the mistake of having his geriatric die of starvation for not eating during the night. The ceremonial relevance of the missing food, however, is absolutely essential and perfect.

The allusion to *King Lear* is worth exploring as well for the corroboration it provides of the implied relationship between Mortimer and Herbert. Critics have been wont to identify Herbert with Lear because they both are the fathers of a caring daughter.[93] But Herbert has none of Lear's magnificence, and he especially lacks the affective power displayed by Lear on the stormy heath. Rather, Herbert is comparable to Gloucester. He shares the blindness and the pathos of Gloucester, unknowingly being lead about by his mad and disguised son Edgar on the heath, just as Herbert is being led about by the deranged Mortimer, his probable son, on the heath. Gloucester's description of his painful situation is as apt for Herbert's: "'Tis the time's plague, when madmen lead the blind" (*King Lear*, Act IV, Scene i, l. 46).

To state River's motivation now more comprehensively: he has a need to express remorse through the repetition of sacrifice and he arranges that sacrifice in a setting where he senses incest. He himself prepares the way for the sacrifice of Herbert with another dramatically senseless act, the killing of Herbert's dog, which becomes meaningful, however, if the dog is seen as totemic. The following speech of Mortimer intriguingly associates the dog with its master:

> *Mort*: You are sure that dog of his
> Could not come after us—he must have perished—
> The torrent would have dashed an oak to splinters—
> You said that you did not like his looks—that he
> Would trouble us; if he were here again
> I swear the sight of him would quail me more
> Than twenty armies.
>
> (Act II, Scene iii, ll. 34-40)

As the Freudian totem, the father's dog embodies the affective power of the father against the combined force of his sons, Mortimer's "twenty armies."

Mortimer makes the association, but remains unknowing of the action's symbolic power and its influence over his coming, equally senseless aggression against Herbert:

> *Mort*: You should not, Rivers,
> Have hurled the innocent animal from the precipice,
> You should not—there was no occasion for it—
>   (Act II, Scene iii, ll. 43-45)

If executing the dog is Rivers's token of the sacrifice of Herbert, Mortimer himself must commit the literal deed.

The unconscious motivation of Rivers's dramatic action has been to dismantle Mortimer's romantic relationship with Matilda to prevent sibling incest. To do so with complete psychological force, Mortimer must be duped into killing the father in order to rediscover the force of civilization's primal guilt for his band of brothers, the borderers. Rivers has become a true brother to Mortimer, in Freud's sense, by teaching Mortimer the function of brother-leaders on the borderland of history and civilization. But to what larger end?

As we reviewed above, political readings of *The Borderers* inevitably associate the play with Wordsworth's reaction to the French Revolution. This historical connection holds here as well, because the play explores the psychodynamics of the primitive and brutal democracy as described by Freud. However, when we leap to the macropolitics suggested by the play, a startling inversion occurs. The personal fates of Rivers, the Sea Captain, his daughter, Mortimer, Herbert, and Matilda are discovered to be frustratingly irrelevant as the weakness of the play's conclusion reflects. The play may indeed be about "the perils of the soul in its passage toward individuation, . . . or from a morality based on 'nature' to one based on the autonomous self," as Geoffrey H. Hartman argues,[94] but Mortimer's is finally a pathetic soul groping for some proof of its mettle in condemning itself to an heroic alienation that no one else could be strong enough to endure, he hopes:

> *Mort*: No prayers, no tears, but hear my doom in silence!
> I will go forth a wanderer on the earth,
> A shadowy thing, and as I wander on
> No human ear shall ever hear my voice,
> No human dwelling ever give me food
> Or sleep or rest, and all the uncertain way
> Shall be as darkness to me, as a waste

Unnamed by man! and I shall wander on
Living by mere intensity of thought,
A thing by pain and thought compelled to live,
Yet loathing life, till heaven in mercy strike me
With blank forgetfulness—that I may die.
(Act V, Scene iii, ll. 264-75)

And thus the play ends, with Mortimer, like Milton's Satan, imagining a psychological drift through Chaos.[95] And thereby the poet refracts his fear that the crises of his personal life will be correspondingly minimized in historical context. Though he has escaped the dangers of France, he yet can be used and discarded by the inscrutable course of history.

The Borderers thus provides an historical context for the exploration of psychobiographical vicissitudes, only to find either their resolution or their continuance to be personally inconsequential. Perhaps there was some relief in learning that the sources of guilt in one's life could be overshadowed by ominous historical forces with which one could feel in correspondence, but it is more likely that this retraction of the individual ego was a part of "the soul's lowest ebb." William Hazlitt's assessment of the state of the drama for his generation is thus to the point of Wordsworth's play and its discovered frustrations:

> We participate in the general progress of intellect, and the large vicissitudes of human affairs; but the hugest private sorrow looks dwarfish and puerile. In the sovereignty of our minds, we make mankind our quarry; and, in the scope of our ambitious thoughts, hunt for prey through the four quarters of the world. In a word, literature and civilization have abstracted man from himself so far, that his existence is no longer *dramatic*; . . .[96]

Wordsworth discovered in writing *The Borderers* that the first task of a poet who had experienced the crush of history like a seed between the grinding wheels of England and France and who had observed as well a corresponding diminishment of individual lives in an increasingly urban, industrial, capitalist society—that poet's first task would have to be the reconstruction of selfhood prior to assuming responsibility for the rejuvenation of community. *The Borderers* thus has something to do with the poet's purgation of incestuous desire, but more to do with Wordsworth's readiness for the influence of Coleridge.

Part Two

"this dialogue of one"
(Donne, "The Exstasie")[1]

Out of Mortimer's ashes arose a new poet, but how is difficult to say. Whatever it was that catalyzed Wordsworth's self-renewal and new poetic orientation occurred by March 1798, when, Dorothy reports, William's faculties "seem to expand every day . . . his ideas flow faster than he can express them" (*EY*, p. 200). If the closing argument of Part One is correct, then we should look for experiences that now enhanced the building of Wordsworth's self-confidence as a poet. Coleridge's presence per se could not be the sole catalyst of Wordsworth's transformation, because the Wordsworths and Coleridge had been together on a daily basis since July 1797 when Coleridge had convinced them to move closer to his residence in Nether Stowey. It may be, however, that as Coleridge's unusual challenges to relationship and vocation became apparent, Wordsworth found his strength in successfully competing for prominence. We noted in Part One that the sparkle of *The Borderers'* Lord Clifford lightly suggests Coleridge's rivalry for Dorothy's respect and affection. Here we will consider the odd, but far more important vocational threat, that Coleridge introduced. While Wordsworth was revising his play, Coleridge was appropriating significant vocational moments of Wordsworth's biography for highlighting in his own autobiographical verse. In needing now to vie for influence over his sister and his own life's story, Wordsworth was awakened from the solipsism of the Mortimer-Rivers relationship to engage an inspired fellow-poet. Wordsworth's poetic character was reconstructed, if not entirely created, through the process of a poetic exchange that made his earlier impotence an affective power.

1. "many recognitions dim and faint"
(*Tintern Abbey*, l. 60)

The most important compositional interaction of the annus mirabilis—July 1797–July 1798—was Wordsworth's *Ruined Cottage* with Coleridge's *Rime of the Ancyent Marinere,* tandemly composed during winter 1797–spring 1798.[2] But this creative dialogue was preceded by the biographical borrowings of Coleridge's first major poem of summer 1797, "This Lime-Tree Bower My Prison," with the realistic threat of future appropriations.

In a recent conversation poem, "To the Rev. George Coleridge" (1797),[3] Coleridge had used trees to allegorize supportive male relationships. In one of his desperate earlier letters on the pain he had wrought with his wild behavior at Cambridge University, Coleridge referred to his brother George as the generic paternal tree "beneath the shade of whose protection [Coleridge] grew up" (*STCL,* Vol. I, p. 63). Now in the poem to George, brother-in-law Robert Southey fares less well as the poet's "False and fair-foliaged" Manchineel ("To George Coleridge," l. 26), who had been a "sturdy Republican" (*STCL,* Vol. I, p. 84), when Coleridge had been floundering morally, but who finally proved disappointing when he betrayed the ideals of Pantisocracy, Coleridge's name for the ideal communal state they dreamed of founding on the banks of the Susquehenna River in Pennsylvania. Local friend and prosperous businessman Thomas Poole, however, is figured as an heroic oak of "impervious covert" ("To the Rev. George Coleridge," l. 33) for providing economic security, domestic stability, and guidance at a time when Coleridge was beside himself with anxieties over first fatherhood. With moral and economic demons now at rest, or temporarily at bay, Coleridge reflects hopefully in his poem to George, on the vocational fantasy of George's "divine and nightly-whispering Voice, / Which from my childhood to maturer years / Spake to me of predestinated wreaths, / Bright with no fading colours!" ("To the Rev. George Coleridge," ll. 36–39). Now in "This Lime-Tree Bower My Prison," composed just a month after "To the Rev. George Coleridge," the allegorical arboretum of friends-in-need provides a subtext for Coleridge's quiet appropriation of Wordsworth's autobiographical epiphanies that represent a vocational identification with the poet he now admired to a fault.

The central poetic vision of "This Lime-Tree Bower" is Coleridge's exaltation of a sunset scene from Wordsworth's *Evening Walk.* Here is the relevant section of Coleridge's poem from a letter of July 1797 to Robert Southey, which offers the text that Wordsworth would know:

> —Ah slowly sink
> Behind the western ridge; thou glorious Sun!
> Shine in the slant beams of the sinking orb,
> Ye purple Heath-flowers! Richlier burn, ye Clouds!
> Live in the yellow Light, ye distant Groves!

And kindle, thou blue Ocean! So my friend
Struck with joy's deepest calm, and gazing round
On the wide view, may gaze till all doth seem
Less gross than bodily, a living Thing
That acts upon the mind, and with such hues
As cloathe the Almighty Spirit, when he makes
Spirits perceive His presence!

                              (*STCL*, Vol. I, p. 335)

Wordsworth's transforming—though hardly transcendental—sunset scene
as found in the 1794 manuscript of *Evening Walk* is Coleridge's ur-text,
although no one besides the Wordsworths would know of it, because the
text remained unpublished until 1836:

How pleasant, as the sun declines, to view
The total landscape change in form and hue!
Here, vanish, as in mist before a flood
Of bright obscurity, hill, lawn, and wood;
These objects, by the searching [beams] betrayed,
Come forth, and here retire in purple shade.
. . . .
The shepherd, all-involved in wreathes of fire,
Now shows a shadowy spot, and now is lost intire.

     Into a gradual calm the Zephyrs sink;
A blue rim borders all the lake's still brink:
And now, on every side, the surface breaks
Into blue spots, and slowly-lengthening streaks;
Here plots of sparkling water tremble bright
With thousand thousand twinkling points of light;
There, waves that, hardly weltering, die away
Tip their smooth ridges with a softer ray,
And now the universal tides repose,
And, bright with gold, the burnished mirror glows
          (*EW*, 1794, pp. 136-37, ll. 155-60; 169-80)

The ability to value what W. J. B. Owen has called "time-notes," or the
record of "variation in natural appearances which ensues from variations
in the light-source, as the day drifts towards evening and night,"[4] was a
telling point of imaginative discrimination for Wordsworth. In a manu-

script passage from the expanded version of *EW* that remained unpublished, he writes:

> Blest are those spirits tremblingly awake
> To Nature's impulse like this living lake,
> Whose mirrour makes the landscape's charms its own
> With touches soft as those to Memory known.
> (EW, 1794, p. 137, ll. 191-94)

Such "favoured souls" glow with sensitivity over natural minutia: "With them the sense no trivial object knows; / Oft at its meanest touch their Spirit glows / And, proud beyond all limits to aspire, / Mounts through the fields of thought on wings of fire" (*EW*, 1794, p. 138, ll. 207-10). Through the conflagration of love-fire permeating "This Lime-Tree Bower," Coleridge proves a favored soul.

Coleridge's poem then reveals that twilight has intensified the darkening presence of objects in his bower:

> I watch'd
> The sunshine of each broad transparent Leaf
> Broke by the shadows of the Leaf or Stem,
> Which hung above it: and that Wall-nut Tree
> Was richly ting'd: and a deep radiance lay
> Full on the ancient ivy which usurps
> Those fronting elms, and now with blackest mass
> Makes their dark foliage gleam a lighter hue
> Thro' the last twilight.
> (STCL, Vol. I, pp. 335-36)

The descriptive emphasis of this passage derives from an important perception both in *The Vale of Esthwaite* and *Evening Walk* that Wordsworth recalls as the first sign of his poetic uniqueness. Here is its rendering in *The Vale of Esthwaite*:

> While in the west the robe of day
> Fades, slowly fades, from gold to grey,
> The oak its boughs and foliage twines
> Marked to the view in stronger lines,
> Appears with foliage marked to view,

> In lines of stronger, browner hue,
> While every darkening leaf between,
> The sky distinct and clear is seen.
> (Hayden, Vol. I, pp. 52-53, ll. 95-102)

And then its recurrence in *Evening Walk*, both the published version of 1793 and the expanded version of 1794 quoted below addressed to his friend, presumably Dorothy, to join him in enjoying the perceptive uniqueness he has brought to poetry:

> Now while the solemn evening-shadows sail,
> On red slow-waving pinions down the vale,
> And, fronting the bright [west], in stronger lines,
> The oak its darkening boughs and foliage twines,
> Come with thy Poet, come, my friend, to stray,
> Where winds the road along the secret bay;
> Come, while the parting day yet serves to show
> Thy cheek that shames the water's crimson glow
> > (*EW*, 1794, p. 144, ll. 410-17)

Wordsworth's remembrance of this image of trees darkening against the evening sky emphasizes its lasting vocational importance:

> I recollect distinctly the very spot where this first struck me. It was in
> the way between Hawkshead and Ambleside, and gave me extreme
> pleasure. The moment was important in my poetic history; for I date
> from it my consciousness of the infinite variety of natural appearances
> which had been unnoticed by the poets of any age or country, so far
> as I was acquainted with them: and I made a resolution to supply in
> some degree the deficiency. I could not have been at that time above
> 14 years of age.
> > (*EW*, p. 54, n. to ll. 193-94)

Coleridge discovers in his own present experience a comparable epiphany, overladen with the moral value in nature that he and Wordsworth now shared:

> > Henceforth I shall know
> That nature ne'er deserts the wise & pure,

No scene so narrow, but may well employ
Each faculty of sense, and keep the heart
Awake to Love & Beauty
                    (*STCL*, Vol. I, p. 336)

A small but significant detail that corroborates the poetic exchange between Wordsworth's texts and Coleridge's poem is actually an unusual Wordsworth borrowing from Coleridge. Wordsworth's description of a shepherd in the landscape being a "shadowy spot" in the 1794 version of *Evening Walk*— "The shepherd, all-involved in wreathes of fire, / Now shows a shadowy spot, and now is lost intire"—is changed to a "shadowy speck" in the 1836 version of *An Evening Walk*. Although it is unclear what makes a "shadowy speck" a more accurate description than a "shadowy spot," *speck* is Coleridge's perception of a rook crossing the light in "This Lime-Tree Bower":

        when the last Rook
Beat it's straight path along the dusky air
Homewards, I bless'd it; deeming, it's black wing
Cross'd, like a speck, the blaze of setting day,
While ye stood gazing.
                    (*STCL*, Vol. I, p. 336)

But this Wordsworthian borrowing and even Coleridge's appropriation of Wordsworth's poetic epiphany and its poetic renderings all pale in significance to what was to occur several months later when Coleridge's verse becomes thematically and even stylistically indistinguishable from Wordsworth's. Although Coleridge had earlier expressed his skepticism over transcendental inclinations in "Frost at Midnight," composed February 1798, by April he had so completely conceded to Wordsworth's poetic belief that his "The Nightingale" becomes a notable achievement of poetic ventriloquism.

The argument of the first published form of "Frost at Midnight" holds that there is a basic human need to relate psychologically to the world, which thereby precludes the possibility of perception uncontaminated by projection:

        the living spirit in our frame,
That loves not to behold a lifeless thing,
Transfuses into all its own delights,
Its own volition, sometimes with deep faith,

And sometimes with fantastic playfulness.
(1798; *CPW*, p. 240, note to ll. 19-25)

Whether the perceiver has "deep faith," as Wordsworth does, or "fantastic
playfulness," as Coleridge does, the life of nature's "lifeless thing[s]" is
bestowed by the perceiver.

In musing hopefully on the spiritual awakening of his infant son,
Coleridge argues that while nature might provoke a desire for transcendent
experience, nature finally cannot be the experience or even the medium of
the experience itself:

> But *thou*, my babe! shalt wander like a breeze
> By lakes and sandy shores, beneath the crags
> Of ancient mountain, and beneath the clouds,
> Which image in their bulk both lakes and shores
> And mountain crags: so shalt thou see and hear
> The lovely shapes and sounds intelligible
> Of that eternal language, which thy God
> Utters, who from eternity doth teach
> Himself in all, and all things in himself.
> Great universal Teacher! he shall mould
> Thy spirit, and by giving make it ask.
> (*CPW*, p. 242, ll. 54-64)

Nature's context of "companionable forms," in this case, the clouds' recipro-
cation of the landscape's features, will cause the boy to yearn for appropriate
relationship with a being similar to his essential spiritual self, here "wandering like a breeze," but he will find no companionable spiritual form in nature.
But that is the intent of the "Great universal Teacher." Much as Milton's God
prepared Adam to desire a suitable companion by creating a world of mated
animals for Adam to muse upon,[5] the "Teacher" will "mould" the boy's spirit
in the milieu of companionate natural imagery to the end of showing that
the earth cannot provide a satisfactory spiritual mate. In short, nature
inspires the desires that she cannot satisfy. The pantheist or spiritual natu-
ralist thus misperceives the opportunity for true spiritual life.

In the poem's conclusion, Coleridge provides an analogue of divine
influence as the formative power of temperature on physical states. God is
a force outside of natural objects, shaping His creation into correspondence.
Just as "the secret ministry of cold / Shall hang [eavesdrops] in silent icicles,
/ Quietly shining to the quiet moon" (*CPW*, p. 242, ll. 72-74), so Hartley's

soul will be developed by the secret ministry of God to quest for its fulfillment of spiritual desires in silent meditation. It's a strongly responsive argument to the ambivalence of "Eolian Harp," which came out on the side of biblical Revelation, but not without tantalizing the reader with a beautifully imaginative rendering of pantheism. Here the tension is resolved in showing the proper and functional harmony between physical and metaphysical experience.

However, Wordsworth's poetic achievement in a series of experimental psychological fragments caused Coleridge to suspend his disbelief in natural spirituality. In passages such as the following, Wordsworth develops what Paul D. Sheats calls his "presentational style," which "seeks to reproduce the presentation of phenomena to the mind in experience,"[6] by a syntactical breakdown which imitates the dissolution of boundaries between nature and consciousness to prove nature a means as well as end to spiritual experience. Pauses (//) and repetitions, italicized below for emphasis, pace the breathing to coincide with the systolic and diastolic rhythm of a palpably new experience for poetry:

> *I lived* // without the knowledge that *I lived* //
> Then // by those beauteous forms brought back *again* //
> To lose myself *again* // as if my life
> Did ebb and flow // with a strange mystery.
> (Hayden, Vol. I, p. 269; emphasis added)

Other fragments continue the rhythmic and rhetorical patterning of similar psychological experience, valued now for a passivity that ascends to moral power as consciousness *experiences*, rather than merely "see[s] and hear[s] / The lovely shapes and sounds intelligible / Of that eternal language," which nature's silent objects bespeak:

> Not useless do I deem
> These quiet sympathies with things that hold
> An inarticulate language, for the man
> Once taught to love such *objects* as excite
> *No* morbid passions, *no* disquietude,
> *No* vengeance and *no* hatred, needs must *feel*
> The *joy* of that *pure* principle of *love*
> So deeply that, unsatisfied with aught
> Less *pure* and exquisite, he cannot choose
> But seek for *objects* of a *kindred love*

In fellow-natures, and a *kindred joy.*
Accordingly he by degrees perceives
His *feelings* of aversion softened down,
A holy tenderness pervade his frame,
His sanity of reason not impaired,
Say rather all his thoughts now *flowing clear*
—From a *clear* fountain *flowing*—he looks round,
He seeks for *good* and finds the *good he seeks* . . .
(Gill, p. 678, ll. 1-18; emphasis added)

Wordsworth's word repetitions fix the focus of thought, while the rhythm of their rhetorical patterning arouses the aesthetic experience of a dreamy coalescence between nature and the perceiving subject. The first sentence above, "Not useless I deem . . . kindred joy," contains six repetitions of key words in its latter eight lines—*objects, no, pure, love, kindred, joy*—with closure reached with the repetitions of the final two lines: "kindred love," "kindred joy." The repetition of *feel, feelings* joins the first with the second sentence. The chiasmic density of the final three lines of the second sentence then brings strong feeling and thought into tighter relationship: "flowing clear" and "clear . . . flowing"; "He seeks . . . good" and "good he seeks." One further point bears mentioning. This experience of natural morality will not come unsought. The uninitiated will have to be literally taught, not somehow prepared by spiritual osmosis by the "Great universal Teacher": "for the man [i.e., not child] / . . . taught to love such objects."

In "The Nightingale,"[7] Coleridge proves an adept pupil in employing repetition as effectively as Wordsworth in key passages of formative experience to chastise the "poor Wretch" who "fill[s] all things with himself / And [makes] all gentle sounds tell back the tale / Of his own sorrows" ("Nightingale," ll. 19-21); that is, the projective poet. The poet who wishes to follow nature will submit to nature's discipline by resting his self-concerns through wise passiveness. He will not accept the mythology of the Nightingale's woeful lamentation, like the traditional poet who

        had better far have stretch'd his limbs
    Beside a brook in mossy forest-dell
    By sun or moonlight, to the influxes
    Of shapes and sounds and shifting elements
    Surrendering his whole spirit, of *his song*
    And of *his fame* forgetful! so *his fame*

Should share in *nature's* immortality,
A venerable thing! and *so his song*
Should make all *nature lovelier,* and itself
Be *lov'd,* like *nature!*
                    (Brett and Jones, pp. 41-42, ll. 25-34; emphasis added)

Simple diction densely patterned in repetition, especially the final chiasmus, is pure Wordsworth, spring 1798: "his song" and "his fame" with "so his fame" and "so his song"; "nature's" and "nature lovelier" with "lov'd . . . nature." In "This Lime-tree Bower" Coleridge assumes Wordsworth's biographical pattern; in "The Nightingale," Coleridge echoes Wordsworth's poetic voice.

Of course, while these instances of biographical and stylistic appropriation may be novel, an argument that illustrates Coleridge's notorious propensity for psychological identification—in any of its forms—cannot surprise. Whether it be joining the Dragoons as a confused young man in imitation of his soldier brothers; or marrying or desiring the sisters of best friends, to wit, marrying Sara Fricker, the sister of Robert Southey's wife, and later, hopelessly longing for Sara Hutchinson, the sister of Wordsworth's wife; or whether it be brazen intellectual identification in its most notorious form of plagiarizing from Friedrich Schelling and other German philosophers in *Biographia Literaria;* or whether it be, as here, the appropriation of Wordsworth's vocational narrative and poetic style, repetition and imitation are central to our understanding of Coleridge's biography and poetry. This propensity would have been quite novel to Wordsworth, however, and his reaction to the threat still needs to be considered.

In *Coleridge and Wordsworth: A Lyrical Dialogue,* Paul Magnuson argues for an opposing perspective on Wordsworth's vocational concerns; that Wordsworth would have feared his own tendency to absorb too much of Coleridge's work and style, especially in being attracted to Coleridge's meditative blank verse poems, "Eolian Harp," "This Lime-Tree Bower, and "Frost at Midnight." Wordsworth's fear of amalgamation with Coleridge's work thus caused him to misread Coleridge's meditative nature poems in the Bloomian sense so as to establish grounds for a belief in a myth of his poetic autogenesis.[8] The reading provided here, however, finds the primary poet in Wordsworth, who would have to battle for his creative life against the remarkable gifts of originality and imitative prowess that Coleridge possessed.

2. "the burthen of the mystery"
(*Tintern Abbey*, l. 39)

Originally thinking that their work and thought could readily and support-ively dovetail, Wordsworth and Coleridge intended *Rime of the Ancyent Marinere* to be a co-authored poem. And although, as Norman Fruman has relentlessly detailed,[9] much of the poem's imagery and narrative event were suggested by Wordsworth (and others), the friends soon discovered that they were psychologically mismatched for this common enterprise. We might infer from the compositional development of *Ancyent Marinere* with *Ruined Cottage*, especially with respect to the poems' narrators, that their creative relationship became irresistibly agonistic. Both the Mariner of *Ancyent Marinere* and the Pedlar of *Ruined Cottage* have experienced great weaknesses in their lives, which each transmutes into narrative power over an auditor. Furthermore, these weaknesses are of psychobiographical impor-tance to the authors, so that, quite apart from the quality of the poems themselves, the quest for power over a threatening past becomes a daring but necessary gamble on behalf of a vocational future.

The psychobiographical context for *Ancyent Marinere* draws upon Cole-ridge's continuing desire for rebirth in the face of his life's already wearisome pattern of crises and recoveries. His manic-depressive cycles eventually left him wary of hoping for emotional stability, but, more importantly for a reading of *Ancyent Marinere* and *Ruined Cottage*, even more wary of the validity of attitudes, beliefs, transformations, and perceptions derived from the contexts of emotional experience. As autobiographical figures, then, the Albatross and the Mariner are shadowy glimpses of Coleridge's self, as George Whalley maintained, but rather than associating the Albatross with the poet's imagination, as Whalley, following Robert Penn Warren,[10] had done, this reading will suggest that the docile bird represents weaknesses that Coleridge found embarrassingly reflected in himself as man and poet. In this light, the Mariner's behavior against the Albatross becomes a release of aggression against self and similar others prompted by self-aversion. The biographical event that most likely prompted this poetic impulse was Coleridge's recent reaction against his own *Poems* (1797), co-authored with friends Charles Lamb, Charles Lloyd, and Robert Southey, in his so-called Higginbottom sonnets.

Although Coleridge tries to make light of the nasty Higginbottom incident in *Biographia Literaria*,[11] it is difficult to put a good face on it. Besides being co-authored by friends, Poems (1797) was published by friend Joseph

Cottle, who had taken extraordinary effort and expense to make the volume a success out of affection for Coleridge. Indeed, Coleridge's motto for the volume was a touching tribute to friendship and poetry: "We have a double bond: that of friendship and of our linked and kindred Muses: may neither death nor length of time dissolve it" (*STCL*, Vol. I, p. 390, n. 3). Yet within a month of publication, Coleridge turned into a raucous critic of self and friends in the scornful sonnets published under the pseudonym of Nehemiah Higginbottom. As he explained to Cottle, who must have been distressed and befuddled:

> I sent three mock Sonnets in ridicule of my own, & Charles Lloyd's, & Lamb's, &c &c—in ridicule of that affectation of unaffectedness, of jumping & misplaced accent on common-place epithets, flat lines forced into poetry by Italics (signifying how well & *mouthis[b]ly* the Author would read them) puny pathos &c &c—the instances are almost all taken from mine & Lloyd's poems—I signed them Nehemiah Higginbottom. I think they may do good to our young Bards.
>
> (*STCL*, Vol. I, pp. 357-58)

Charles Lamb had been Coleridge's dear friend from their schoolboy days at Christ's Hospital. Coleridge's sycophant, Charles Lloyd, had lived through a trying time of his life in the Coleridge household, and Coleridge had once expressed pride and delight in Lloyd's subsequent moral, economic, and poetic development as his tutee. But, more to the point, the co-authors undoubtedly had discussed and shared mutual approbation for their works. It was late in the day for even reasoned public criticism, let alone a courting of humiliation.

Coleridge's friends suspected that his relationship with the Words-worths was responsible for the assault—and it was—but it is unlikely that they could appreciate (or care for) its motivation. Simply stated, Coleridge now found the collaborative volume a stylistic embarrassment when compared with the poetry of Wordsworth and with the poetry he now found himself capable of writing, and he sought to distance himself from its mediocrity with scorn. After the publication of the Higginbottom sonnets, Lamb, Lloyd, and Cottle obliged in widening the breach with Coleridge by convincing Southey that his work was intended for ridicule as well. Coleridge denied it, but Lamb argued on Southey's behalf that "It was a lie too gross for the grossest ignorance to believe" that Southey did not share in the ridicule (*STCL* Vol. I, p. 358, n. 1). The sonnet ostensibly directed at Southey is "On a Ruined House in a Romantic Country," which Coleridge claimed to be an attack on his own "indiscriminate use of elaborate and swelling language and imagery":[12]

Still on his thighs their wonted brogues are worn,
And thro' those brogues, still tatter'd and betorn,
His hindward charms gleam an unearthly white;
As when thro' broken clouds at night's high noon
Peeps in fair fragments forth the full-orb'd harvest moon!
(CPW, p. 211, ll. 10-14)

In retaliation, Southey, Lamb, and Lloyd colluded on the novel Edmund Oliver (1798), a caricature of Coleridge's life—with a sideswipe at the Words-worths—and Cottle published it. Though not scurrilous, the novel vindic-tively details the truth of Coleridge's life and ideas: the passionate disorder of his youth, including the circumstances of his hopeless loves; his youthful debaucheries; his hapless military experience at the nadir of his fortune, and the family bribe to the military officials to release him from his commitment for being "Insane"; and then the extremities of Coleridge's moral positions on the evil of private ownership, on marital fidelity, on universal benevo-lence, on the primary importance of Revelation, and on the utopian ideal represented by Pantisocracy. William and Dorothy Wordsworth were as pointedly satirized in Edmund Oliver's relationship with his sister.

Each day we would wander through some interesting scene near our dwelling, watch the floating clouds, pore in the passing stream, observe the various foliage of each tree, animate the meadow with our innocent and pure feelings, and give to each object of nature a tribute of grateful sensation—the overflowings of a humanized soul![13]

In fact, the connection between the first names of Edmund Oliver and William Wordsworth's nickname, Edmund, suggests that the novel's hero was an amalgamation of William Wordsworth and Coleridge, and thus constituted an attack on their relationship.[14]

There is no record of William Wordsworth's response, except to say that he hadn't read the novel, but he reports that Dorothy "read it through [and] thinks it contains a great deal a very great deal of excellent matter but bears the marks of a too hasty composition" (EY, p. 218). Dorothy's non-reaction would not have surprised the master satirist, Jonathan Swift, who writes in Battle of the Books (1704) that "Satyr is a sort of Glass, wherein Beholders do generally discover every body's Face but their Own,"[15] but Coleridge saw the face of his life embarrassingly reflected and was sorely distressed. Referring to the close friendships he had once with Lamb and Southey especially, Coleridge writes dolefully: "I have had many sorrows;

and some that bite deep, calumny & ingratitude from men who have been fostered in the bosom of my confidence!" (*STCL*, Vol. I, p. 407). Thus, although biographical events seem to offer an unpromising pretext for one of the greatest and strangest poems of the English language, Coleridge's reaction to the violation of friendship and intimacy requires that we analogously view the Mariner's equally venial sin and its astonishing consequences.

The Mariner's crime and unrelievable guilt reflect the burden of a human mystery: Why would one seek to destroy an innocent creature, especially one beloved?[16] Because it was painful for Coleridge to consciously account for his public outburst against his friends, there is murkiness on points of greatest relevance to this question, the bird's love for the Mariner, the Mariner's motivation, and his character. These can be fleshed out, however, with direction provided by this biographical context.

The personal qualities allegorized in the image of a trusting, dependent Albatross hardly seem to be faults of character, but they are the qualities Coleridge found incongruous with the personal strengths required of a strong poet. Wordsworth embodied strength of purpose, independence, a stern morality, and emotional reticence. Coleridge's personal traits were opposite: he was excessively dependent upon the aid, love, and approval of others; he was inclined to moral laxity; he felt largely without resolve, effusive, weak, and vulnerable; and, as the Higginbottom sonnets reveal, he could act aggressively on impulse. As we saw in the preceding section, Coleridge sought to align himself with Wordsworth's poetic strengths. Here his concern is character. His present idealization of Wordsworth is related: "Wordsworth is a very great man—the only man, to whom *at all times* & in *all modes of excellence* I feel myself inferior" (*STCL*, Vol. I, p. 334). Coleridge's insight into the role of projection in perceiving others reveals what he learned from his experience with Wordsworth:

> When a man is attempting to describe another's character, he may be right or he may be wrong—but in one thing he will always succeed, in describing himself. If he express simple approbation, he praises from a consciousness of possession—If he approve with admiration, from a consciousness of deficiency.
>
> (*STCNB*, Vol. I, entry 74)

Obviously, Coleridge's praise of Wordsworth derives from "consciousness of [his own] deficiency."

Besides suggesting the principal emotional impulse of dominant symbols, the biographical background also helps to explain the obscurity of the
Mariner's motivation. The Mariner's inexplicable assault on the Albatross
suggests the mystery of human evil in the manner of traditional ballads, such
as "Edward," "Lord Randall," "Barbara Allan," "The Wife of Usher's Well," all
of which employ hopelessly vague or absent motivation.[17] However, revealing the intellectual weakness identified by Keats as Coleridge's inability to
live in mystery,[18] Coleridge leaves the matter unresolved, but not unresolvable. We learn that the Albatross loved the Mariner ("'The spirit who 'bideth
by himself / In the land of mist and snow, / He lov'd the bird that lov'd the
man / Who shot him with his bow,'" [*AM*, ll. 407-10]),[19] but by the time we
learn of this affection, it seems thematically gratuitous, possibly posited as
an afterthought by the Mariner to account for his lasting punishment.
Curiously, though telling his tale in retrospect, the Mariner does not admit
to being aware of the bird's love when he shot it, and then we learn later in
the narrative that "Two voices in the air" discuss his punishment for killing
an important spirit's beloved bird. He says this message came in a "swound,"
brought on by a rush of blood to his head when the boat bursts forth powered
by the avenging Polar Spirit:

> How long in that same fit I lay,
> I have not to declare;
> But ere my living life return'd,
> I heard and in my soul discern'd
> Two voices in the air.
> (*AM*, ll. 398-402)

He awakens nine stanzas later with the ship "sailing on / As in a gentle
weather" (*AM*, ll. 435-36). During the period of his unconsciousness—
"swound," "fit," or "trance"—the ship bolts forward unnaturally fast and he
hears the spirits "in [his] soul." These inner voices tell him that the bird loved
him; therefore, they reveal what he knew at some level of consciousness all
along, in the experiential present, so to speak, and surely what he knows and
always knows when he narrates, to wit, that the bird either did love him and
he intuited it, or he suspected it loved him. Is he being coy, evasive, obtuse,
or merely artless in withholding information about the bird's love for him
when he shot it? The wary reader is led to conclude that the Mariner shot
the Albatross knowing of, or, more likely, because of, this real or suspected
love, which tentatively represents Coleridge's outbreak against his friends.[20]

Furthermore, the many instances of spontaneity in the poem reveal the unsettling influence of emotional phenomenology on the belief and action of all the humans and events of the poem: the mariners spontaneously welcome the bird; the Ancient Mariner spontaneously kills the bird; the sailors curse the Mariner for killing the Albatross and just as readily celebrate him for killing it; he feels unreflecting aversion for the watersnakes and then he loves the watersnakes; he selects his auditors with no more than a glance of the eye when the spell is upon him. Such vagaries of response indicate that objects do not have a fixed psychological value—such as Oedipal correspondences at an unconscious level—but rather take on temporary or situational meaning and value in response to the fluidity of circumstances and emotional conditions. The Mariner is no more a killer than Coleridge was a duplicitous friend, yet both behaved so when the fit was upon them, and they may do so again.

Wordsworth expressed displeasure with *Ancyent Marinere*. His note to the poem in the 1800 edition of *Lyrical Ballads* specifies the deficiencies he perceived, I would think, even as the poem was being composed, rather than as an afterthought, or servile gesture towards the poem's negative critical reception:[21] the Mariner "has no distinct character"; "he does not act, but is continually acted upon"; "the events having no necessary connection do not produce each other"; and "the imagery is too laboriously accumulated."[22] *Ruined Cottage* pointedly avoids these faults in style, narrative economy, and characterization. In doing so, Wordsworth transforms the affective impotence of his biographical past into narrative strength.

In the spring of 1797 (March-June), Wordsworth had been chiefly concerned with three elements of Margaret's story: the decline of her husband Robert, Margaret's own decline, and the motivation of Robert's abandonment of Margaret and their children. Contrasting and even directed development between the Mariner and Pedlar now become the chief outcome of the compositional experience of January-March 1798, which is then completed by Wordsworth's refinements and revisions in 1799.[23] The following comparisons strongly suggest that the poets were consciously engaged in an evolving debate on epistemology[24] as it related to poetic vision and power.

The motive for narration in both poems seems, at first, to be pedagogical therapy: the Pedlar and the Mariner recognize auditors with some need to learn from their tales, but they also share a therapeutic need to tell their tales. The Mariner says an "anguish comes" to make him "tell / [His] ghastly aventure" (*AM*, ll. 617-18), which apparently sensitizes him to identify a needful auditor: "The moment that his face I see / I know the man that must hear me; / To him my tale I teach" (*AM*, ll. 621-23). Likewise, the Pedlar emphasizes his auditor's need in a concluding passage written in March 1798—"no longer read / The forms of things with an unworthy eye"[25]—but his narration just as surely gives release to the painful, obsessive memories that he muses upon as narrative:

> Sir, I feel
> The *story* linger in my heart. I fear
> 'Tis long and tedious, but my spirit clings
> To that poor woman. . . .
> (*RC*, p. 65, ll. 362-65; emphasis added)[26]

The relationships between narrators and auditors thus begin with the narrators' intuitive recognition of their similarity, which confirms a human desire and ability to find or to create Coleridge's "companionable forms."

The cause of the Mariner's anguish and his need for narrating is a recurring experience of guilt: he destroyed the Albatross that loved him, probably because it loved him. What obsesses the Pedlar? From Thomas De Quincey on, readers have believed that the Pedlar ought to feel more than impotence for being so useless to Margaret, but it is difficult to name his culpability. It is not irresponsibility, or lack of compassion. What does one think of someone who refrains from visiting a lonely, loving friend after sensing her death is imminent, and then minutely describes a pathetic, painful end he imagines she endured? Jonathan Barron and Kenneth R. Johnston answer that the Pedlar is a kind of impotent lover who abandons Margaret for lacking both the power to bring her the news she wants about her missing husband and the language to console her when they are together. He thereby becomes a source of disappointment to her and thus guilty, and then more guilty for failing to return to her cottage until she dies.[27] Following this line of argument, one is lead to conclude that if Margaret had not died, the Pedlar would not have returned.

But I think that the Pedlar is unlike Robert, or the Sailor from *Adventures on Salisbury Plain* for that matter, for he does not identify masculine worth with material usefulness to spouse and offspring. The Pedlar is more like Mortimer and far too much like Margaret, displaying the obsessive tenacity she displays in relationships. Although he has chosen a profession of permanent transience, and thereby avoids the risks and costs of intimacy, his longing for relationship causes him to seek filial love from virtual strangers. He classifies the emotional bonds he shared with Margaret as familial on both of their parts: "when I appeared, / A daughter's welcome

gave me, and I loved her / As my own child" (RC, p. 50. ll. 148-50). His
memory of Margaret later remains as clinging and potentially disabling as
her memory of Robert:

> . . . my spirit clings
> To that poor woman: so familiarly
> Do I perceive her manner, and her look
> And presence, and so deeply do I feel
> Her goodness, that not seldom in my walks
> A momentary trance comes over me; . . .
> (RC, p. 65, ll. 364-69)

They also both wander and (eventually) return, which is unlike the behavior
of Robert, who simply leaves. Margaret says, "I've wandered much of late /
And sometimes, to my shame I speak, have need / Of my best prayers to
bring me back again" (RC, p. 64, ll. 399-401). Because of such fatal similarities, the Pedlar fears their passion and the end it portends unless he can find
a defense, which he does in his turn away from Margaret to nature. It is
pertinent then to compare the Pedlar's motivation for discontinuing his visits
to Margaret with the Mariner's motivation for killing the Albatross: each
reacts against one who loves him because he senses a fatal flaw of the loved
one reflected in himself.

The guilt feelings of the Mariner and Pedlar swell and subside upon
their employing strategies of relief: fantasies of rebirth, turns to higher
powers, and narration. The turn from death to new life in *Ancyent Marinere*
begins with the Mariner's identification with the loathsome sea snakes:

> The many men so beautiful,
>   And they all dead did lie!
> And a million million slimy things
>   Liv'd on—and so did I.
>   (AM, 228-31)

The death of the men is unbearable to him. He accounts for their fate by
shifting from a Christian motif, which had colored the mariners' experience
with the Albatross, to a pagan motif of vengeance exacted without regard
for real culpability, carried out by nether spirits and fantastic spectres. But
after an extended period of isolation, the Mariner feels a change towards the
creatures of the sea:

> O happy living things! no tongue
>   Their beauty might declare:
> A spring of love gusht from my heart,
>   And I bless'd them unaware!
> Sure my kind saint took pity on me,
>   And I bless'd them unaware.
>   (AM, ll. 274-79)

If the Mariner had earlier found the million slimy things morally compatible with his condition, now they exceed his estimate of self-worth. When he forgets his miserable self under the charm of moonlight, however, love overcomes him, he feels renewed, and experiences his renewal as rebirth. Feeling reborn, he sees the crew arise:

> I mov'd and could not feel my limbs,
>   I was so light, almost
> I thought that I had died in sleep,
>   And was a blessed Ghost.
> . . . .
> The strong wind reach'd the ship: it roar'd
>   And drop'd down, like a stone!
> Beneath the lightning, and the moon
>   The dead men gave a groan.
>
> They groan'd, they stirr'd, they all uprose,
>   Ne spake, ne mov'd their eyes:
> It had been strange, even in a dream
>   To have seen those dead men rise.
>   (AM, ll. 297-300; 319-26)

Their rejuvenation and his relief are short-lived. The curse remains in their eyes and his spell or illusion is ended:

> The pang, the curse, with which they died,
>   Had never pass'd away:
> I could not draw my een from theirs
>   Ne turn them up to pray.
>   (AM, ll. 443-46)

Upon his landing, the agony of guilt returns with a need to confess his tale in what becomes a never-ending effort to obtain absolution.

A comparable despondency falls upon the Pedlar at the outset of *Ruined Cottage* when he announces that Margaret is dead while lesser life prevails in her spot:

> She is dead,
> The worm is on her cheek, and this poor hut,
> Stripped of its outward garb of household flowers,
> Of rose and jasmine, offers to the wind
> A cold bare wall whose earthy top is tricked
> With weeds and the rank spear-grass. She is dead,
> And nettles rot and adders sun themselves
> Where we have sat together while she nursed
> Her infant at her bosom.
>   (*RC*, p. 50, ll. 157-65)

In direct comparison with *Ancyent Marinere*, Wordsworth includes passages on the Pedlar's changing perception of spear grass comparable to the Mariner's perception of the water snakes. The "rank spear-grass" of the following passage contrasts with the visionary peace offered the Pedlar by the so-called reconciling addendum of March 1798:

> ["]I well remember that those very plumes,
> Those weeds, and the high spear-grass on that wall,
> By mist and silent rain-drops silver'd o'er,
> As once I passed did to my heart convey
> So still an image of tranquillity,
> So calm and still, and looked so beautiful
> Amid the uneasy thoughts which filled my mind,
> That what we feel of sorrow and despair
> From ruin and from change, and all the grief
> The passing shews of being leave behind,
> Appeared an idle dream that could not live
> Where meditation was. I turned away
> And walked along my road in happiness."[28]
>   (*RC*, p. 75, ll. 513-25)

It is important to recognize that his first description of the spear grass being "rank" is not a memory, but a reaction in the narrative present. The perception of its visionary glaze belongs to the narrative past: "As once I passed." In other words, the value of the spear grass is contextual or situational. The Pedlar's turn to nature is a memory of reconciliation, much as the Mariner's, that must be achieved anew whenever the psychological experience of Margaret's demise and death is relived, as now in narration.

The Pedlar's turn to nature is comparable to the Mariner's turn to religion, and both are related to their poets' predispositions: Wordsworth's, to nature, and Coleridge's, to Christianity. The Mariner claims that "sweeter than the Marriage-feast, / 'Tis sweeter far to me / To walk together to the Kirk / With a goodly company" (ll. 634-37), for there "all together pray" and "each to his great father bends, / Old men, and babes, and loving friends, / And Youths, and Maidens gay" (ll. 639-42). Despite the communal solace of worshipping with believers, however, the Mariner seems not to realize that his tale's moral—"He prayeth best who loveth best, / All things both great and small: / For the dear God, who loveth us, / He made and loveth all" (ll. 647-50)—is irreconcilable with his recurring agony. Likewise, the Pedlar's natural relief is temporary.

Margaret's literal death is yet an imagining of the Pedlar because he did not witness the event. It may be a truism that one must see the loved one interred to fully accept the emotional reality of death; his references to her being asleep suggest that he has not. This is Margaret's problem as well. She remains "a wife, and widow," out of uncertainty. She cannot entirely give up her love; she cannot entirely grieve. So with the Pedlar. After providing what seems an eyewitness accounting—"And so she sate, etc."—and then unflinchingly acknowledging her end—"and here she died, / Last human tenant of these ruined walls" (RC, p. 72, ll. 516-28)—within twenty lines he says, "She sleeps in the calm earth" (RC, p. 75, l. 512) as he had mused earlier that she had been "By sorrow laid asleep or borne away" (RC, p. 67, l. 371).[29]

The Pedlar experiences a feeling of rebirth when the memory of Margaret affects him most acutely. At one point of particular grief, when he recalls how poignantly Margaret described her anguish—"I have slept / Weeping, and weeping I have waked; my tears / Have flowed as if my body were not such / As others are, and I could never die" (RC, p. 64, ll. 407-10)—the Pedlar describes his correspondent fantasy of her immortality:

> so familiarly
> Do I perceive her manner, and her look
> And presence, and so deeply do I feel

> Her goodness, that not seldom in my walks
> A momentary trance comes over me;
> And to myself I seem to muse on one
> By sorrow laid asleep or borne away,
> A human being destined to awake
> To human life, or something very near
> To human life, when he shall come again
> For whom she suffered.
>
> $\qquad\qquad\qquad$ (RC, pp. 65, 67; ll. 365-75)[30]

In other words, he cannot believe that she is entirely dead; in fact, to him she is as alive as nature—a "presence" that is not to be put by—and so she is undead much like the heroine of a macabre fairy tale, awaiting comatose for the return of her prince. The auditor attests to the power of the Pedlar's narration to effect an active fantasy of rebirth akin to the Mariner's fantasy of the crew's awakening: "He had rehearsed / Her homely tale with such familiar power, / With such a countenance of love, an eye / So Busy, that the things of which he spake / Seemed present, . . ." (RC, p. 56, ll. 266-70). Through narration Margaret comes alive to the imagination of the Pedlar and to the corroborating witness of another. Like the Mariner, the Pedlar must tell his tale to memorialize, to unburden his soul, to deny a horrible reality, but finally and most importantly to give the deceased new life, a resurrection, as it were, to assuage guilt, through the impact of his tale upon another.

The wedding guest in *Ancyent Marinere* departs a stunned man, but "A sadder and a wiser man / He rose the morrow morn" (*AM*, ll. 657-58). However, his need for the Mariner's tale is left unspecified. One can infer a specific need of the Narrator of *Ruined Cottage*. He is vulnerable to the vicissitudes of human relationship, as are Robert, Margaret, her dead baby, and the Pedlar himself:

> The old Man ceased: he saw that I was mov'd;
> From that low Bench, rising instinctively,
> I turned aside in weakness, nor had power
> To thank him for the tale which he had told.
> I stood, and leaning o'er the garden-gate
> Reviewed that Woman's suff'rings, and it seemed
> To comfort me while with a brother's love
> I blessed her in the impotence of grief.
>
> $\qquad\qquad\qquad$ (RC, p. 73, ll. 493-500)[31]

Having been weakened by the Pedlar's narrative power, the narrator is prepared now to be strengthened by the lesson: "enough to sorrow have you given, / The purposes of wisdom ask no more; / Be wise and chearful, and no longer read / The forms of things with an unworthy eye. / She sleeps in the calm earth, and peace is here" (*RC*, pp. 73, 75, ll. 508-12).[32] Though the following reaction of Wordsworth's Narrator does not find its way into the completed texts, manuscripts indicate that he has absorbed the tale as deeply as the Wedding Guest of *Ancyent Marinere*: "I turned to the old man, & said my friend / Your words have consecrated many things / And for the tale which you have told I think / I am a better and a wiser man" (*RC*, pp. 257, ll. 13-14; p. 259, ll. 3-4). A "better," not a "sadder," man implies a teacher who can make matters "All gratulant if rightly understood" (1805 *Prelude*, Book XIII, l. 385).

Finally, Wordsworth shows that nature can offer no respite if it can only be a vessel for projected human weaknesses. Indeed, Nature's *otherness* is its potential for emotional solace. The early manuscript of *Ruined Cottage* includes an important passage on projection and two kinds of poetry:

> The Poets in their elegies and songs
> Lamenting the departed call the groves
> They call upon the hills & streams to mourn,
> And senseless rocks, nor idly; for they speak
> In these their invocations with a voice
> Obedient to the strong creative power
> Of human passion.
> (RC, p. 49, ll. 73-79)[33]

But yet there are other ways of corresponding with nature that more wisely take advantage of its therapeutic value:

> Sympathies there are
> More tranquil, yet haply of a kindred birth,
> That steal upon the meditative mind
> And grow with thought.
> (*RC*, pp. 49, 51; ll. 79-82)

In contrast to the elegists, this poet's plea is for man to turn away from human misery in order to accept the blessed indifference nature offers, rather than to intensify grief through pathetic fallacy.

Conversely, Coleridge shows through the Mariner's experiences that we as perceivers cannot confidently discern when psychological fabrications have shaped our seeing, so imperceptible and satisfying are their coming upon us.[34] In addition to the Mariner hearing voices in his "swound" that told him why he would continue to suffer, we might also consider the visitation of the specter ship as an imagined occurrence. Textual evidence at important points fails to show that anyone but the Mariner sees the ship or its weird crew of two.

The Mariner is wearing the Albatross about his neck with manifestly good and personal reasons for wanting to proclaim salvation for the crew, lying about thirsting to death with "glazed" eyes, as the 1817 text makes explicit.[35] He alone beholds the hope of "something in the Sky" (AM, l. 139), moving through a series of transformations from distant speck to mist to a "certain shape" (AM, l. 144). He finally announces his vision to the crew with a cry of "A sail! a sail!" (AM, l. 153). The crew's only reaction is a grin of joy and a sigh of expectation at the Mariner's hopeful cry: "Agape they hear'd me call: / Gramercy! they for joy did grin / And all at once their breath drew in / As they were drinking all" (AM, ll. 155-58). He cries out once more to interpret the good fortune that is approaching: "She doth not tack from side to side— / Hither to work us weal" (AM, ll. 159-60). The 1817 text emphasizes that he alone sees the vessel: "See! see! (I cried) she tacks no more! / Hither to work us weal" (1817, ll. 167-68). The editorial commentary or gloss that Coleridge added to the 1817 text also queries the reality of the ship: "And horror follows. For can it be a *ship* that comes onward without wind or tide?"[36] After that, there is no indication that the crew sees or hears with the Mariner; indeed, his responses become privately parenthetical: "And strait the Sun was fleck'd with bars / (Heaven's mother send us grace)" (AM, ll. 169-70). "Alas! (thought I, and my heart beat loud)" (AM, l. 173). "[T]hought I" indicates that the coming vision of Death and Life-in-Death are interior and singular phantasms rather than a communal hallucination. This skepticism about what "really" happened is supported by the poem's later gloss, which indicates that even the sympathetic Glossist believes the Mariner to be alone in his imaginings. Thus: "As it nearer approach, it seemeth him [i.e., not them] to be a ship"; "It seemeth him but the skeleton of a ship."[37] The 1798 text does not make clear what the crew does as the Mariner "witnesses" the dice game for their fates; however, the later text implies that they, including him at some point, have been looking down all along—"We listened and looked sideways up!"—till the ship disappears with a whisper (1817, l. 207). The men then die, possibly all at once, but more likely, individually, as they die of thirst.

How much more of the tale is hallucinatory? It may help to begin with the certain events. While stuck in an ice jam, the Mariner shot an albatross the crew had befriended; the superstitious crew feels this will have negative consequences, it doesn't and then it does, and they vacillate, not entirely sensibly, on the morality of killing the bird; during a period of dreadful calm at the equator, they hang the bird around his neck, feeling now it was surely a wrong thing to have killed the Albatross; to a man they die of thirst; although he somehow survives, he sees and hears many things in states of delirium and unconsciousness; he returns to land, understandably guilt-ridden and thus needing to justify what seems to him his ironic survival. We conclude that he makes narrative out of fact and private fiction to account consecutively for poignantly meaningless, unrelated events.

Furthermore, in imitation of medieval and Anglo-Saxon works, such as *Beowulf*,[38] which illustrate the historical grafting of Christianity upon pagan religions by their blending of Christian and pagan myth to account for epic events,[39] Coleridge has his Mariner create an artful pastiche of Christian and pagan explanatory events and symbols, but not so much to represent a transitional state of culture as to focus upon the act of consciousness in creating meaning. Thus, in his retrospective reconstruction of events, the Mariner employs a Christian metaphysic to account for the good and a pagan metaphysic to account for the bad. An exemplary indication of the former is the blessing of the water snakes "unawares." Literally, let us say, he felt moved by the beauty of living things in his depressed and isolated state and felt correspondingly rejuvenated. In retrospect, reflecting upon the religious meaning of his transformation from alienation to unity with living things, the Mariner decides that divine intervention *must* have occurred—"Sure my kind saint took pity on me," he protests—else, he wonders, how could he have been reborn? The Mariner thus asserts that he must have unknowingly blessed the snakes, despite the fact that blessing is an intentional act. On the other hand, the most important instance of switching belief systems to account for bad events is the imposition of a dice game to account for the awful fate of the mariners, for how could he assume that the loving Judeo-Christian God of the poem's moral was responsible? While the dice game could easily suggest to the Mariner the throwing of the die for Christ's clothing at the foot of the cross, Coleridge has him ignore this relevant association to emphasize the selective process he artfully employs to construct the Mariner's solipsistic fabrication. These explanatory projections of the Mariner, then, make the poem's critical issue not deciding the nature of the Mariner's universe, but rather interpreting the Mariner's self-serving projections, for whether he employs pagan or Christian motifs, both serve to dignify with cosmic significance a series of unfortunate, but not uncommon, literal events of a vessel lost at sea.

The tandem arguments of Wordsworth and Coleridge on the relationship of projection to guilt thus reach a bipolarity by March 1798: on one hand, there is the Pedlar's claim that the wisely meditative mind can, at times, under certain conditions, preclude self-projection and, on the other, there is the psycho-narrative of Coleridge's Mariner to illustrate the culturally-determined, hardly perceptible, shaping force of projection. Throughout this compositional period of *Ruined Cottage*, Wordsworth continued to experiment with poetry that represented more directly the states of consciousness the Pedlar was suggesting. "Wise passiveness" soon became more consciously formulated as an hypothesis of the selfless perceiver "Wrapped in a still dream [?of] forgetfulness."[40]

3. "let the moon / Shine on thee"
(*Tintern Abbey*, ll. 135-36)

Although nature in *Ruined Cottage* lacks a transcendental aura, Wordsworth had been speculating about the spirituality of his psychological experience in exploratory fragments. In support of Coleridge's "Frost at Midnight," Dorothy's journal descriptions of daily natural observation become a second voice of muted opposition to her brother's first attempts to make a quasi-religious phenomenon out of experience at hand.

In late December 1797, Coleridge began jotting verses on evanescent celestial landscapes in his Notebook:

> Twas not a mist, nor was it quite a cloud,
> But it pass'd smoothly on towards the Sea
> Smoothly & lightly betwixt Earth & Heaven.
> So thin a cloud—
> It scarce bedimm'd the Star that shone behind it.
> . . . .
>   And Hesper now
> Paus'd on the welkin's blue & cloudless brink,
> A golden circlet! while the Star of Jove,
> That other lovely Star, high o'er my head
> Shone whitely in the center of his Haze.
> . . . .
>   —one black-blue Cloud

> Stretched, like the heavens o'er all the cope of Heaven
> (*STCNB*, Vol. I, entries 315-18)

Dorothy's Alfoxden Journal and William's Alfoxden Notebook begin concurrently in January 1798. Following Coleridge's lead as if he had given her the assignment, Dorothy creates both literal and classically allusive skyscapes that color the sky with romance.

William's use of Dorothy's journal entry in the composition of "A Night-Piece" is a familiar matter,[41] but her subtle responses to her brother's immanent vision in subsequent lunar entries are not. Dorothy's description of the sky her brother would use in his first important poem of the winter is suggestive, but she stops short of interpretation:

> The sky spread over with one continuous cloud, whitened by the light of the moon, which, though her dim shape was seen, did not throw forth so strong a light as to chequer the earth with shadows. At once the clouds seemed to cleave asunder, and left her in the centre of a black-blue vault. She sailed along, followed by multitudes of stars, small, and bright, and sharp. Their brightness seemed concentrated, (half-moon). (*DWJ*, p. 2)

William transforms this description into a private vision:

> He looks around—the clouds are split
> Asunder, and above his head he views
> The clear moon & the glory of the heavens.
> There in a black-blue vault she sails along
> Followed by multitudes of stars, that small,
> And bright, & sharp along the gloomy vault
> Drive as she drives. How fast they wheel away!
> Yet vanish not! The wind is in the trees;
> But they are silent. Still they roll along
> Immeasurably distant, and the vault
> Built round by those white clouds, enormous clouds,
> Still deepens its interminable depth.

When the vision closes:

> the mind

> Not undisturbed by the deep joy it feels,
> Which slowly settles into peaceful calm,
> Is left to muse upon the solemn scene.[42]

The traveler has gone from pensiveness (through surprise, deep joy, and calm) to enlightened pensiveness as he is left to reflect upon the solemn sign of his vault that leads to infinity.

It might be expected that future lunar scenes in Dorothy's journal would recall the vision of her brother's poem. The entry for January 27, two days later, indeed does, but features an immediate shift from the light of his transcendental sky to its enhancement of the earth's intense loveliness:

> 27th. Walked from seven o'clock till half-past eight. Upon the whole an uninteresting evening. Only once while we were in the wood the moon burst through the invisible veil which enveloped her, the shadows of the oaks blackened, and their lines became more strongly marked. The withered leaves were coloured with a deeper yellow, a brighter gloss spotted the hollies; again her form became dimmer; the sky flat, unmarked by distances, a white thin cloud. The manufacturer's dog makes a strange, uncouth howl, which it continues many minutes after there is no noise near it but that of the brook. It howls at the murmur of the village stream. (*DWJ*, p. 3)

Wordsworth's poetic response to the same scene provides an instructive contrast:

> Solemn dreams,
> Dreams beautiful as the fair hues that lie
> About the moon in clouds of various depth,
> In many clouds about the full-orb'd moon.
> Why cannot they be still those barking curs
> That so disturb the stillness of the moon
> And make the [   ] restless?
> (Hayden, Vol. I, p. 311)

Literal accuracy aside, three differences are telling: 1) the clouds of the verse are suggestive of the aggregated mounds of "A Night-Piece," while Dorothy's are diffused ("clouds of various depth" vs. "the sky flat . . . a white thin cloud"); 2) the verse describes colors in the clouds about the moon; the journal highlights the colors of the earth ("fair hues that lie / About the moon in clouds" vs. "withered leaves were coloured, with a deeper yellow, a brighter gloss spotted the hollies"); 3) the verse responds to the dog's or dogs' barking with annoyance as the dreaming imagination is disturbed, while the journal notes the barking disinterestedly ("Why cannot they be still those barking curs" vs. "It howls at the murmur of the village stream").

On January 30, Dorothy records that William focused on yet another lunar scene:

> William called me into the garden to observe a singular appearance about the moon. A perfect rainbow, within the bow one star, only of colours more vivid. The semi-circle soon became a complete circle, and in the course of three or four minutes the whole faded away. Walked to the blacksmith's and the baker's; an uninteresting evening.
>
> (*DWJ*, p. 3)

Dorothy gives the scene its descriptive due without betraying any interest in speculation. A final journal entry on the lunar scenes of January 1798 again underscores the visual supremacy of earthly reality for Dorothy:

> 31st. Set forward to Stowey at half-past five. A violent storm in the wood; sheltered under the hollies. When we left home the moon immensely large, the sky scattered over with clouds. These soon closed in, contracting the dimensions of the moon without concealing her. The sound of the pattering shower, and the gusts of wind, very grand. Left the wood when nothing remained of the storm but the driving wind, and a few scattering drops of rain. Presently all clear, Venus first showing herself between the struggling clouds; afterwards Jupiter appeared. The hawthorn hedges, black and pointed, glittering with millions of diamond drops; the hollies shining with broader patches of light. The road to the village of Holford glittered like another stream. On our return, the wind high—a violent storm of hail and rain at the Castle of Comfort. The Heavens seemed in one perpetual motion when the rain increased; the moon appearing, now half-veiled, and now retired behind heavy clouds, the stars still moving, the roads very dirty.
>
> (*DWJ*, pp. 3-4)

The features of earth are given the sharpest notice in this entry. The stars were sparkling above, yet Dorothy anticipates "Frost At Midnight" in calling

attention to their earthbound correspondent forms, "glittering with millions
of diamond drops." The hollies were shining, the road glittered like a stream,
as the light of the moon reflected on wet surfaces. The elements of "A Night-
Piece" are present at the close—the veil of clouds, the moon half-veiled, the
moving stars—but rather than the motion of the heavens inspiring a grand
speculation, the passage ends ingloriously with "the roads very dirty."

Thus, Dorothy's natural descriptions seem unintended to reinforce her
brother's transcendental inclinations. The unpleasant conclusions to the
moon passages—the dog's howl and the dirty roads—even seem purposeful
distractions from the correspondences she herself creates. From a common-
sense point of view, such hard-headedness should not be entirely surprising.
When one considers that Wordsworth himself did not perceive a religious
quality in nature prior to 1797 or so—as Jonathan Wordsworth has argued,
there is very little evidence of a nature to support transcendental leanings in
the poetry of 1793-97 (*Descriptive Sketches, Salisbury Plain, Adventures on Salisbury
Plain, The Borderers* and *The Ruined Cottage*)[43]—one should not expect that
Dorothy would, or could, simply accept her brother's metaphysical assertions out of deference. It is difficult to imagine her challenging William
overtly, for what would be served by seeking to undermine this evolving
vision (or fantasy) that was beginning to provide a sense of poetic purpose?
She could quietly and effectively support their poetic endeavor by providing
descriptions of natural phenomena, without as yet being expected to leap
to faith.

Experimental fragments suggest that Wordsworth was not deflected
from his developing argument but that he also began to place considerable
stress upon the need to accept his insights as a precondition for an ideal
intimacy:

> never for each other shall we feel
> As we may feel, till we have sympathy
> With nature in her forms inanimate,
> With objects such as have no power to hold
> Articulate language. In all forms of things
> There is a mind
>
> (Hayden, Vol. I, pp. 268-69)[44]

Query: Why should anyone believe this assertion? Response: Because of its
corollary. There are,

> unknown modes of being which on earth,

Or in the heavens, or in the heavens and earth
Exist by mighty combinations, bound
Together by a link, and with a soul
Which makes all one.

> (Hayden, Vol. I, p. 269; *RC*, p. 123)

"Wise passiveness" becomes the code phrase for the egoless condition required of the perceiver to experience the truth of such assertions:

They rest upon their oars
Float down the mighty stream of tendency
A most wise passiveness in which the heart
Lies open and is well content to feel
As nature feels and to receive her shapes
As she has made them.

> (*RC*, p. 115)

H. W. Piper remarks that,

for Coleridge, Nature was symbolical, by which he meant that its appearances were designed to impress the mind of man and to bring him to know God. For Wordsworth the forms of nature were expressive of an independent life which was to be known and loved for its own sake and this love brought with it illumination and benevolence towards all life.[45]

Stephen Maxfield Parrish also observes that "Wordsworth's reading of a 'holy plan' behind the surfaces of nature . . . troubled Coleridge as much as any other practice of his partner's."[46] "Frost at Midnight" shows it is fair to surmise that Coleridge denies our ability to experience or perceive a pantheistic universe, even if it were the deepest truth, because Coleridge's experience and thought taught that one could only see through the self darkly.[47] However, Wordsworth was experiencing the salubrious effects of natural forms through reverie or trance, and as we noted above, Coleridge's "Nightingale" reveals that he could and would eventually capitulate, at least temporarily, to Wordsworth's beliefs.

In particular, Wordsworth was sharing reveries with Dorothy and boldly describing them as a kind of psycho-conjugal intimacy experienced in romantic settings of moonlight and "beds of forest moss":

In many a walk

> At evening or by moonlight, or reclined
> At midday upon beds of forest moss,
> Have we to Nature and her impulses
> Of our whole being made free gift, and when
> Our trance had left us, oft have we, by aid
> Of the impressions which it left behind,
> Looked inward on ourselves, and learned, perhaps,
> Something of what we are.

We recall William's earlier expression of intimacy expressed in his dream for a future with Dorothy: "How much do I wish that each emotion of pleasure and pain that visits your heart should excite a similar pleasure or a similar pain within me, by that sympathy which will almost identify us when we have stolen to our little cottage!" (*EY*, pp. 101-02). Psychological experience now becomes a substitute for sexual intimacy, which is pleasurably rehearsed again and again:

> Nor in those hours
> Did we destroy [   ]
> The original impression of delight,
> But by such retrospect it was recalled
> To yet a second and a second life,
> While in this excitation of the mind
> A vivid pulse of sentiment and thought
> Beat palpably within us, and all shades
> Of consciousness were ours.[48]

Dorothy Wordsworth also colored her natural descriptions with romantic desire, but directed at Coleridge. The journal entry for February 26, 1798 begins quietly to suggest emotions that she had not written about since her impassioned letters to Jane Pollard:

> walked with Coleridge nearly to Stowey after dinner. A very clear afternoon. We lay sidelong upon the turf, and gazed on the landscape till it melted into more than natural loveliness. The sea very uniform, of a pale greyish blue, only one distant bay, bright and blue as a sky; had there been a vessel sailing up it, a perfect image of delight. Walked to the top of a high hill to see a fortification. Again sat down to feed upon the prospect; a magnificent scene, *curiously* spread out for even

minute inspection, though so extensive that the mind is afraid to calculate its bounds. A winter prospect shows every cottage, every farm, and the forms of distant trees, such as in summer have no distinguishing mark. On our return, Jupiter and Venus before us. While the twilight still overpowered the light of the moon, we were reminded that she was shining bright above our heads, by our faint shadows going before us. We had seen her on the tops of the hills, melting into the blue sky.

(DWJ, 8)

Landscape "melt[ing] into more than natural loveliness," the moon "melting into the blue sky," with Jupiter and Venus in attendance, suggest an impassioned emotional communion. Coleridge used the term *melting* in this sense when he spoke of his initial response to his future wife: "I certainly love her. I think of her incessantly & with unspeakable tenderness—with that inward melting away of Soul that symptomatizes it" (*STCL*, Vol. I, p. 103). Dorothy now shares the experience with Colerige, just as it is Dorothy who replaces Sara as the reigning female presence of Coleridge's recent and coming poetry ("My Sister & my Friends" from "Lime-Tree Bower"; "My Friend, and thou, our Sister" from "The Nightingale"). Coleridge addressing Dorothy as sister allows for the kind of permissible infatuation that she once experienced with her brother.[49] Indeed, Dorothy's relationship with the married Coleridge was as brotherly as her relationship with William in that both required the desired denial of sexual experience. The classical gods and goddesses of Dorothy's night sky suggest an inevitable imaginative outlet, however, for the suppression.

Dorothy's use of pagan deities indicates that she was more inclined to romanticize than transcendentalize the night sky, which was a way of preferring Coleridge's skyscapes to her brother's. We can recall here Coleridge's notebook entry of December 1797 as a kind of authorizing document for Dorothy's romantic heavens:

> And Hesper now
> Paus'd on the welkin's blue & cloudless brink,
> A golden circlet! while the Star of Jove,
> That other lovely Star, high o'er my head
> Shone whitely in the center of his Haze.
> (*STCNB*, Vol. I, entry 317)

Hesper is the name for the planet Venus after sunset. The Star of Jove/Jupiter is the moon, or Diana, his daughter, who became committed to celibacy after seeing her mother in the throes of giving birth to Apollo, her brother. When prayed to by women in childbirth, Diana is known as Lucina. Part of the mythology of Diana's romantic life is that she eventually became the lover of the human shepherd Endymion.[50]

Dorothy dramatizes her celestial descriptions throughout January-February 1798 with the same panoply of pagan divinities, though, curiously, she never refers to the moon by name: "Venus first showing herself between the struggling clouds; afterwards Jupiter appeared" (January 31, 1798; *DWJ*, p. 3); "Full moon. She rose in uncommon majesty over the sea, slowly ascending through the clouds. Sat with the window open an hour in the moonlight" (February 1, 1798; *DWJ*, p. 4); from an experience witnessed alone with Coleridge, "I never saw such a union of earth, sky, and sea. The clouds beneath our feet spread themselves to the water, and the clouds of the sky almost joined them" (February 3, 1798; *DWJ*, p. 5); "Walked after dinner beyond Woodlands. A sharp and very cold evening; first observed the crescent moon, a silvery line, a thready bow, attended by Jupiter and Venus in their palest hues" (February 18, 1798; *DWJ*, p. 7); "On our return, Jupiter and Venus before us. . . . We had seen her [the moon] on the tops of the hills, melting into the blue sky" (February 26, 1798; *DWJ*, p. 8); in the final entry of the month, the sea swells: "The sea big and white, swelled to the very shores, but round and high in the middle. Coleridge returned with me, as far as the wood. A very bright moonlight night. Venus almost like another moon. Lost to us at Alfoxden long before she goes down the large white sea" (February 27, 1798; *DWJ*, pp. 8-9). Coleridge was also looking on the moon with an erotic wink: "Such light as Lovers love—when the <waxing> Moon steals in behind a black black Cloud, Emerging soon enough to make the Blush visible, which the long Kiss had kindled.—" (*STCNB*, Vol. I, entry 333). After this series of February entries, many describing solitary walks with Coleridge, no more is said of gendered celestial deities, and future skies are described less romantically.

The chief point to be observed in Dorothy's fragmented narrative is the relationship between Venus and Jupiter and the tension between the figures of Venus and the always unnamed moon goddess, Diana. According to Plato, Venus is Jupiter's daughter by the nymph Dione. Cicero identifies her more popular origin as arising from the froth of the sea. Because of her extraordinary beauty, Venus was carried into the heavens, where Jupiter unsuccessfully attempted to woo her. It wouldn't matter if Venus were Jupiter's unrequited love or his daughter, because, as a good Greek god, he exhibited no prejudice against incestuous relationships by marrying his sister, Juno. Venus herself is known for her many amours, the most famous with Mars, with whom she begot Cupid, but also with Mercury, Bacchus, Neptune, Adonis, Anchises, and the ugly and lame son of Jupiter, Vulcan, whom Jupiter forced her to marry because of her obstinacy to his advances. The goddess of love is thus the adulterous goddess of many lovers and the mother of many. In Dorothy's sky, Venus and Jupiter are still getting on well together, spending much of their time gazing upon the moon: "[we] first observed the crescent moon, a silvery line, a thready bow, attended by Jupiter and Venus in their palest hues"; "On our return, Jupiter and Venus before us. . . . We had seen her [the moon] on the tops of the hills, melting into the blue sky."

As noted above, Diana is the celibate daughter of Jupiter, who is referred to as Lucina when called upon by women in childbirth. She is a huntress as well. Dorothy's reference to a "silvery line, a thready bow," is a pretty explicit reference to her archer's bow. As a huntress, John Lempriere says, Diana is imaged as a rugged, manlike woman: "She is represented taller by the head than her attendant nymphs, her face has something manly, her legs are bare, well-shaped, and strong, and her feet are covered with a buskin, worn by huntresses among the ancients" (Lempriere, p. 201). She hunts to avoid men. However, as noted above, she did spend time with Endymion, and also with Pan, the bestial god of shepherds and hunters, and with Orion, whom she slew with arrows for his attempted rape of either her or one of her nymphs. Diana never lost her virginity.

Looking at Dorothy looking at the moon and Jupiter and Venus, we infer that she could readily identify with Diana to whatever extent she was aware of her myth. But what does Dorothy's night sky mean? Diana's celibacy, her physical ruggedness, and her strong, but diverted, romantic desires, are hardly esoterica. And then, across Dorothy's night sky is Diana's antithesis, Venus, the beautiful and erotic goddess of love and fertility, accompanied by the lascivious Jupiter. When we re-read Dorothy's final journal entry on the romantic heavens—"The sea big and white, swelled to the very shores, but round and high in the middle. Coleridge returned with me, as far as the wood. A very bright moonlight night. Venus almost like another moon"—we might understand the mythological subtext to mean that another Venus-goddess is yearning to emerge from the swelling sea, after this bright moonlit night in Coleridge's company, but the new Venus will be "almost like another moon." Though beautiful and desirable, she will yet retain the consciousness of Diana and thus fearful of pursuing her desires.

Dorothy's romantic allegory culminates with a corroborative para-praxis. While staying with Sara Coleridge at Stowey, like a supportive Lucina to be of assistance if Sara should go into labor (with Berkeley) during one of Coleridge's absences, Dorothy commits a textual slip in her journal entry's interchange of *Mr* for *Mrs*: "In the evening went to Stowey. I staid with Mr Coleridge. Wm went to Poole's. Supped with Mr Coleridge."[51] This unconscious slip occurs after about a month of nonromantic journal entries, as if it were a trickle of relief. Thus, we might conclude with Anne K. Mellor that "Dorothy's *Journals* linguistically represent a self that is not only rela- tional, formed in connection with the needs, moods and actions of other human beings, but also physically embodied. . . ."[52] But we will also appreciate the force behind her imaginative sublimations in expressing her love for both her brother and Coleridge.

By March 10, William Wordsworth experienced four important achieve- ments related to competition with Coleridge for poetic precedence and for influence over Dorothy. We have already considered the outcome of the dialogic interplay between *Ruined Cottage* and *Ancyent Marinere* and then Cole- ridge's capitulation to Wordsworth's program for natural morality in "The Nightingale." Regarding the latter, Coleridge was especially impressed by Wordsworth's argument that relating appropriately to nature's passive forms could affect a moral renewal partly through passive affection and partly through the resulting dormancy of aggression. He wrote to brother George:

> I love fields & woods & mounta[ins] with almost a visionary fondness—
> and because I have found benevolence & quietness growing within me
> as that fondness [has] increased, therefore I should wish to be the means
> of implanting it in others—& to destroy the bad passions not by
> combating them, but by keeping them in inaction.
>
> (*STCL*, Vol. I, p. 397)

In March, Coleridge wrote Cottle of his "evenness of benevolent feeling" and the "new & tender health" which is "all over me like a voluptuous feeling" (*STCL*, Vol. I, p. 401). The third point to be considered is the intellectual support Wordsworth found for his inclination to read nature spiritually in his new nature lyrics. The last, and summative point, is Wordsworth's reclamation of his sister's life and affections in *Tintern Abbey*.

4. "the language of the sense"
(*Tintern Abbey*, l. 109)

Although Coleridge's positive response to Wordsworth's ideas and poetry added to a resurgence of creative confidence, March 1798 also held its bad news. The Wordsworths learned early in the month that occasional visitors, such as John Thelwall; their lifestyle, such as moonlight ramblings and searching for origins of streams; and the radical reputations of Coleridge and even Thomas Poole, combined to make neighbors wary of their presence. During this period of threatened French invasion, the fewer democrats around the better, and thus the Wordsworths' lease on Alfoxden was not to be renewed.[53] Their immediate prospect, as Dorothy wrote to Mary Hutchinson on March 5, was unpleasant:

> It is decided that we quit Allfoxden—The house is lett. It is most probable that we shall go back again to Racedown, as there is little chance of our getting a place in this neighbourhood. We have no other very strong inducement to stay but Coleridge's society, but that is so important an object that we have it much at heart. . . . William was very unwell last week, oppressed with languor, and weakness.
>
> (*EY*, pp. 199-200)

On March 6, Dorothy reports visiting Coleridge, who was also "very ill" (*DWJ*, p. 9), with a toothache. While testifying to his greater need for Poole, Coleridge believed that the future of English verse actually depended on maintaining his relationship with Wordsworth, and he was right!

> he has written near 1200 lines of a blank verse, superior, I hesitate not to aver, to any thing in our language which any way resembles it. Poole (whom I feel so consolidated with myself that I seem to have no occasion to speak of him out of myself) thinks of it as likely to benefit mankind much more than any thing, Wordsworth has yet written.
>
> (*STCL*, Vol. I, p. 391)

Later, Coleridge would write of a combined attempt with Poole to find Wordsworth a residence in Stowey, for "Poole and I cannot endure to think of losing him" (*STCL*, Vol. I, p. 403).

Within a week, however, a plan was hatched for all, except Poole, to travel to Germany. Wordsworth was very pleased:

> We have a delightful scheme in agitation, . . . We have come to a resolution, Coleridge, Mrs. Coleridge, my Sister and myself of going into Germany, where we purpose to pass the two ensuing years in order to acquire the German language, and to furnish ourselves with a tolerable stock of information in natural science.
>
> (March 11, 1798: *EY*, p. 213).

Supported by the recent award of the Wedgwood annuity of £150 per annum, Coleridge now could afford to listen to the "nightly-whispering Voice" ("To the Rev. George Coleridge," l. 36) that reminded him of ambitions to fulfill. At work on a philosophical project to be called *The Recluse*, Wordsworth could readily convince himself that the study of natural science was essential to a poem on man, nature, and society. His recent reading of Erasmus Darwin's two-volume, 1300-page, medico-psychological treatise *Zoonomia: or the Laws of Organic Life* (1794-96) was proving to be extraordinarily productive for his poetry and for his intellectual independence.

Wordsworth's first great lyric of the spring, "Lines written at a small distance from my House, and sent by my little Boy to the Person to whom they are addressed,"[54] composed by March 10, 1798, reflects his recovery from "languor, and weakness" and the benefit of his recent reading of *Zoonomia*, which will be discussed here as the catalyst of Wordsworth's new poetry of nature. The "Person . . . addressed" is Dorothy; "[M]y little Boy" is Basil Caroline Montagu, now five years old. The extended title, "sent . . . to the Person to whom they are addressed," implies that the reader will learn of William's internalized sense of Dorothy as audience. In encouraging her compliance with his wish to share in a pantheist sentiment of early spring, William uses an argument sensitive both to the dynamics of their personal relationship and to Dorothy's affective responses to nature.

The poem affectionately but with confident persistence challenges Dorothy's indifference to natural supernaturalism, and her concern for more practical things—breakfast dishes, caring for little Basil, reading—as the poet-brother repeatedly implores her to join him outside. After describing the "blessing in the air, / Which seems a sense of joy to yield / To the bare trees, and mountains bare, / And grass in the green field" ("To My Sister," ll. 5-8), and sensing that his joy may not be sufficiently alluring, he quietly (parenthetically) uses a personal ploy—"('Tis a wish of mine)" (l. 9). Anticipating begrudged acquiescence, but undaunted, the poet becomes a bit louder in the next stanza—the parentheses are gone—in "pray[ing]" that "with speed" she put on her "woodland dress" (ll. 13-14), and furthermore "bring no book" (l. 15), as if she had done so previously and would again, in case there really wasn't anything to see or experience. Then follow the most lovely stanzas Wordsworth had yet written to describe the emotional rewards of spring idleness:

> Love, now an universal birth,
> From heart to heart is stealing,

From earth to man, from man to earth,
—It is the hour of feeling.

One moment now may give us more
Than fifty years of reason;
Our minds shall drink at every pore
The spirit of the season.

Some silent laws our hearts may make,
Which they shall long obey;
We for the year to come may take
Our temper from to-day.

And from the blessed power that rolls
About, below, above;
We'll frame the measure of our souls,
They shall be tuned to love.
                    (ll. 21-36)

This complete rejuvenation—epiphany for their minds, laws for their hearts, an expansive border for the metrical ("measure") and lyrical ("tuned") harmony of their souls—ought surely to please Dorothy. The poem concludes with a repetition of the earlier exhortation, excitedly imploring Dorothy to come outside, telling her again what to wear, and reminding her again what not to bring:

Then come, my sister! come, I pray,
With speed put on your woodland dress,
And bring no book; for this one day
We'll give to idleness.
                    (ll. 37-40)

In light of the poem's injunction against books, it is ironic that Wordsworth was reading quite purposefully at this time, as all of his nature ballads, including "To My Sister," reveal. After having requested Cottle for "very particular reasons" to send Darwin's *Zoonomia*, *"by the first carrier,"* most likely in late February (*EY*, pp. 198-99), Dorothy writes in mid-March, or shortly after this poem's composition, that the volumes had "already completely answered the purpose for which William wrote for them" (*EY*, pp. 214-15). Acquiring knowledge for *The Recluse* was most likely Wordsworth's main

motivation for reading Darwin, as James H. Averill has argued, but Averill
finds that only several relatively minor passages on the Pedlar's development
were a product of Darwin's influence. Averill emphasizes instead the good
use Wordsworth made of Darwin's case studies on obsession, madness, and
depression in developing experimental lyrics analogous to Darwin's "fear-
less" experimentalism—"Goody Blake and Harry Gill," "The Last of the
Flock," "The Thorn," "The Mad Mother," "The Idiot Boy," and "The Com-
plaint of the Forsaken Indian Woman."[55]

But Averill and others who have considered Darwin's influence have
missed the profounder impact of *Zoonomia* on Wordsworth's biological
understanding of life, which exceeds anecdotal inspiration for specific
poems. The corporal texture of Wordsworth's images, his confirmed position on nature's mental life, and his emphasis upon the symbiotic depen-
dence of the human body to nature in reaching its optimal state of physical
and mental health, all bespeak the far-ranging biomedical influence of
Darwin. Darwin's ideas on nature had been in the air since *The Botanic Garden*
(1791), which many scholars have noted as an influence on Coleridge,
though not on Wordsworth; however, the point here is that *Zoonomia* is a
direct influence—Wordsworth had it in his hands now—and, furthermore,
it far exceeds *The Botanic Garden* in its articulation of a scientific description
of the human body's systems and relationship to nature. It is arguable that
even the conceptual division of Wordsworth's *Lyrical Ballads* between nature
lyrics and experimental ballads, if these are perceived as poems of healthy
and degenerate states of being, conforms to the general emphases of *Zoonomia's* two volumes—the first offering a theory of the body's systems, including the relationship of body to nature, and the second giving a classification
of diseases that result when body systems or the mind go awry. To gauge
the extent of the influence of *Zoonomia* on Wordsworth's ballads, it will be
necessary to summarize in some detail Darwin's theory of health and disease.

Darwin's dedication "to all those who study the Operations of the
Mind" introduces a fundamental premise of his treatise: that diseases of the
body's physical systems lead to mental disturbance. *Mens sana in corpore sano.*
His strategy for altering the inchoate condition of early medical science is
"to reduce the facts belonging to ANIMAL LIFE into classes, orders, genera,
and species; and, by comparing them with each other, to unravel the theory
of diseases." The assumption that makes this ambition plausible is that "the
great CREATOR of all things has infinitely diversified the works of his
hands, but has at the same time stamped a certain similitude on the features
of nature, that demonstrates to us, that *the whole is one family of one parent.* On
this similitude is founded all rational analogy; . . ."[56]

Darwin's analogues of vegetable to animal and human life are that:

> the roots of vegetables resemble the lacteal system of animals; the sap-vessels in the early spring, before their leaves expand, are analogous to the placental vessels of the foetus; that the leaves of land-plants resemble lungs . . . that the digestive power of vegetables is similar to that of animals converting the fluids, which they absorb into sugar; that their seeds resemble the eggs of animals, and their buds and bulbs their viviparous offspring. And, lastly, that the anthers and stigmas are real animals, attached indeed to their parent tree, like polypi or coral insects, but capable of spontaneous motion; that they are affected with the passion of love, and furnished with powers of re-producing their species, and are fed with honey like the moths and butterflies, which plunder their nectaries.
>
> (*Zoonomia*, Vol. I, pp. 104-105)

Because vegetables have functional properties analogous to the five senses, Darwin speculates on the possibility that vegetables may also have "ideas of external things," which leads directly to a more extensive discussion of natural love:

> Besides these organs of sense, which distinguish cold, moisture, and darkness, the leaves of mimosa, and of dionaea, and of drofera, and the stamens of many flowers . . . are sensible to mechanic impact; that is, they possess a sense of touch, as well as a common sensorium; . . . Lastly, in many flowers the anthers, when mature, approach the stigma; in others the female organ approaches to the male. . . . I ask, by what means are the anthers in many flowers, and stigmas in other flowers, directed to mind their paramours? How do either of them know that the other exists in their vicinity? Is this curious kind of storge produced by mechanic attraction, or by the sensation of love? The latter opinion is supported by the strongest analogy, because a reproduction of the species is the consequence; and then another organ of sense must be wanted to direct these vegetable amourettes to find each other, one probably analogous to our sense of smell, which in the animal world directs the new-born infant to its source of nourishment, and they may thus possess a faculty of perceiving as well as of producing odours.
>
> (*Zoonomia*, Vol. I, p. 106)

Darwin concludes his discussion "Of Vegetable Animation" with a summary of the grand similitude between vegetable and animate life:

> Thus, besides a kind of taste at the extremities of their roots, similar to that of the extremities of our lacteal vessels, for the purpose of selecting their proper food; and besides different kinds of irritability residing in the various glands, which separate honey, wax, resin, and other juices from their blood; vegetable life seems to possess an organ of sense to distinguish the variations of heat, another to distinguish the varying degrees of moisture, another of light, another of touch, and probably another analogous to our sense of smell. To these must be added the indubitable evidence of their passions of love; and I think we may truly conclude, that they are furnished with a common sensorium belonging to each bud, and that they must occasionally repeat those perceptions either in their dreams of waking hours, and consequently possess ideas of so many of the properties of the external world, and of their own existence.
>
> (*Zoonomia*, Vol. I, pp. 106-107)

It is not difficult to see that Darwin's romantic biology underlies the faith of Wordsworth's "doctrinal poems"[57] "that every flower / Enjoys the air it breathes," and that "The budding twigs spread out their fan / To catch the breezy air" in "pleasure" (from "Lines Written in Early Spring"). The hypothesis that plant life has a mental component to stimulate its attraction towards its kind for the survival of species underlies what seem fantastic assertions in Wordsworth's blank verse fragments of March 1798: "All beings have their properties which spread / Beyond themselves, a power by which they make / Some other being conscious of their life, / Spirit that knows no insulated spot, / No chasm, no solitude, from link to link / It circulates the soul of all the worlds" (Gill, p. 676, ll. 6-11). The quiet love-force suffusing the plant kingdom could be experienced or felt at the deepest levels of human consciousness, if that consciousness could lie as passively receptive to its natural environment as a flower.

Wordsworth's transcendent culminations do exceed Darwin's speculations, though Darwin anticipates the step. Darwin's image of life is a network of biological systems autonomically ingesting the universe in pleasure and pain with a corresponding, physiologically-based mental system. He does not argue against a spiritual component to life. In fact, in an important analogue he allows that just as the force of gravity is immaterial in that it is "supposed to exist in or with matter, but to be quite distinct from it, and to be equally capable of existence, after the matter, which now possesses it, is decomposed" so might there be a "spirit of animation . . . capable of existing as well separately from the body as with it." However, his concerns, as he says, are more modest: "By the words spirit of animation or sensorial power, I mean only that animal life which mankind possesses in common with brutes, and in some degree even with vegetables, and leave the consideration of the immortal part of us, which is the object of religion, to those who treat of revelation" (*Zoonomia*, Vol. I, p. 109). He then begins a disquisition on the physiological "Production of Ideas," which moves through each of the senses from most to least primitive in building a metaphysical mind in/of the physical mass of cells called a brain.

At about this time of Wordsworth's greatest interest in Darwin, Coleridge was scribbling in his Notebook a cryptic comment about "the absurdity of the Darwinian System—Birds—Allegators" (*STCNB*, Vol. I, entry 330). Kathleen Coburn is probably correct in suggesting that Darwin's dismissive disregard of epistemology troubled Coleridge most:[58] "So true is the observation of the famous Malbranch, 'that our senses are not given us to discover the essences of things, but to acquaint us with the means of preserving our existence' . . . a melancholy reflection to philosophers" (*Zoonomia*, Vol. I, p. 108). One might expect that such anti-intellectualism would offend Wordsworth as well, yet having recently cast off Godwin's systematizing for not having its feet on the ground, Wordsworth was more likely to be seduced by Darwin's empiricism, especially by its implied challenge to track physical reality to the brink of transcendental speculation.[59]

Darwin begins his discussion of the sensory foundation of mental life with touch, the most ubiquitous and primary sense for being diffused throughout the entire body and being the source of our earliest experience, "for the foetus must experience some varieties of agitation, and exert some muscular action, in the womb; and may, with great probability, be supposed thus to gain some ideas of its own figure, of that of the uterus, and of the tenacity of the fluid that surrounds it" (*Zoonomia*, Vol. I, pp. 109-10). The nonmaterial force of our existence, understood as the Spirit of Animation, is materialized by Darwin in the medulla, with which it shares an identical figure:

> I appeal to common sense! the spirit of animation acts, Where does it act? It acts wherever there is the medulla above mentioned; and that whether the limb is yet joined to a living animal, or whether it be recently detached from it; as the heart of a viper or frog will renew its

contractions, when pricked with a pin, for many minutes of time after
its exsection from the body.—Does it act any where else?—No; then
it certainly exists in this part of space, and no where else; that is, it hath
figure; namely, the figure of the nervous system, which is nearly the
figure of the body.

(*Zoonomia*, Vol. I, p. 111).

Darwin continues with a discussion of animation in a passage that will soon
influence Wordsworth's "motion and a spirit" sensed in ocean, "living air,"
and "light of setting suns" in *Tintern Abbey*:

Hence the spirit of animation at the time it communicates or receives
motion from solid bodies, must itself possess some property of solidity.
And in consequence at the time it receives other kinds of motion from
light, it must possess that property, which light possesses, to commu-
nicate that kind of motion; and for which no language has a name,
unless it may be termed Visibility.

(*Zoonomia*, Vol. I, p. 115).

Darwin describes the body as a magnificent

muscular system . . . considered as one organ of sense, and the various
attitudes of the body, as ideas belonging to this organ, of many of which
we are hourly conscious, while many others, like irritative ideas of the
other senses, are performed without our attention. When the muscles
of the heart cease to act, the refluent blood again distends or elongates
them; and thus irritated, they contract as before. The same happens to
the arterial system, and I suppose to the capillaries, intestines, and
various glands of the body. . . . All these motions of the muscles, that
are thus naturally excited by the stimulus of distending bodies, are also
liable to be called into strong action by their catenation, with the
irritations or sensations produced by the momentum of the progressive
particles of blood in the arteries, as in inflammatory fevers; or by acrid
substances on other sensible organs, . . .

(*Zoonomia*, Vol. I, pp. 123-24).

This body image of inner and outer sensation, which Wordsworth obviously
took to heart in claiming interior body consciousness in *Tintern Abbey*—"felt
in the blood, and felt along the heart," "even the motion of our human blood
/ Almost suspended"—additionally has appetites or painful desires felt when

deficiency occurs, as the desire for heat, extension, animal love, and fresh air (*Zoonomia*, Vol. I, p. 125).

Darwin also provides a substantial physiological analogue between the association of ideas and body movements. Patterns or catenations of body movements have an associative bonding parallel to the association of ideas. Furthermore, body catenations and idea catenations can proceed independently of each other, which is of consequence for the reverie state of "wise passiveness":

> When we are employed with great sensation of pleasure, or with great efforts of volition, in the pursuit of some interesting train of ideas, we cease to be conscious of our existence, and inattentive to time and place, and do not distinguish this train of sensitive and voluntary ideas from the irritative ones excited by the presence of external objects, though our organs of sense are surrounded with their accustomed stimuli, till at length this interesting train of ideas becomes exhausted, or the appulses of external objects are applied with unusual violence, and we return with surprise, or with regret, into the common track of life. This is termed reverie or studium.
>
> (Zoonomia, Vol. I, p. 220)

Pattern suggests repetition as a separate experience of pleasure. In the chapter, "Of Propensity to Motion, Repetition and Imitation," Darwin theorizes that physiological economy is responsible for our pleasure in the repetition of body motion, thought, sound, language, or larger patterns: "This kind of pleasure arising from repetition, that is from the facility and distinctness with which we perceive and understand repeated sensations, enters into all the agreeable arts; and when it is carried to excess is termed formality" (*Zoonomia*, Vol. I, p. 253). Pleasure in language repetition is due to "the greater ease and energy with which our organ is excited by the combined sensorial powers of association and irritation" (*Zoonomia*, Vol. I, p. 252).

Just as arguments formed in unpublished manuscripts led to the confident assertions of published lyrics, so unpublished verse also nurtured the equivalent stylistic feature that gave an experimental cast to the verse of spring 1798: "To the bare trees, and mountains bare"; "And fiercely by the arm he took her"—"And fiercely by the arm he shook her"; "the shadow of a babe you trace, / A baby and a baby's face"; "For joy he cannot hold the bridle / For joy his head and heels are idle, / He's idle all for very joy"; "I said and took him by the arm"—"I said and held him by the arm"—"While still I held him by the arm", etc.

The combined effect of Darwin's empirical evidence and medical science—the mental and emotional life of nature; the autonomic integrity of body systems, with the supporting descriptions of their interior motions; the responsiveness of body to external stimuli and its consequent condition of mental and physical being; the independent life of body and mind deriving from patterned behavior; the pleasure that body and mind experience in repetition—all have some bearing on the world view, experience, imagery, diction, and rhythms Wordsworth now employed in his poetry. Together they significantly gloss Dorothy's comment that *Zoonomia* had served Wordsworth's purpose, which we may infer was an empirical foundation for natural morality and an essentially new vision for poetry. It may not be too speculative to conclude that, if Wordsworth derives his nature from Erasmus Darwin and Alfred Lord Tennyson (1809-92) derives his nature from Charles Darwin, the grandson of Erasmus, the Darwins do indeed divide and define a century of poetic art through the greatest Romantic and the greatest Victorian poet of nineteenth-century England.

Wordsworth will argue later in "Tables Turned" and "Expostulation and Reply" that ratiocination is irrelevant because useless as a formative power in moral development. Real power, like formative sensation, bypasses consciousness entirely. Spirit enters "mind" via pores of the body; the heart, acting independently, makes its own compact with nature. Their morning meal being done, Wordsworth invites his sister outside to feel the sun, but more to feed their spirits, as the consistent analogue for Wordsworth's natural morality is the influence of food upon the body. One decides what to eat; the poet, what sensations to expose himself to. After that, the results are inevitable: "Our minds shall drink at every pore / The spirit of the season" ("Lines Written at a Small Distance From My House," ll. 27-28); "we can feed this mind of ours, / In a wise passiveness" ("Expostulation and Reply," (ll. 23-24); "in this moment there is life and food / For future years" (*Tintern Abbey*, ll. 65-66). As Wordsworth was to argue in his "Essay on Morals," written sometime between September 1798 and February 23, 1799:

> I know no book or system of moral philosophy written with sufficient power to melt into our affections, to incorporate itself with the blood and vital juices of our minds, and thence to have any influence worth our notice in forming those habits of which I am speaking. . . . Can it be imagined by any man who has deeply examined his own heart that an old habit will be foregone, or a new one formed, by a series of propositions . . . ?[60]

When Coleridge complained to Hazlitt in the summer of 1798 that there was "a something corporeal, a *matter-of-factness*, a clinging to the palpable"[61] in Wordsworth's poetry, he was speaking literally and critically of Darwin's biological influence.

It can be no surprise that Coleridge's assent to the healing and moral power of Wordsworth's nature proved transient. On May 14, 1798, Berkeley Coleridge was born. Coleridge reacted again with great anxiety to the birth of a child and expressed his need, not for natural forms, but for "practical religion." Coleridge wrote to his friend, the Unitarian preacher, John Prior Estlin:

> I have been too neglectful of practical religion—I mean, actual & stated prayer, & a regular perusal of scripture as a morning & evening duty! May God grant me grace to amend this error; for it is a grevious one!— Conscious of frailty I almost wish (I say it confidentially to you) that I had become a stated Minister: for indeed I find true Joy after a sincere prayer; but for want of habit my mind wanders, and I cannot *pray* as often [as] I ought.... Prayer & distinct confession I find most serviceable to my spiritual health when I can do it. But tho' all my doubts are done away, tho' Christianity is my *Passion*, it is too much my *intellectual* Passion: and therefore will do me but little good in the hour of temptation & calamity.—
>
> (*STCL*, Vol. I, p. 407)

Poole received a similar letter in which Coleridge admitted that nature had been replaced by "Religion & *commonplace* Religion too," which was now his "restorer & [his] comfort—giving [him] gentleness & calmness & dignity!" Wordsworth probably was annoyed, if not distressed, with Coleridge's apostasy from natural religion. When it mattered most, Coleridge was no disciple.

5. "healing thoughts"
(*Tintern Abbey*, l. 145)

The Wordsworths vacated Alfoxden by the end of June 1798 and decided to enjoy a walking tour before venturing to Germany with, they then thought, the Coleridge family. They stayed with the Coleridges in Nether Stowey for several days and then left for Bristol and the Wye valley in

Wales, where they enjoyed a walking tour that would prove to be one of William's finest creative experiences. Speaking of *Lines Written A Few Miles Above Tintern Abbey*, he wrote: "No poem of mine was composed under circumstances more pleasant for me to remember than this. I began it upon leaving Tintern, after crossing the Wye, and concluded it just as I was entering Bristol in the evening, after a ramble of 4 or 5 days, with my sister." (*LB*, p. 357)

Though this note was dictated to his ardent friend Isabella Fenwick more than forty years after the event, there is good reason to trust Wordsworth's memory. During the course of this walking tour, he was physically invigorated,[62] creatively fulfilled (*Lyrical Ballads* was in press in Bristol), alone with his sister, and thus confident enough to deal with the issues that mattered most. As they walked, it must have come upon him that the time was opportune to reflect upon, indeed to interpret, the flow of his life for Dorothy, obviously in the face of what she knew and believed of it herself. He also wanted to respond critically to Coleridge's work and thought, inasmuch as it conflicted with his own, again in Dorothy's presence, and perhaps with renewed hope of winning something more than Coleridge's "suspension of disbelief for the moment, which constitutes poetic faith" (*BL*, Vol. II, p. 6). And he had yet to transform the rents in his life over death, guilt, and abandonment into an optimistic narrative, one that, as *The Prelude* would later phrase it, was "in the end / All gratulant if rightly understood" (*Prelude*, Book XIII, ll. 384-85).

Reading *Tintern Abbey* as an evolving speech act that seeks to achieve a recollective synthesis of persuasive force helps one to understand its verbal tensions, its tentativeness, and even its rents. The tonal unease of *Tintern Abbey*, especially, which has seemed to so many readers a sign of the poet's doubt in his optimistic narrative,[63] can also, and I think preferably, be read as the poet's sensitivity to his sister as a wary auditor, who, together with Coleridge, represents the skepticism of the wider audience Wordsworth began to confront in the credal lyrics of *Lyrical Ballads*, most notably in "Expostulation and Reply" and "Tables Turned." Although Thomas McFarland discusses *Tintern Abbey* quite differently, he describes the poem as I will discuss: "the poem is somewhat restless and uncertain at its beginning, [but] settles down to a broad and deep current of Wordsworthian certainty, and concludes . . . in some of the most pure and limpid verse Wordsworth ever wrote."[64] In my terms, this poet has not changed his beliefs in the two months since composing his hortatory ballads of May 1798; rather, he has changed his relationship with his immediate audience—Dorothy and Coleridge—because he is aware of its possible skepticism towards the life story he will unfold.

I will concede that a reading with biographical and rhetorical premises such as these promises to be evasive of the poet's and poem's relationship to the historical and political moment, though, in passing, an imbalance may be corrected. In particular, Marjorie Levinson's argument on the relevance of the historical and political information that *Tintern Abbey* suppresses is a large, but half-empty, pitcher. Levinson says that the "textual maneuver" of *Tintern Abbey* is "Wordsworth's erasure of the occasional character of the poem," that is, the quadrupled cluster of mid-July events that the dating of the poem suggests, but which the poem ignores: the ninth anniversary of Bastille Day, the eighth anniversary of the poet's trip to Revolutionary France, the fifth anniversary of Marat's assassination, and the fifth anniversary of the poet's first visit to the Abbey. Levinson states, further, that "the success or failure of the visionary poem turns on its ability to hide its omission of the historical," in other words, the socioeconomic conditions of the Wye valley that peopled the picturesque ruins of the Abbey grounds with tragically ruined lives—the dispossessed, the unemployed, and the vagrants from the war with France.[65] This now (in)famous argument has aroused spirited and even vituperous opposition,[66] all impatient with its ploy of arguing for the importance of the text's meaningful "silences"[67] and even more so for its idiosyncratic selection of material that is predetermined to be relevant. As McFarland has charged: "Levinson's licence for intervention [of repressed material] is so broad that she has no right to exclude anything"; nevertheless, she does so for political and ideological reasons.[68]

To begin with Levinson's critique: If *Tintern Abbey* is read as the culmination of *Lyrical Ballads*, it is unfair to accuse the poet of socioeconomic effacement for not yet again stressing the plight of the dispossessed, the homeless, and the vagrants. In other words, the reader has been prepared to listen for the "still, sad music of humanity" (*Tintern Abbey*, l. 92) through the strategic placement of eleven previous poems on idiot boys, deranged and abandoned mothers, paupered shepherds, and finally convicts.[69] Neither is it quite accurate to accuse the poet of historical effacement for apparently ignoring the "occasional character of his poem," that is, the historical anniversaries of Bastille Day and the assassination of Marat as well as the personal anniversaries of a first trip to France and his last trip to the Abbey. Apart from whatever political allusions one might argue for in the poem, the poem's opening lines emphasize that winters, rather than

summers, have prolonged the psychological time of his absence from the
Wye valley:

> Five years have passed; five summers, with the length
> Of five long winters!
>> (*Tintern Abbey*, ll. 1-2)

The biographical significance of winter and December for the Wordsworth family was profoundly more distressing than that of summer and
July, though both seasons and months are biographically significant.
Recollecting the morose events of winter considered in Part One of this
study helps one to relate the form of the lengthened line and its redun-
dancy ("length"—"long") to the content of the repetitious pattern of ill-
fortune associated with the "the length / Of five long winters!" It has gone
unmentioned, but it is of some importance here, that Wordsworth's failing
to mention spring and fall provides indirect evidence of the biographical
relevance of winter and summer.

Here is a review of the biographical events from the winter of 1778
to the historical present of the winter of 1798; twenty years rather than five,
it is true, but the "five long winters" of *Tintern Abbey* have brought the
recollections of the preceding fifteen now into the darkest relief: William
and Dorothy's mother, Ann Wordsworth, died in late winter 1778; shortly
thereafter their father, John Wordsworth, dissolved his household, sending
the brothers to Hawkshead Grammar School and Dorothy to the home of
distant relatives, thus separating Dorothy from her brothers from December
1777, until their reunion a decade later in 1787. John Wordsworth died in
December 1783, leaving the children completely dependent upon relatives
because his employer, Lord James Lowther, refused to pay the family the
£5,000 owed for his services. Wordsworth's first separation from his French
mistress, Annette Vallon, and the birth of their daughter, Anne-Caroline,
occurred in December 1792. England and France declared war on each other
in the winter of 1793, ruining William's plans for returning to Annette and
provoking his hatred of his fatherland. William's surreptitious return to
Annette and their parting (until 1802) occurred in a snowy French October
of 1793. Wordsworth's benefactor, Raisley Calvert, whom Wordsworth
nursed as he died of consumption in January 1795, provided another infusion
of guilty conscience for self-interest prevailing over altruism. Wordsworth
experienced his deepest depression over revolutionary politics and personal
responsibilities in the winter of 1795-96, when he "Yielded up moral questions in despair" (*Prelude*, Bk. X, l. 900). Even *The Borderers* being rejected for

the London stage in December 1797, belongs to this biographical litany as the failed emblematic work of its psychological summation. All of these, and the summers of Levinson, prepare one for reading *Tintern Abbey* as an artifice of poetic intensity, deeply troubled not by history per se, but history as experienced, which is biography.

The poem's overt auditor, Dorothy Wordsworth, was more than aware of this troubled family and personal pretext. Indeed, as we have seen, her isolation and youthful anguish exacerbated her brother's pain and became the controlling guilt of his life. Thus, from its grosser structural features to the very specific moments of its nervous transitions, the poem's argument anticipates the implied reaction of its auditor to moments of a distressing biographical record. The poem's implied auditor, Coleridge, becomes implicated intertextually, because Wordsworth chose Coleridge's "Eolian Harp" as a formal guide and oppositional inspiration for this synthetic and sensitive enterprise of poetic persuasion. These combined voices, texts, and pressures of immediate and implied audience, sharpened by specific biographical, aesthetic, and philosophical differences, give *Tintern Abbey* a quality of tonal complexity that Wordsworth would never match. Therefore, I think that it is nigh futile to continue reading this poem as if the poet were arguing with himself. Don H. Bialostosky admonishes wisely: "If we expect Wordsworth's voice to be involved with other voices, if we hear how his voice is indeed constituted in and as an interplay of voices, we will stop complaining of interruptions or condescending to ideologies and move on to examine interactions and resistances."[70] To paraphrase Pope's line on the sensitivity of the spider to its life in the web, Wordsworth's poem, too, becomes "exquisitely fine!" for "feel[ing] at each [biographical] thread, and liv[ing] along the line."[71]

In order to understand the subtext that Coleridge's "Eolian Harp" became for *Tintern Abbey*, we first will consider what Coleridge's poem would have meant to Wordsworth.[72] We recall from Part One that its "soft floating witchery of sound" most likely inspired the creation of the voluptuary, Lord Clifford, of *The Borderers* as a way of dealing with the passing jealousy Wordsworth felt over Dorothy's attraction to Coleridge. Furthermore, Coleridge considered "Eolian Harp" the "favorite of [his] poems" (*STCL*, Vol. I, p. 295), which would have vexed Wordsworth for its opposition to the critical positions he held or would take on biography, religious experience, and poetic purpose: to wit, "Eolian Harp" plays the easier tune in rejecting a troubled past as a period to be repented, rather than accepting it as the formative period of the present; it rejects personal religious vision as a prideful, negative way of indolence, mental vagrancy, and misplaced libido;

it affirms a necessity to accept Revelation as given, rather than a personal, recurrent experience; finally, it verges on humiliation of the visionary poet in preferring the stifling humility of its auditor above the quest for imaginative religious experience. Though beautiful, it is manipulative.

Wordsworth also recognized "Eolian Harp" as a clever formal construction in adapting the parts of a classical oration to its allegedly "effusive" development. Its original title in *Poems* (1796) was "Effusion XXXV." The parts of the classical oration both poems employ are the *exordium*, or introduction; the *propositio*, or view to be maintained, which in *Tintern Abbey* also contains a division of the proposition into *partitiones*; the *narratio*, or presentation of experiences and facts that lead to the proposition; the *argumentatio*, or confirmation of the proposition through arguments of reason and emotion, which considers opposing arguments; and the *peroratio*, or exhortation to the audience—or auditor, in the case of both poems—to adopt the speaker's position. Wordsworth also uses an optional sixth part of an oration, the appeal to emotion.[73] A classically based educational system made this rhetorical structure a familiar and congenial pattern for arguing on one's feet, and thus likely to be employed—perhaps even expected—whenever extemporaneousness or its illusion was desired or required. It is likely that Coleridge employed this hortatory form for poetry because his conversation poems were essentially arguments, in intent and thus in rhetorical form. Also, their origin was contemporaneous with a fervid period of lecturing. He composed six lectures on his own and assisted Robert Southey in the composition of another dozen in 1795, the year of "Eolian Harp." Coleridge's later meditative lyrics or conversation poems also employ the form and Wordsworth got the point.[74]

The *exordium* of *Tintern Abbey* is its first verse paragraph (ll. 1-22). The landscape description prepares for the poem's later movement towards relational perfection with the auditor. The poet describes a landscape of objects without boundaries, though objects retain separate identity; a present time that blends with past time; and a welcoming from nature for human dwellers. In contrast to Coleridge's "distant Sea" providing a "stilly murmur" to *tell* "of silence" (ll. 11-12), the gentle Wye rolls from its "mountain springs / With a soft inland murmur," to bespeak an hardly audible communication about peacefulness. "Wreaths of smoke" are "Sent up, in silence," as if in purposeful sign of welcome from "vagrant dwellers" in nature, or from a cave "where by his fire / The Hermit sits alone" (ll. 22-23).

Nevertheless, this smoke, as Mary Moorman and others have pointed out, has a peculiarly unromantic smell to it, deriving both from the charcoal factories on the Wye and from William Gilpin's *Observations on the River Wye*

. . . *made in the Summer of 1770* (1771), which the Wordsworths carried with them on this four- or five-day jaunt. Here is the passage from Gilpin: "Many of the furnaces, on the banks of the river, consume charcoal, which is manufactured on the spot; and the smoke, which is frequently seen issuing from the sides of the hills; and spreading its thin veil over a part of them, beautifully breaks their lines, and unites them with the sky."[75] Kenneth R. Johnston has also argued that *Tintern Abbey* demands a political reading for transmuting the extended attention Gilpin gives to the impoverished vagrants on the Abbey's grounds and throughout the vicinity with the remarkably picturesque phrase: "vagrant dwellers in the houseless woods."[76] Interestingly, however, the approval to ignore the sociopolitical implications of a beautiful landscape is also to be found in Gilpin. In his *Three Essays: On Picturesque Beauty; on Picturesque Travel; and On Sketching Landscape* (1792) he writes:

> We are most delighted, when some grand scene, tho perhaps of incorrect composition, rising before the eye, strikes us beyond the power of thought . . . and every mental operation is suspended. In this pause of intellect, this *deliquium* [eclipse] of the soul, an enthusiastic sensation of pleasure overspreads it, previous to any examination of the rules of art. The general idea of the scene makes an impression, before any appeal is made to the judgement. We rather *feel* than *survey* it.[77]

John Thelwall, the greatest radical of the day, made a comment even more to the point on the power of this particular landscape to distract one from the socio-historical. Though it turns out that he was mistaken, because his neighbors turned out to be hateful boors, Thelwall chose the Wye valley as a retreat from public life because, "Such a retreat could not but appear, to an enthusiastic imagination, as a sort of enchanted dormitory, where the agitations of political feeling might be cradled to forgetfulness, and the delicious day dreams of poesy might be renewed."[78] The Wordsworths visited the Thelwall residence in Llys Wen during their July walking tour, but *Tintern Abbey* represents neither the naivete of Thelwall's dreamy retreat nor his embattled reality.

Analogous to the transitional function of Coleridge's wind harp ("Eolian Harp," ll. 26-35), the hermit in *Tintern Abbey* provides a bridge between both the poem's imagery and the poet's experience as well as between the *exordium* and the *propositio*. As Coleridge has lain, like the wind harp, receptive to passing sensory inspiration, so Wordsworth has withdrawn into hermetic states of consciousness "oft, in lonely rooms, and mid the din / Of towns and cities" (*Tintern Abbey*, ll. 26-27), where for lack of human relationship, he has dwelt on memories of the Wye and its landscape. The associations that the hermit arouses are as central to the movement of *Tintern Abbey* as the wind harp is in "Eolian Harp." The abbey of the poem's title suggests that a hermit is the new monk of nature, living outside of traditional religious structures, within a primitive wood of holiness. Yet the poet does not prefer isolation. Though *alone* resoundingly concludes the positive, first verse paragraph, when it is echoed three lines later in the biographical experience of "lonely rooms" we begin to expect that human relationship in the poem will become prominent. For it is a distressed man who in his loneliness has received the benefits of psychological defense that he now forms as the tripartite *partitio* of the poem's proposition (*Tintern Abbey*, ll. 22-49): he has owed to the "beauteous forms" of memory 1) "sensations sweet, / Felt in the blood, and felt along the heart" (ll. 28-29); 2) "feelings too / Of unremembered pleasure" (ll. 31-32); and 3) "another gift, / Of aspect more sublime" (ll. 37-38), a "blessed mood" of mystical union:

> In which the affections gently lead us on,
> Until, the breath of this corporeal frame,
> And even the motion of our human blood
> Almost suspended, we are laid asleep
> In body, and become a living soul:
> While with an eye made quiet by the power
> Of harmony, and the deep power of joy,
> We see into the life of things.
>   (*Tintern Abbey*, ll. 43-49)

In a meaningful contrast with Coleridge's sexual metaphor of the harp aroused by breeze and his parallel imaginative experience ("Eolian Harp," ll. 12-25; 26-35), Wordsworth's sensations and emotions flow towards an ultimate mood of passivity in a progression controlled by the associative links of memory, rather than external sensation. The mind brings forth only what is desired for the needs of the moment.

    On some level of consciousness, the poet also has quietly assimilated his auditor into the experience he describes to counter a lack of intimacy. The unobtrusive change of first-person pronoun from singular to plural is his verbal gesture. The description begins with solitary reflection—"Nor less, I trust" and "I may have owed"—but when the process of losing self-consciousness is reached, a pronoun shift is made: "The affections gently lead *us* on"; "the motion of *our* human blood"; "*we* are laid asleep / In body"; and, "*We* see into the life of things" (emphasis added). The colon and extended dash following "Is lightened:—," and after which the pronoun shift is made, may signal a turn to the auditor for response. Coleridge's auditor being his betrothed, the sexual metaphor of wind and harp is an inevitable figure of amorous desires; Wordsworth's auditor and partner in experience being a sibling, another order of intimate experience is required. Their bodies must be put to rest as minds interact; their emotions are best tranquilized; until "We," that is, William and Dorothy, brother and sister, "are laid asleep / In body, and become a living soul."

John Donne, whom Wordsworth had been reading in the past few months,[79] would have provided a literary precedent in "The Extasie" for understanding how "We" can become a single "soul." While Donne's lovers lie silent and motionless on a river bank together, "hands . . . firmely cimented / With a fast balme" (ll. 5-6), "bodies like sepulchrall statues" (l. 18), they experience a comparable spiritual unification:

> When love, with one another so
>   Interinanimates two soules,
> That abler soule, which thence doth flow,
>   Defects of lonelinesse controuls.
> Wee then, who are this new soule, know,
>   Of what we are compos'd, and made,
> For, th'atomies of which we grow,
>   Are soules, whom no change can invade.
> . . . .
> And if some lover, such as wee,
>   Have heard this dialogue of one,
> Let him still marke us, he shall see
>   Small change, when we'are to bodies gone.
>   (ll. 41-48; 73-76)[80]

Wordsworth's distinction from Donne was his "presentational style," which was described earlier in the discussion of his fragments on psychological intimacy ("reclined / At midday upon beds of forest moss, / Have we to Nature and her impulses / Of our whole being made free gift, and when / Our trance had left us . . ."). Dorothy as auditor would have recollected and understood her brother's allusion, as well as the will for love and domination that impelled it during this their "dialogue of one."

The narrative section of *Tintern Abbey* (ll. 49-111) conforms to the classical pattern in supporting the proposition by drawing on past experience and in taking organizational shape from the order of its three-part *partitio*. Yet it also seems subliminally influenced by the poet's consciousness of his auditor. Opening the narrative section are the unexpected and troubling lines of transition, "If this / Be but a vain belief" (ll. 49-50). Because of proximity, we tend to read the preceding line—"We see into the life of things"—as the referent of "vain belief," though we know that the logical referent is fifteen lines above in the "trust" the poet has expressed in owing "another gift, / Of aspect more sublime" to his memories of the Wye (ll. 36-37). If we heed the immediately preceding pronoun shift, however, the "vain belief" can have as its referent that "*We* see into the life of things" (emphasis added), which would place proper doubt on the mutuality of transcendental experience. I believe that readers have always heard and felt the apposition in the preceding line, as any auditor would have done, but we have not thought to place emphasis upon the pronoun, rather than the fact of the poet's experience, which, of course, could not be a "vain belief."

The appropriate meaning of *vain* in the phrase is also at issue. It cannot primarily be taken to mean "valueless" or "pointless" because, as a matter of judgement, the poet can have his say about the worthiness of his beliefs. However, it can be taken as a matter of "vanity" to believe that "we" see something that I believe in, but perhaps you do not. "Vain belief" has then two mutually exclusive referents, each grammatically and logically acceptable, the first of which belongs to the poem's surface, the second of which incorporates the poet's consciousness of his auditor. As we shall see, the final part of the narrative section will also allude to Wordsworth's underlying preoccupation with Dorothy.

The first component of the proposition indicates that memories of nature provided "in hours of weariness, sensations sweet" that were felt as physiological reality "in the blood" and "along the heart" till finally passing into the brain to restore the "purer mind" (ll. 27-29). This body inscape, inspired by Darwin's *Zoonomia*, is followed by the diagnosis of the heart's disturbance in "hours of weariness" (l. 27), "when the fretful stir / Unprofitable, and the fever of the world, / Have hung upon the beatings of my heart" (ll. 53-55), which introduces an unusual formal problem for the poem. Why the mixed metaphor of illness with economics in "fretful stir / Unprofitable, and the fever of the world"? And, to be literal, when would Wordsworth have been so palpably vexed by events connecting profit and disease?

Readers have been wont to provide interpretations of either the profit or the fever, but not of their peculiar relationship. Kenneth R. Johnston, for example, has colored these lines with a political palette in seeking to account for the "fretful stir" as Wordsworth's urban experience of "heated discussions, intense arguments, differences of editorial opinion[,] pressures of deadlines and securing copy, peer pressure and rivalries, . . ." involved with the poet's probable involvement with publishing *The Philanthropist* in the revolutionary 1790s, especially in 1795. Mark Jones has approached the issue introduced by these lines as another intersection between Wordsworth's usurious business streak and the spiritual economics of *Tintern Abbey*, which "rather than displac[ing] or sublimat[ing] material capitalism in spiritual capitalism, . . . promotes a capitalism both material and spiritual."[81] But to return to the original question, Why the *mixed* metaphor?

If we understand in answering such questions that the poet's spontaneous verbal associations might well be compressed, modified, and displaced, we might profitably recall from Part One the discussion of Wordsworth's troubled conscience for nursing a consumptive Raisley Calvert to receive a £600 bequest, which was then raised to £900, doubtless with some quiet joyfulness from his penniless nurse. After Calvert's death Wordsworth left for London, drifting aimlessly from flat to flat over an eight-month period in 1795, and certainly living through an experience something like that suggested by Johnston. As far as the metaphor's dependency on medical reality goes, however, John Keats clearly saw the medical, though not the economic, point of Wordsworth's displacement in *Ode to A Nightingale*, when he echoed lines 52-54 in reference to nursing his brother Tom, also dying from tuberculosis: "The weariness, the fever, and the fret / Here, where men sit and hear each other groan; / . . . / Where youth grows pale, and spectre thin, and dies. . . ."[82]

Relatedly, in the next verse paragraph, the second part of the proposition section, Wordsworth recalls the visual voraciousness of his 1793 visit to the Wye valley in lines equally disturbed by a strangely applied economics:

> The sounding cataract
> Haunted me like a passion: the tall rock,
> The mountain, and the deep and gloomy wood,
> Their colours and their forms, were then to me
> An appetite: a feeling and a love,
> That had no need of a remoter charm,
> By thought supplied, or any interest
> Unborrowed from the eye.—
>
> (ll. 77-84)

This second economics metaphor ("interest / Unborrowed") is also associated with the wealthy Calvert brothers.[83] In July of 1793, during another period of economic destitution, Wordsworth accompanied Raisley Calvert's older brother William across Salisbury Plain, until their carriage was destroyed in an accident and the men separated, Calvert on horseback, Wordsworth on foot. Wordsworth then ventured into the Wye Valley for his first visit to the Abbey, or the one referred to as occurring five years earlier in *Tintern Abbey*. An otherwise inexplicable metaphor, "[I]nterest / Unborrowed from the eye," carries the trace or the residue of a second experience with the Calvert family colored by economic motivations.

The contention of the second part of the proposition that feelings associated with "unremembered pleasure" (l. 32) also attend the holistic restorative process is developed in lines 58-83:

> And now, with gleams of half-extinguish'd thought,
> With many recognitions dim and faint,
> And somewhat of a sad perplexity,
> The picture of the mind revives again:
> While here I stand, not only with the sense
> Of present pleasure, but with pleasing thoughts
> That in this moment there is life and food
> For future years.
> (ll. 59-66)

The poet stands between past and future. But now, his successfully and unexpectedly remembering of his memories ("The picture of the mind revives again") promotes some hope that the pleasant experience of the present will be a permanently available sustenance for future need. Physical and emotional change, again which he recalls only generally, and though it may continue to be drastic, will not impair memory. "And so I dare to hope, / Though changed, no doubt, from what I was, when first / I came among these hills . . ." (ll. 66-68). The retrieval of specific events seems unnecessary, for the past in general has formed a good, thoughtful man, "hearing often-times / The still, sad music of humanity" (ll. 91-92)—music that, unlike the joyously impassioned music of "Eolian Harp," has led to a new and quieter sublimity.[84]

The third part of the proposition describes an "eye made quiet by the power / Of harmony, and the deep power of joy" that can "see into the life of things" (ll. 48-50). The related development in lines 94-112 describes what is seen, felt, and believed about such experience:

And I have felt
A presence that disturbs me with the joy
Of elevated thoughts; a sense sublime
Of something far more deeply interfused,
Whose dwelling is the light of setting suns,
And the round ocean, and the living air,
And the blue sky, and in the mind of man,
A motion and a spirit, that impels
All thinking things, all objects of all thought,
And rolls through all things.
                              (ll. 94-103)

It is important to realize that the poet has not *"learned / To look on nature"*
(ll. 89-90; emphasis added) in a spiritual way until after his last visit to the
valley of the Wye. Then—that is, five years ago—he experienced "a feeling
and a love," for objects, such as the "sounding cataract," which "haunted him
like a passion." He was, we will soon be told, as Dorothy is now—"Oh! yet
a little while / May I behold in thee what I was once" (ll. 120-21). Significantly, lines 94-103, describing not psychological experience, but rather the
interpretation of that experience, revert to the first person pronoun. The
poet and his sister may have shared experience, but they do not yet share
interpretation. She, under the domination of "aching joys" and "dizzy
raptures," cannot, perhaps, even care for his thoughtfulness. Only the poet-
narrator has "felt" the presence; only he has "a sense sublime / Of something
far more deeply interfused"—"And *I* have felt. . . ." The auditor's development
will be the next concern of the poem.

There is also an implied corrective to Dorothy's preference, noted
earlier, for earthly rather than celestial landscapes. Following his statement
of faith that finds a presence in the unsubstantial physical images of the
sky—"the light of setting suns," the roundness of the ocean at the horizon,
"the living air," and "the blue sky"—and in the "mind of man," the poet
concludes:

Therefore am I still
A lover of the meadows and the woods,
And mountains; and of all that we behold
From this green earth; of all the mighty world
Of eye, and ear. . . .
                              (ll. 103-107)

For the poet, the world—the green earth—is beautiful, but his love for it now derives from the evidence of transcendence gleamed from above. Educated ("For I have learned . . .") in spiritual meaning from above, the eye and ear can create a new sublunar world; they "half create" with spiritual value.

Wordsworth's vital experience contrasts with Coleridge's denial of his past and the rejection of his religious vision in "Eolian Harp." It also assimilates and responds to the later vision described by Coleridge in "This Lime-Tree Bower My Prison," which falters with equivocation: the poet gazes till "all doth *seem* / Less gross than bodily"; "till all doth *seem* / . . . of such hues / As veil the Almighty Spirit . . ." ("Lime-Tree Bower," ll. 40-42; emphasis added). To say more is to confront the religious pride stifled in "Eolian Harp." A more important deficiency, however, is that belief is brought to experience, not found therein—the poet knows there is an "Almighty Spirit" who "makes / Spirits perceive his presence" ("This Lime-Tree Bower," l. 43) and the transformation of the physical earth by light is an example of its influence upon the spirit. In short, the poet says to auditor: here is what to see; here is what it means; now have the experience, as you have been taught.

The *narratio* of *Tintern Abbey* ends with confidence, as if it were the conclusion of the argument as well as the poem:

> well pleased to recognize
> In nature and the language of the sense,
> The anchor of my purest thoughts, the nurse,
> The guide, the guardian of my heart, and soul
> Of all my moral being.
>   (ll. 108-12)

In "Frost at Midnight" Coleridge presents a language of earth as the voice of God, the "Great universal Teacher" of Hartley, his child and poem's auditor. Wordsworth finds the reading of nature less directed, more participatory, inductively achieved. Nature is the object; sensory organs translate the objects of nature into a mental world. Nature is "what [is] perceive[d]"; "language of the sense" is the medium of "half creat[ion]" (*Tintern Abbey*, ll. 107-08). In this universe free of Coleridge's tutelary deity, the poet as teacher will be necessary. Thus, the poem does not end, for its shaping and interpretation of personal experience has only established the poet's authority to teach as one who has earned and learned his vision through the experience of a difficult, though guided, life. He now will apply his educative vision to the level of his auditor.

The argument section of the poem (ll. 112-35) begins tentatively, though the narrative has just concluded with indisputable confidence, because the auditor's personal belief and knowledge of the poet's life imply serious counterarguments to his affirmations. She could not have listened with indifference to his moving description of his life and their experience, but there was much room for meaningful, even disturbing, disagreement. The subtheme of identity and similarity now reaches the surface of the text as the poet seeks to overcome her separateness by describing her present as his past, thereby hoping to predetermine her future and to achieve his argumentative purpose. He was once like her, and, thus it follows that, when (if?) she reaches a comparable level of maturity, she will be like him. He opens by stressing the psychological and biological nature of their similarity. As he read the language of nature above, so he now "catch[es] / The language of [his] former heart, and read[s] / [His] former pleasures in the shooting lights" of his sister's "wild eyes" (ll. 117-20). Momentarily, it seems he succumbs to his former impassioned self: "Oh! yet a little while / May I behold in thee what I was once, / My dear, dear Sister!" (ll. 120-22). Of course there is ambivalence about growing older and these lines betray an intensity of desired identification beyond nostalgia. However, like the *Intimations Ode*, this poem too is about growing up; even more clearly than the *Ode*, it "is not only not a dirge sung over departing powers but actually a dedication to new powers."[85] One of those powers is being revealed as the ability to argue and to persuade by addressing the point of view of the opposition. More directly concerning the auditor, as Friend she has been rationally chosen for social and psychological compatibility; as Sister, she is of natural similarity. There seems little reason now to doubt her future development, that is, agreement with her brother's metaphysical position.

There is also a private allusion that again calls to mind the biographical crisis of the summer of 1793, when the poet took his original trip through the Wye valley. Several months before he made his clandestine trip to France to see Annette Vallon and their child. He had then underscored in a letter his commitment to Dorothy with the exact repetitive emphasis of *Tintern Abbey*: "Oh my dear, dear sister with what . . . rapture shall I again wear out the day in your sight. I assure you so eager is my desire to see you that all obstacles vanish. I see you in a moment running or rather flying to my arms" (*EY*, p. 102). It was a line that Dorothy quoted proudly to friends. Five years later, he can claim fidelity to the love recalled by the allusion.

Only from the point of contrast with "Eolian Harp" does one appreciate the next turn Wordsworth takes to assure identity with his auditor, yet still remain justified in instructing her. He will not adjust his position to reach her; that is his past. Her future experience, he prays, will rather bring her closer to him:

> this prayer I make,
> Knowing that Nature never did betray
> The heart that loved her; 'tis her privilege,
> Through all the years of this our life, to lead
> From joy to joy: for she can so inform
> The mind that is within us, so impress
> With quietness and beauty, and so feed
> With lofty thoughts, that neither evil tongues,
> Rash judgments, nor the sneers of selfish men,
> Nor greetings where no kindness is, nor all
> The dreary intercourse of daily life,
> Shall e'er prevail against us, or disturb
> Our chearful faith, that all which we behold
> Is full of blessings.
>
> (122-35)

"[C]hearful faith" does not sound like much, at least not in comparison with the commitment and depth of vision described in the proposition and narrative sections, but there the poet was speaking of his personal response to nature and of his personal belief. Here he describes only that which is shared now with his friend and sister. He would stress that they are of a single life ("this our life"), that they are of a single mind ("The mind that is within us"), and that they are of a single faith that, generally, things turn out for the better. After all, despite the separations, the confusion, and the losses of their past, and because of the difficult choices that William had made on their behalf, they are together now.

It is difficult not to hear a response to Coleridge's line from "This Lime-Tree Bower," "Nature ne'er deserts the wise and pure" (l. 60) in the following lines from *Tintern Abbey*: "this prayer I make / Knowing that Nature never did betray / The heart that loved her" (ll. 122-24). But the primary point seems addressed to Dorothy. The intensive, "never did betray," counters the auditor(s)' knowledge of contrary evidence,[86] such as the poet's parental experience that "entrust[ing] himself / To Nature for a happy end of all" (*Prelude*, Book IX, ll. 602-603) was harmfully naive. On the occasion of his first visit to the Wye, Wordsworth was tormented over the plight of his mistress and child in France, "more like a man / Flying from something that he dreads than one / Who sought the thing he loved" (*Tintern Abbey*, ll. 71-

73), experiencing guilt and ambivalence over his French affair. Dorothy was aware of the near-disastrous psychological effect of the experience on her brother as well as the fact that it easily could have separated them forever. It was near preposterous to believe that all of this was for the best. And yet, he is happy now for trusting to nature. Indeed, strange are the ways of nature to incline him towards his sister, rather than towards his child and its mother.

The peroration of *Tintern Abbey* (ll. 135-60) is triumphant in its invocation of the process, the outcomes, and the mysterious influences of nature, which is to say, following one's natural inclinations. With confidence the poet concludes that his sister should let that transcendental moon "Shine on thee in thy solitary walk; / And let the misty mountain winds be free / To blow against thee . . ." (ll. 136-38). Memories of the freedom and sensory exhilaration nature offers will provide imaginative restoration when reality becomes oppressive. Even more importantly, the memory of the poet's response to nature at this very moment of educative passion will give his auditor confidence to trust:

> Oh! then,
> If solitude, or fear, or pain, or grief,
> Should be thy portion, with what healing thoughts
> Of tender joy wilt thou remember me,
> And these my exhortations!
> (ll. 143-47)

When "Frost at Midnight" concludes so beautifully to predict the receptivity of the poet's child to nature's ministrations— "Therefore all seasons shall be sweet to thee, / Whether the summer clothe the general earth / With greenness, . . ." (ll. 65-67)—it is the culmination of the father/poet's transferral of responsibility for the moral rearing of his child. Unhappily raised, the father finds it best to displace himself with the "Great universal Teacher" ("Frost at Midnight," l. 63). Wordsworth's response is that the poet's role as teacher is an acceptance of responsibility for loved ones who may readily stray without the testimony of his experience.

In the final lines of "Eolian Harp," Coleridge reaffirms his own faith in Christianity as the wellspring of healing waters and renders thanksgiving for the benefaction that granted to his benighted soul "Peace, and this Cot, and thee, heart-honour'd Maid!" (l. 64). Wordsworth also closes with the language and rhythm of benediction to join his auditor, but so as to interweave their experience and to imprint the pattern of his life and development upon hers, for it is her development, not his faith, that is at issue:

> Nor, perchance,
> If I should be, where I no more can hear
> Thy voice, nor catch from thy wild eyes these gleams
> Of past existence,—wilt thou then forget
> That on the banks of this delightful stream
> We stood together; and that I, so long
> A worshipper of Nature, hither came,
> Unwearied in that service: rather say
> With warmer love—oh! with far deeper zeal
> Of holier love. Nor wilt thou then forget,
> That after many wanderings, many years
> Of absence, these steep woods and lofty cliffs,
> And this green pastoral landscape, were to me
> More dear, both for themselves and for thy sake.
>   (ll. 147-60)

Dorothy here becomes the emotional inspiration of her brother's landscape as Sara had been the inhibiting conscience of Coleridge's.

Wordsworth's opportunism in working against the favorite poem of Coleridge's to clarify his opposing beliefs and to win back his sister's admiration left him pleased. Although he does not claim in the poem that he successfully wins over Dorothy's mind and heart in comparison, say, with his Pedlar, who had moved his more malleable young auditor to intellectual and emotional assent, he could say that he is now a much stronger narrator for sensitivity to the nuances of a real, rather than staged, rhetorical situation.

We do not have Dorothy's immediate reaction to the poem, but we know from a later response that it affected her deeply. During a moment of lucidity that broke the long mental agony of her midlife, she wrote in "Thoughts on My Sick-Bed" (1832):

> When loving Friends an offering brought,
> The first flowers of the year,
> Culled from the precincts of our home,
> From nooks to Memory dear.

> With some sad thoughts the work was done,
> Unprompted and unbidden,
> But joy it brought to my *hidden* life,
> To consciousness no longer hidden.

I felt a Power unfelt before,
Controlling weakness, languor, pain,
It bore me to the Terrace walk,
I trod the Hills again;—

No prisoner in this lonely room,
I *saw* the green Banks of the Wye,
Recalling thy prophetic words,
Bard, Brother, Friend from infancy!

No need of motion, or of strength,
Or even the breathing air;
—I thought of Nature's loveliest scenes;
And with Memory I was there.[87]

And yet, it is difficult to say of the compositional present of *Tintern Abbey* whether Wordsworth's argument finally achieved the single-mindedness of Donne's "dialogue of one" that derives from the perfect fusion of souls, or whether it remained, as it began, a "dialogue of one" point of view.

Part Three

A Winter's Tale

It seems necessary here to recapitulate and to offer a demurral before proceeding. Part One described the refraction of family history in Wordsworth's earliest works to *The Borderers*, with a particular emphasis upon his recently discovered love for his sister and the psychological entanglements this introduced: the guilt that Dorothy aroused in him over his vengeful wish for their father's death for breaking up their family home; and then the fantasy of the father's return and his second death in the character of Baron Herbert of *The Borderers* whose psychological function is to prevent an incestuous relationship between the virtual siblings, Mortimer and Matilda. We also read the doppelganger of Rivers and Mortimer as the poet's attempt to reintegrate his conflicting selves. Part One concluded with a poet at an impasse, distraught over the irrelevance of his ego's distress in the revolutionary world allegorized in his tragedy. Part Two represented Wordsworth as finding vocational direction and confidence in a dialogic and competitive interplay with Coleridge as rival poet and lover, culminating with the grand argumentative synthesis of *Tintern Abbey*, which reveals a poet now masterfully sensitive to the biographical challenges placed before him by his sister's skepticism and the poetic and epistemological challenges anchored in Coleridge's poetry. This final part of the psychobiographical narrative will find Wordsworth returning to the intense emotional and vocational dilemmas of both France and Racedown, almost as if Alfoxden had never happened. Alone again with Dorothy in Germany, during a dangerously frigid winter, Wordsworth will confront the particular problems of erotic love exacerbated by foreign residence, not unlike the permissiveness of his French experience with Annette Vallon. He will also deal with a reawakening of familiar fears associated with incestuous desire. Although the psychobiographical constellation of sister-love and father-death is dispersed throughout a series of poems rather than handled unitedly as in *The Borderers*, their separation allows for individual resolutions. The boy-child's aggression infuses the natural landscape of Part One of the 1799

Prelude as the prototype and incipient force that will explode into the French Revolution and the Reign of Terror. Meditations upon family loss and the father's death close the experimental autobiography at the brink of the poet's self-awareness of his moral and political culpability. By the time the poet and his sister escape Germany for England, their love and its romantic desires will have been domesticated, bringing to mind the distinction drawn in Part One between the human lovers of *Descriptive Sketches* and the animal mates of *Evening Walk*. In *Home at Grasmere*, Wordsworth will complete the bio-allegory by identifying the fraternal love he shares with his sister with the mated swans of Grasmere Lake. His acceptance of the patriarchal politics of the Lake District will reveal his attempt to identify with the father in comparison with the unsuccessful attempt in *The Borderers* to forge a world in the confused image of the tribal brothers.

I will hesitate, however, before proceeding to Germany, because as almost every reader will have anticipated, we approach the place and time of the Lucy poems, and their mysterious masterpiece, "A Slumber Did My Spirit Seal," lately identified, and not entirely fancifully, as "Archimedes' fulcrum for the discipline of English studies."[1] The history of the criticism of the poems alone, and again "A Slumber" in particular, has recently been the subject of Brian G. Caraher's *Wordsworth's "Slumber" and the Problematics of Reading* (1991) and Mark Jones's *The "Lucy Poems": A Case Study in Literary Knowledge* (1995), neither of which has been duly impressed with the bio-graphical/psychobiographical approach. Caraher objects to deriving readings of poetry from preparatory contextualizing; Jones objects to the closure of biographical readings. These are not disabling charges; however, it seems appropriate to prepare the ground for what is to come.[2]

To begin with the charge of closure: I would like to make a distinction between biographical and psychobiographical readings. The case of Lucy is not a matter of identifying a corpse still tangled up in the poetic lines that undid her; notifying the surviving relatives in Grasmere, Oxford, or near the springs of Dove; and burying the matter as a literary issue— cold-case closed. In fact, going to our literary morgue would be pointless, because as we almost all suspect, there never has been a body. There is only a series of meditations on Lucy's death by her too-human lover, who says that very few or none knew of the deceased's life and no one can now care that she is dead. Of course he was wrong about who might care, and from the beginning.

Coleridge copied "A Slumber Did My Spirit Seal" in a letter from Germany to Thomas Poole, with an oft-quoted prefatory comment worthy of serious consideration: "Some months ago Wordsworth transmitted to me a most sublime Epitaph / whether it had any reality, I cannot say.—Most probably, in some gloomier moment he had fancied the moment in which his Sister might die" (*STCL*, Vol. I, p. 479). Coleridge does not break the case open, but he offers the type of response that matters to a psychobiographical reading. Indeed, seen in the light of a few common observations, Coleridge's response almost reaches the status of evidence: Coleridge knew the Wordsworths very well; he knew Wordsworth's poetry and his poetic mind perhaps even more completely; Coleridge's poetic and aesthetic insights are acclaimed as perhaps the best of the nineteenth century, and on Wordsworth's poetry—his particular specialty—the best ever written; any reader of his letters realizes that he was no less astute at psychological insight. Knowing all of this, one might wonder why Coleridge would have ventured his provocative speculation to Thomas Poole, unless; 1) he found the death referred to in the poem an issue that he thought about, to 2) conclude that it was more likely to have been imagined rather than real, because 3) it was almost inevitably about the poet's sister, Dorothy, whom he knew meant everything to William. Therefore, the poem, although sublime, was a "fancy."

Considered thusly, no approach other than the psychobiographical has so *much* to go on in dealing with the issues specified above and from this best, most proximate, and intimate of witnesses to Wordsworth's life, to his relationship with his sister, and to his poetry. It goes without saying that the poet of *Dejection: An Ode* also knew a great deal about the relationship of mood—that is, fancy and gloom—to creative experience.

We also might come at this matter of identification from another direction by asking a more obvious question: Why didn't Coleridge ask Wordsworth about the referent of his "sublime Epitaph"? He had had ample opportunity both in letters and in person. Coleridge had been visited by the Wordsworths several times and possibly for several weeks prior to their departure from Germany (*CEY*, p. 264). Isn't it likely that Coleridge refrained because he knew the answer and suspected that querying Wordsworth would be both awkward and naive? Coleridge knew from his own poetic experience that loved ones routinely die mysteriously in ballads and lyric poetry.

Coleridge's letter on "A Slumber" begins by discussing the real death of his infant son Berkeley, who died while Coleridge was in Germany. Coleridge had once imagined the death of his firstborn, Hartley, in his sonnet "Composed on a Journey Homeward; the Author having received Intelligence of the Birth of a Son, Sept. 20, 1796," in language and psychological experience that apparently fascinated Wordsworth, because he made

use of both in *Intimations Ode,* as well as in "Strange Fits of Passion." Here is
Coleridge's early sonnet:

> Oft o'er my brain does that strange fancy roll
> Which makes the present (while the flash doth last)
> Seem a mere semblance of some unknown past,
> Mixed with such feelings, as perplex the soul
> Self-questioned in her sleep; and some have said
> We liv'd, ere yet this robe of flesh we wore.
> O my sweet baby! when I reach my door,
> If heavy looks should tell me thou art dead,
> (As sometimes, through excess of hope, I fear)
> I think that I should struggle to believe
> Thou wert a spirit, to this nether sphere
> Sentenc'd for some more venial crime to grieve;
> Did'st scream, then spring to meet Heaven's quick reprieve,
> While we wept idly o'er thy little bier!
> (*CPW*, pp. 153-54)

Coleridge had received the poems we now call "She Dwelt Among the
Untrodden Ways" and "Strange Fits of Passion" months earlier. Although he
doesn't mention their relationship to "A Slumber" in his letter, he would have
noted the influence of his sonnet on Wordsworth's "Strange Fits" and "A
Slumber"—the journey homeward, the "soul self-questioned in her sleep,"
the idle weeping over a fancied death. Thus, the presumption that Coleridge
speaks with authority on the identity of Lucy and her imagined death is not
only a concession to his psychological and poetic insight; he saw as well
Wordsworth's dialogue with the psychological curiosity of his own poem,
including the daring risk in its manner of stating what is being hoped for
and feared: "If heavy looks should tell me thou art dead, / (As sometimes,
through excess of hope, I fear)." The lines read with an ambiguity entirely
in accord with the tremendous fits of debilitating anxiety that Coleridge
suffered prior to the birth of Hartley over his moral worthiness to be a father,
over his feared inability to provide the sustenance of life for his dependents,
over the impact of all of this on his vocation, and his telling misdiagnosis of
Sara's miscarriage.[3] In short, he uses language ambiguously to permit an
outlet for wish-fulfillment. His letter draft of *Dejection: An Ode* will later
overtly confront the temptation to (half)wish for the loss of his children:

> Those little Angel Children (woe is me!)

There have been hours, when feeling how they bind
And pluck out the Wing-feathers of my Mind,
Turning my Error to Necessity,
I have half-wish'd, they never had been born!
                    (*STCL,* Vol. II, p. 797)

But to return to the issue of closure: Why continue if Coleridge's insight on the identity of Lucy is as close to definitive as one can hope for? The answer is that Dorothy Wordsworth being the referent opens wide rather than closes the possibilities for interpretation. It matters considerably for treating the formal properties of the poems that the deceased referent is the poet's beloved sister; it matters as much for discussing the effect of the poems that the death is imagined rather than real. In other words, to read the Lucy poems most meaningfully, we cannot hypothesize that Lucy's absence means she is merely language or symbol.[4] We also cannot discuss the poems as if there were a literal death, even an imagined literal death, rather than a fancied death.

I have been following Coleridge in employing *fancied* for the inspirational phenomenon he recognized in "A Slumber," rather than *imagined.* We should wonder why he used the pejorative term.[5] Perhaps, feeling the effects of the real death of his son, Coleridge would be dismissive towards a meditation on a death that never happened. An aesthetic emotion is not inferior, but it is different from a real emotion.[6] Wordsworth's secondary emotion had yielded a "most sublime Epitaph," yet the poem was, Coleridge suspected, prompted by the passing emotion of "some gloomier moment," when the poet's sister "might have died," as if to say that he might have expected a different kind of poem from Wordsworth if his emotions had been intensified and disciplined by a fully imagined loss—as in *Ruined Cottage*—or the real loss of a beloved—as would later come in *Elegiac Stanzas* on the death of the poet's mariner brother John, or the great sonnet, "Surprised by Joy," on the death of the poet's young daughter. Apparently, Coleridge recognized something amiss, something unreal, or more literary than real, about "A Slumber." It will be one of the objectives of Part Three to try to fully understand Coleridge's response.

One might look upon a good deal of what follows, then, as a massive explanatory footnote to Coleridge's comment. Why would Wordsworth fancy his sister's death? What of this gloomier moment? What difference does understanding the literal context of the poems make for reading and interpretation? How does the emotional motivation matter for reading the poems? And, though not anticipated by Coleridge's comment, How does the bulk of the poetry Wordsworth composed in Germany, most of it elegiac, relate to the Lucy poems and their context?

1. "all in each other"[7]

Their passage from England to Germany was predictive of the experience the Wordsworths and Coleridge, with his traveling companion, John Chester, would have abroad: the Wordsworths, seasick and largely to themselves; Coleridge, healthy, happy, and gregarious. "Chester was ill the whole voyage," Coleridge wrote to his wife, and "Wordsworth shockingly ill, his Sister worst of all—vomiting, & groaning, unspeakably!" (*STCL*, Vol. I, p. 416). If Coleridge is reliable, then William was either in denial or inclined to produce some of the most facetious commentary he ever penned. Wordsworth wrote to an unfamiliar correspondent that they had a "very pleasant voyage, of three days and three nights" (*EY*, p. 231). Dorothy's version of the experience describes a queasy blending of body and landscape:

> Before we heaved the anchor I was consigned to the cabin, which I did not quit till we were in still water at the mouth of the Elbe on Tuesday morning at 10 o'clock. I was surprised to find, when I came upon the deck, that we could not see the shores, though we were in the river. It was to my eyes a still sea, but oh! the gentle breezes and the gentle motion! I thought of returning to the cabin in the evening with a mingled sensation of shuddering and sickness.[8]

One cannot resist noting that the exclamatory highlight expressed in her brother's diction and style—"but oh! the gentle breezes and the gentle motion"—make for a light parody on nausea sometimes being the outcome of gentle breezes rather than poetry!

After a short stay in Hamburg, the Wordsworths and Coleridge (accompanied by his lackey, John Chester) divided into two parties, due to the high cost of living and traveling in Germany. The plan for the itinerary had never been set in stone, but no one had anticipated a separation. The original plan called for the Wordsworths and the Coleridges (including Sara and both children) to stay in a university town within the vicinity of Hamburg to avoid the expense of traveling in-country (*EY*, p. 213); after learning that living in university towns was prohibitively expensive, the plan was modified for them to reside in some small town in the vicinity of Hamburg till they learned the language, and then, after a year, to move to a university town for a second year of study (*EY*, p. 221). By early August, Sara Coleridge and the children were excluded, because it would necessitate borrowing, which Coleridge wisely judged "an imprudent, perhaps an immoral thing," and the trip was consequently reduced to three or four months to learn the language (*STCL*, Vol. I, p. 414); after visiting and conferring with the younger brother of the German poet Friedrich Gottlieb Klopstock (1724-1803), Coleridge's on-site decision was to follow the plan of living in a small town, such as Ratzeburg, and then moving to the university town of Göttingen. The Wordsworths, however, distressed at the avarice of German shopkeepers and tradesmen, felt it necessary to take an alternative route. They ventured south in search of the cheapest, most pleasant locale they could find, and finally located in Goslar, a village at the foothills of the Harz Mountains, arriving on October 6, 1798, and remaining until February 23, 1799 (*CEY*, p. 255).

The Wordsworths probably chose Goslar for several reasons besides frugality. Being in a mountain region, Goslar was similar geographically to the north of England. More importantly, it was only fifty miles from Göttingen, where Coleridge intended to move after his preparatory stay in Ratzeburg. It seemed a nice compromise; nevertheless, their experience turned out to be another Wordsworth winter. They finally wrote to Coleridge of their unfortunate situation six weeks after settling in Goslar, an "ominous silence" (*STCL*, Vol. I, p. 445) that understandably left Coleridge in "great Anxiety & inexpressible Astonishment" (*STCL*, Vol. I, p. 440). Wordsworth's excuse for their prolonged silence was "his violent hatred of letter writing" (*STCL*, Vol. I, p. 445), which did not explain Dorothy's silence. Coleridge's terse paraphrase of their letter suggests he was as frustrated and angered with the Wordsworths' neglect of his feelings as they apparently were with their situation:

> Goslar is an old decaying city at the Foot of the Hartz Mountain[s]— provisions very cheap, & lodgings very cheap; but no Society—and therefore as he did not come into Germany to learn the Language by a Dictionary, he must remove: which he means to do at the end of the Month [of November]. . . . Dorothy says—"William works hard, but not very much at the German."—This is strange—I work at nothing else, from morning to night—.
>
> (*STCL*, Vol. I, p. 445)

Plans for moving on at the end of November also fell through. Coleridge wrote several letters to the Wordsworths in early December, several of which exist as undated fragments, discussing the German language, poetry, future residences, and the physical ailments he was suffering for lack of their companionship. In early December 1798, he offered the Wordsworths a specimen of his poetic experimentation:

> William, my head and my heart! dear Poet that feelest and thinkest!
> Dorothy, eager of soul, my most affectionate sister!
> Many a mile, O! many a wearisome mile are ye distant,
> Long, long, comfortless roads, with no one eye that doth know us.
> O! it is all too far to send to you mockeries idle:
> Yea, and I feel it not right! But O! my friends, my beloved!
> Feverish and wakeful I lie,—I am weary of feeling and thinking.
> Every thought is worn *down*,—I am weary, yet cannot be vacant.
> Five long hours have I tossed, rheumatic heats, dry and flushing,
> Gnawing behind in my head, and wandering and throbbing about me,
> Busy and tiresome, my friends, as the beat of the boding night-spider.

Coleridge concludes the letter with the comment that he has forgotten the remainder of the poem, but not the final couplet. "The last line which I wrote I remember, and write it for the truth of the sentiment, scarcely [sic] less true in company than in pain and solitude":

> William, my head and my heart! dear William and dear Dorothea!
> You have all in each other; but I am lonely, and want you!
>   (*STCL,* Vol. I, pp. 451-52)

Regardless of tribulations or consequences, Coleridge understood that it would always be William *and* Dorothy.

Within a month, Coleridge received a graphic account of Words-worth's sympathetic ailments, as if there were a seasonal flu afflicting visiting poets with restlessness, fever, and a kind of internal agitation. William writes, "As to your hexameters—I need not say how much the sentiment affected me"; informs Coleridge that Dorothy will transcribe for him "two or three little Rhyme poems which I hope will amuse you," to wit, "She Dwelt Among the Untrodden Ways" and "Strange Fits of Passion"; and then proceeds to describe his own psychosomatic condition:

> As I have had no books I have been obliged to write in self-defence. I
> should have written five times as much as I have done but that I am

prevented by an uneasiness at my stomach and side, with a dull pain about my heart. I have used the word pain, but uneasiness and heat are words which more accurately express my feeling. At all events it renders writing unpleasant. Reading is now become a kind of luxury to me. When I do not read I am absolutely consumed by thinking and feeling and bodily exertions of voice or of limbs, the consequence of those feelings.

(*EY*, pp. 236-37)

Although the restlessness, fever, and fret are shared with Coleridge's listed ailments in "Hexameters," Wordsworth's "writ[ing] in self-defence" suggests a consciousness under siege. He is consumed by thinking and feeling, the latter of which provokes bodily reactions when he isn't reading, or, in other words, distracting himself from himself. Having little to read, he writes instead in self-defense, but when he writes he feels an uneasiness and a heat "hang upon the beatings of [his] heart," to recall what seems a comparable symptom from *Tintern Abbey*, which impedes his writing. If he was thinking about what he was writing about, it would make sense that writing would make for ineffective therapy. For the common topics haunting his consciousness and his Goslar poetry are these: the death of his father, vocational anxiety, penury, ambivalence towards loved ones, impediments to human liberty, insecurity over the constancy of Coleridge's friendship, which translates poetically into meditations on a lifetime of unfortunate separations from male mentors. The confidence of *Tintern Abbey* has subsided. Apparently, remembered images of the Wye are of no use here. The presence of his dear, dear friend is once again a part of the problem rather than the cure.

The poetry included in this letter to Coleridge indicates that Wordsworth was perforce reinventing himself as a poet with experimental lyrics on love and loss and autobiographical blank verse dealing with the central anxiety of vocation, which in practical terms meant concern for Coleridge's approval of the poetry he now felt compelled to write. Besides "Strange Fits of Passion" and "She Dwelt Among the Untrodden Ways," Dorothy transcribed three blank verse narratives describing William's youthful experiences, the first related to the topic of skating that Coleridge most likely introduced in a previous letter, and then two haunting experiences inspired by boyhood mischief.

Dorothy alludes to Coleridge's speaking "in raptures of the pleasure of skating" [*sic*] (*EY*, p. 238) to which she icily responds that "[a] race with William upon his native lakes would leave to the heart and the imagination something more Dear, and valuable than the gay sight of Ladies and countesses whirling along the lake of Ratzeberg" (*EY*, pp. 238-39). The proof is a brief poetic narrative on skating from William's boyhood.

Here is Coleridge's description of ice-skating from a letter to his wife, which is most likely identical to the passage he sent the Wordsworths:

> In skating there are three pleasing circumstances—the infinitely subtle particles of Ice, which the Skate cuts up, & which creep & run before the Skater like a low mist, & in sun rise or sun set become coloured; 2nd the Shadow of the Skater in the water seen thro' the Transparent Ice, & 3rd the melancholy undulating sound from the Skate not without variety; & when very many are skating together, the sounds and the noises give an imp[ulse to] the icy Trees, & the woods all round the lake *tinkle!*—It is a plea[sant] Amusement to sit in an ice-stool . . . and be driven along [the ice] by two Skaters—I have [done] so, faster than most horses can gallop.
>
> (*STCL*, Vol. I, p. 462)

The visual image of the "Shadow of the Skater in the water seen thro' the Transparent Ice" is deflected in Wordsworth's episode to an unusual image of the boy "cut[ting] across the shadow of a star / That gleam'd upon the ice." The auditory sensation of Coleridge's "melancholy undulating sound from the Skate" is given an onomatopoeic expression in Wordsworth and friends being "shod with steel, / . . . hiss[ing] along the polished ice," while the source of "melancholy" is transferred to "distant hills." Coleridge's "sounds and the noises" that "give an imp[ulse to] the icy Trees, & the woods" to "tinkle," expand and converge in Wordsworth's passage to "The leafless trees, and every [icy crag] / Tinkl[ing] like iron, while far distant hills / Into the tumult sent an alien sound / Of melancholy." The speed of being driven along the ice "faster than most horses can gallop" in Coleridge's experience finds its comparison in the boy "wheel[ing] about, / Proud and exulting like an untired horse, / That cares not for his home." And then Wordsworth's boy retreats to solitary experience as an alternative to Coleridge's social delights, as if to say, and here I depart from you to explore my own poetic self:

> And oftentimes
> When we had given our bodies to the winds
> And all the shadowy banks on either side
> Came sweeping through the darkness, spinning still
> The rapid line of motion, then at once

Have I, reclining back upon my heels,
Stopped short; yet still the solitary cliffs
Wheeled by me, even as if the earth had rolled
With visible motion her diurnal round;
Behind me did they stretch in solemn train
Feebler and feebler, and I stood and watch'd
Till all was tranquil as a summer sea.
(EY, p. 239)

Dorothy hoped that these verses she was transcribing, which also included the boat-stealing scene from *The Prelude* and "Nutting," would bring Coleridge back within the sphere of her brother's influence and her adulation:

> wherever we finally settle you must come to us at the latter end of next summer, and we will explore together every nook of that romantic country. You might walk through Wales and Yorkshire and join us in the county of Durham, and I would once more follow at your heels, and hear your dear voices again.
>
> (EY, p. 241)

There was indeed hope that they might reside together. Coleridge had recently written, "I am sure I need not say how you are incorporated into the better part of my being; how, whenever I spring forward into the future with noble affections, I always alight by your side" (*STCL*, Vol. I, p. 453). However, by early January, Coleridge reported to Poole that he had given the Wordsworths far less reason to be sanguine about his residential flexibility: "Wordsworth is divided in his mind, unquietly divided, between the neighborhood of Stowey & the N. of England. He cannot think of settling at a distance from *me*, & I have told him that I *cannot* leave the vicinity of Stowey" (*STCL*, Vol. I, p. 455).

The Wordsworths' plan to leave Goslar at the end of November was delayed because they feared traveling in the cold. As William dictated to Isabella Fenwick regarding "Written in Germany, on one of the coldest days of the Century," which was probably December 25, 1798, Dorothy's birthday:

> A bitter winter it was when these verses were composed, by the side of my Sister in our lodgings at a draper's house in the romantic imperial town of Goslar on the edge of the Hartz Forest. . . . So severe was the cold of this winter, that when we past out of the parlour warmed by the stove, our cheeks were struck by the air as by a cold iron.
>
> (LB, p. 393)

In early February, Dorothy is still describing William as "very industrious," but ill: "his mind is always active; indeed, too much so; he overwearies himself, and suffers from pain and weakness in the side" (*EY*, p. 247). Thus the pain associated with composition has lasted from the beginning until now, the final month of their Goslar residence. It is worth recalling that there are no recorded ailments of painful composition at Alfoxden, and certainly nothing about "self-defence." Dorothy's comment on William's health and writing in March 1798, seven months after moving to Alfoxden House, was:

> He gets up between seven and eight in the mornings and I dare say will continue it [lying in bed] for he is fully convinced of the relaxing tendency of lying in bed so many hours. His faculties seem to expand every day, he composes with much more facility than he did, as to the *mechanism* of his poetry, and his ideas flow faster than he can express them.
>
> (*EY*, p. 200)

Because William was writing poetry rather than studying German, Dorothy remarked to their brother Christopher that, on the whole, their German experience was "not sufficiently" different from their "English way of life" (*EY*, p. 246). Except, of course, for the loss of Coleridge's company and the related decline in William's health. It was not entirely true that the Wordsworths had "all in each other," and as Coleridge had become increasingly acclimated to German society and intellectual life, the Wordsworths became increasingly anxious about his fidelity to their relationship. Coleridge wrote to Thomas Poole in October 1798:

> Every one pays me the most assiduous attentions—I have attended some Conversations at the Houses of the Nobility—stupid things enough.—It was quite a new thing to me to have Counts & Land-dr[osten] bowing & scraping to me—& Countesses, old & young, complimenting & amusing me.—But to be an Englishman is in Germany to be an Angel—they almost worship you.
>
> (*STCL*, Vol. I, p. 435).

Besides his whirling social life, Coleridge assiduously devoted himself to accomplishing his intellectual mission of beginning a life project worthy of the Wedgwood annuity. His dutiful approach to his studies in Germany reveals his vocational commitment, his newfound economic responsibility in carrying out this venture, and even a strength of moral purpose. He came to feel fully adequate on his own, and something of his personal independence must have carried over into his correspondence with the Wordsworths, as it had in correspondence with friends and family. In now studying the life and works of the German man-of-letters Gotthold Ephraim Lessing (1729-81), preparatory to a biographical study, Coleridge experienced a vocational transition. Rather than settling for the vicarious achievement of promoting Wordsworth, who often proved intransigent on matters that mattered a great deal, Coleridge found that he could live through a biography *he* could control in the act of writing it, and in support of the principles and ideas he valued. This psycho-vocational strategy gave Coleridge direction, as he burrowed with single-mindedness through Lessing's works, through biographies composed by others, and through the literature surrounding Lessing's life.[9]

In contrast to Coleridge's intellectual and social life, William describes the disappointing situation he and Dorothy had endured for the past eight weeks in a letter of February 1799 to Josiah Wedgwood:

> [Goslar] was once the residence of Emperors, and it is now the residence of Grocers and Linen-drapers who are, I say it with a feeling of sorrow, a wretched race; the flesh, blood, and bone of their minds being nothing but knavery and low falshood [sic]. We have met with one dear and kind creature, but he is so miserably deaf that we could only play with him games of cross-purposes, and he likewise labours under a common German infirmity, the loss of teeth, so that with bad German, bad English, bad French, bad hearing, and bad utterance you will imagine we have had very pretty dialogues. . . . (*EY*, p. 249)

The correspondence does not survive, but Coleridge says that William began writing regularly in December to breach the void now growing between them over the mistake of bringing Dorothy. He wrote directly to William: "You have two things against you: your not loving smoke; and your sister" (*STCL*, Vol. I, p. 440). He wrote in January 1799 to his wife:

> I hear as often from Wordsworth as letters can go backward & forward. . . . He seems to have employed more time in writing English [tha]n in studying German—No wonder!—for he might as well have been in England as at Goslar, in the situation which he chose, & with his *unseeking* manners. . . . His taking his Sister with him was a wrong Step—it is next to impossible for any but married women or in the suit of married

women to be introduced to any company in Germany. Sister [here] is
considered as only a name for Mistress.

(*STCL,* Vol. I, p. 459)

The blame is entirely on William: it is "the situation which he chose," and
now they all had to live with it. "Still however," Coleridge continues:

male acquainta[nce] he might have had——& had I been at Goslar, I
would [have] had them—but [W., God] love him! seems to have lost
his spirits & [almost his] inclination [for] it. In the mean time his
expences have been almost less than [if he had] been in England. /
Mine have been . . . very great; . . .

(*STCL,* Vol. I, pp. 459-60)

Wordsworth's experiences in France reveal that he surely knew how to get
about in a foreign land, having no trouble in developing intimate relationships with men, such as the soldier-patriot, Michel Beaupuy, and, of course,
the woman of his French experience, Annette Vallon. Perhaps that is why
Coleridge says that Wordsworth seems to have lost "his spirits" and his
"inclination" for society.

Dorothy gently skirts the issue of social innuendo that might consider
her a "mistress" rather than a proper sister by emphasizing the financial
disadvantage of her presence:

we find that when a *man and woman* are received into society, they are
expected, being considered as a sort of family, to give entertainments
in return for what they receive. Now this, in conjunction with the
expence of travelling, is absolutely out of our power, . . .

(*EY,* p. 244)

In the same letter to brother Christopher, Dorothy contrasts their experience with Coleridge's, again emphasizing their economic disadvantage:

Coleridge is in a very different world from what we stir in, he is all in
high life, among Barons counts and countesses. He could not be better
placed than he is at Ratzeberg for attaining the object of his journey;
but his expences are much more than ours conjointly. . . . It would
have been impossible for us to have lived as he does; we should have
been ruined.

(*EY,* p. 245).

And yet, Coleridge reports from the Wordsworths that they were living on less money than they had in England, and even Dorothy once surmises that, if they didn't travel, perhaps they could entertain. Couldn't William have made some contact in town with at least male companions? Imagine how odd the Wordsworths must have seemed and what gossip they must have aroused as a reclusive foreign couple who dropped from out of nowhere and for no apparent respectable reason to dwell alone in a small town.

Dorothy describes the reaction of German burghers to their public presence when they begin to move about after their sunless hibernation:

> The appearance of the people as we passed through the streets was very little favorable, they looked dirty, impudent, and vulgar, and absolutely the whole town being at the windows or in the streets as we unluckily met them coming from church, we were stared completely out of countenance, at least I was; William stoutly denies that he was at all uncomfortable; however this was we had not courage to stop at an inn till we had walked through the whole town, and just on the other side of the city gates, we called at one where they told us they would give us nothing to eat. . . .
>
> (EY, p. 252)

Despite the avarice the Wordsworths complained of in their dealings with German merchants, here they are treated as outcasts who cannot even buy food! "While we stood pondering what we should do," Dorothy continues, a pair of town officials interceded on their behalf, but only after interrogating them about their business and hassling them for quite a while about their lack of passports (EY, p. 252).

On this same day in February when Coleridge's letters informed them that he had finally moved to Göttingen, Dorothy admits that she could hardly contain her joy: "I burst open the seals and could almost have kissed them in the presence of the post-master, but we did not read a word till we got to the inn when we devoured them separately, for at least two hours" (EY, p. 254). William continues the letter, regretting to Coleridge his very different circumstances even now that they have left Goslar:

> We must pursue a different plan. We are every hour more convinced that we are not rich enough to be introduced into high or even literary german society. We should be perfectly contented if we could find a house where there were several young people some of whom might perhaps be always at leisure to converse with us. We do not wish to

read much but should both be highly delighted to be chattering and chatter'd to, through the whole day. As this blessing seems to be destined for some more favoured sojourners, we must content ourselves with pshaw for the ears—eyes for ever!

(*EY*, p. 254)

Does Wordsworth mean that the only words spoken to them were expressions of contempt, rather than delightful "chattering," and that the only looks they received were derisive stares, a kind of "pshaw for the . . . eyes"?

It seems then that the social awkwardness Coleridge identified as founded in sexual assumptions about so-called sisters and brothers rather than finances per se kept the Wordsworths reclusive. When they emerged, they recalled why they had hidden. When hidden, what feelings and emotions were likely to work their way into poetry, especially into love poetry about the death of a beloved? It was a time for "self-defence," as William wrote to his fellow poet following their seven-week silence, during which time he dealt with the emotional and vocational feelings that isolation with Dorothy had brought on.

2. "If Lucy should be dead!"[10]

The Cornell edition of Lyrical Ballads, *and Other Poems, 1797-1800* (1992) makes more obvious than before the great quantity of verse that Wordsworth wrote in Germany. The works most likely composed during the seven silent weeks—between October 6 and December 28, 1798—are: "Strange Fits of Passion I have Known," "She Dwelt Among the Untrodden Ways," "A Slumber Did My Spirit Seal," "'Tis Said That Some Have Died for Love," "Poor Susan," "If Nature, for a Favored Child," "Nutting" (short version), "Written in Germany, On one of the coldest days of the Century," "The Childless Father," "A Poet's Epitaph," "A Character in the Antithetical Manner," "The Farmer of Tilsbury Vale. A Character," "Alcaeus to Sappho," "Remembering how thou didst beguile", "I would not strike a flower," and passages associated with the 1799 *Prelude*, Part I.[11]

The most general comment that can be made about these works is that they are elegiac. Central to their mood of loss are the Lucy lyrics, which have their referent in Dorothy Wordsworth. Culling from the correspondence the immediate causes that made for the "gloomier moment" Coleridge judged as the inspiration for "A Slumber Did My Spirit Seal," and by extension, much of the Goslar poetry, we would list the separation from

Coleridge, the almost enforced isolation brought about by sexual innuendo, Coleridge's insistence on the mistake of Wordsworth's bringing his sister to Germany, and certainly a lack of money. Later, knowledge of Coleridge's starkly contrasting social and intellectual life would enhance the gloom, like "darkness to a dying flame."[12] Drawing from the psychobiographical past considered in the earlier parts to this study, we might create a palimpsest overlaid with family associations of trauma with winter, especially the death of parents; the comparable isolation and boredom of Racedown; and the anxiety Wordsworth associated with overstepping the bounds of intimacy with Dorothy as he had with Annette Vallon, whom we considered earlier as a surrogate for Dorothy. Thus, it seems as clear as these things can be that the poet's love for his sister would undergo a shock of ambivalence, which would bring about a painful change.

"Strange Fits of Passion," probably the first Lucy poem composed, introduces the fantasy, or in Coleridge's term, the fancy, of Lucy's sudden death. The schizoid structure of the poem reflects the inherent ambivalence of a mental experience of dreamy love interrupted by a premonition of death. Until the disappearance of the moon at the poem's close, the first two lines of each quatrain depict the narrator's changing perspective of the moon and the latter two lines indicate either his physical motion, his location, or his progress of mind, with these paired lines divided by emphatic stops. Although there is elision between the first and second lines and between the third and fourth lines of some stanzas, there is no elision between the second and third lines of any stanza. This stanzaic division, which reinforces the discontinuity of the narrative, makes it structurally possible to interject the poem's reversal and psychologically possible to "slide" the strange "fancy"— here the narrator's own term—into his abruptly shifting consciousness, which moves from self, to position, to perspective, to nascent awareness. Dorothy prefaces her transcription of the poem with the poignant comment to Coleridge, "the next poem is a favorite of mine—i.e. of me Dorothy—":

1
Once, when my love was strong and gay,
And like a rose in June,
I to her cottage bent my way
Beneath the evening Moon.

2
Upon the moon I fixed my eye
All over the wide lea:

My horse trudg'd on, and we drew nigh
Those paths so dear [to] me.

3

And now I've reached the orchard-plot,
And as we climbed the hill,
Towards the roof of Lucy's cot
The moon descended still.

4

In one of those sweet dreams I slept,
Kind nature's gentlest boon,
And all the while my eyes I kept
On the descending moon.

5

My horse moved on; hoof after hoof
He raised and never stopped,
When down behind the cottage roof
At once the planet dropp'd.

6

Strange are the fancies that will slide
Into a lover's head,
"O mercy" to myself I cried
"If Lucy should be dead!"

7

I told her this; her laughter light
Is ringing in my ears;
And when I think upon that night
My eyes are dim with tears.
                    (*EY*, pp. 237-38)

Given the drowsiness, the dream, and the "too easy entrance"[13] of the fearful premonition into consciousness, it is hardly possible in considering Lucy's death to refrain from suspecting that a wish has been fulfilled between stanzas 6 and 7. In considering the process of mind that culminates in the fantasy of Lucy's death, there are two psychological phenomena to consider: the identification of Lucy with the falling moon and the lover's somnambulistic state, which is no less important than the identification and no less strange than the fit itself. One does not expect a lover to become torpid when nearing the dwelling of his beloved. Why does he drift off as he nears the cottage, instead of becoming increasingly excited at the prospect of seeing Lucy? And how does this behavior lead to the fatal symbol of the declining moon?

We considered in Part Two that Dorothy's attraction to the moon became a matter of complex identification during her infatuation for Coleridge. Although there is no evidence explicitly referring to Dorothy as Diana, associations between the contemporary understanding of the myth of Diana and Dorothy Wordsworth are striking, and could have been easily made. John Lempriere is here worth quoting again on the associations the myth of Diana would evoke in an eighteenth-century lyric:

> She was born at the same birth as Apollo; and the pains which she saw her mother suffer during her labour, gave her such an aversion to marriage, that she obtained from her father the permission to live in perpetual celibacy, and to preside over the travails of women. To shun the society of men, she devoted herself to hunting, . . . She is represented with a bent bow and quiver, and attended with dogs, . . . [H]er face has something manly, her legs are bare, well-shaped and strong, . . . She was called Lucina . . . when invoked by women in childbed. . . . She was supposed to be the same as the moon, . . .
> (Lempriere, p. 201)[14]

Diana as a manly and celibate hunter, fearful of men and heterosexual love because of the pains of childbirth, sometimes called Lucina, sister of Apollo—none of these alone, but parts of all together, establish an interesting human referent in Dorothy Wordsworth. The independence and ruggedness Dorothy displayed in sauntering about the countryside with William—and for which she was soundly critized by female relatives (*EY*, p. 117)—made her an enlightened rebel of sorts against the contemporary standards of female behavior.[15] Thomas De Quincey put it another way when he met her: Dorothy was "the very wildest person" he had ever known. Some of this wildness is described in one of her brother's introductions to "Nutting," where she becomes the female equivalent—the Diana, Lucina, or Lucy—of his boyhood hunter:

> Ah! what a crash was that! with gentle hand
> Touch those fair hazels—My beloved Maid!

Though 'tis a sight invisible to thee,
From such rude intercourse the woods all shrink
As at the blowing of Astolpho's horn.—
Thou, Lucy, art a maiden "inland bred,"
And thou hast "known some nurture", but in truth
If I had met thee here with that keen look
Half cruel in its eagerness, those cheeks
Thus [   ] flushed with a tempestuous bloom,
I might have almost deem'd that I had pass'd
A houseless being in a human shape,
An enemy of nature, hither sent
From regions far beyond the Indian hills.—
                    (*LB*, pp. 305-06, ll. 1-14)

We considered her fearful attitude towards heterosexuality in Part One, but we might have included there as well her primary function as the "Lucina" of the family, assisting her Aunt Cookson in the birth and caring for four children within the space of several years. She summarized for Jane Pollard her domestic duties when her aunt was recovering from yet another "lying in":

> As I am head nurse, houskeeper, tutoress of the little ones or rather superintendent of the nursery, I am . . . a very busy woman and literally *steal* the moments which I employ in letter-writing. . . . [M]y aunt does not gain strength so fast as I expected; the weather is much against her, as she is languid and delicate. . . . [A]s she sleeps very indifferently at nights I am obliged to lie very long in the mornings for fear of disturbing her.
>
> (*EY*, p. 99)

As sister and kindred spirit of a poet, the relationship to Apollo is apt. There is also a parallel between Diana's "forget[ting] her dignity to enjoy the company" of the likes of Endymion, Pan, and Orion (Lempriere, p. 201) and Dorothy's consorting with Coleridge, especially, and other members of her brother's circle. Finally, Dorothy's attraction to the moon and her celestial mythologizing confirms her as a convincing candidate for Lucina-Lucy.

We can look back upon the sonnet considered in Part One, "Sweet was the walk along the narrow Lane" (*EY*, p. 74), with new eyes, for calling attention to a "clouded Moon" hearkening the poet "forth to stray / Thro' tall, green, silent woods and Ruins gray" (ll. 13-14). A mythological gloss on this lunar imagery suggests, allegorically, not only that Dorothy as Moon is hearkening her brother home, but that the celibate huntress Diana is calling her brother Apollo back to nature and the "Ruins gray" of their youth. The moon would distract him from his French lover Annette on behalf of dreams shared with Dorothy over their living together. But in the narrative recollection of "Strange Fits," the brother and sister *were* living together, at Racedown, in 1795, and William is reflecting back upon the ocular fantasy that lead then to Dorothy's imagined death, transformed now at Goslar, in 1798, into Lucy's real death.

Why is she dying? F. W. Bateson's once-controversial thesis that an attempt to ward off incestuous desires is at stake, and my earlier thesis that ambivalence towards Dorothy for her serious inconvenience motivates her imagined death are both true, but always together, for neither is sufficient to explain alone the motivation of the entire cycle. The principle of *overdetermination* in psychobiography "suggests that actions typically have multiple causes and meanings."[16] I would wish to avoid accumulating all of the possible causes for Lucy's death that can be imagined, in other words, for "overdetermining" the imaginative event, for that way critical anarchy lies; but within the narrative developed herein, with the support of corroborating evidence, patterns have been developing that ought to be acknowledged. For example, as I indicated in the precis to this part, the biographical similarities between France and Goslar and between Racedown and Goslar reawakened in Wordsworth challenges redolent of liberal France and domesticated Racedown with reference to his sister and to an awakening of paternal fears once quelled in *The Borderers*. While Dorothy's death is imagined out of both hostility and love, the emotional outcome of the cycle of the Lucy poems that evolved was to alter the poet's love for his sister and to solve once and for all its dangers and vicissitudes. Thus, as almost everyone acknowledges, the poems are not about Lucy, but about the lover's reaction to her death. It is his reaction that needs alteration. As we observed in the discussion of *Tintern Abbey*, psychological strategies of intimacy had earlier sublimated incestuous desire: the poet and his sister-auditor "are laid asleep in body / And become a living soul." Here in Germany, they occasionally shared comparable experiences for sublimating passions, again as the introductory lines to "Nutting" reveal in their address to a frantic Lucy: "Come rest on this light bed of purple heath, / And let me see thee sink into a dream / Of gentle thoughts, protracted till thine eye / Be calm as water when the winds are gone / And no one can tell whither" (*LB*, p. 306, ll. 15-19). Relatedly, Lucy as a presence becomes disembodied in her poems, which can be read as a sign of the poet's success in dealing with intensities of frustration and passion to reach finally a spiritual level of peace, rarified by lyric beauty.

To return to "Strange Fits of Passion" and evidence for the narrator's problematic love: The emotional inappropriateness of the lover's behavior in becoming torpid rather than excited on his home approach might be partly explained by Shelley's observation in *Julian and Maddalo* that turning "Homeward . . . always makes the spirit tame."[17] The time Julian spends with Count Maddalo is, like the time William spent with Coleridge, all the more valued for being sometimes harmonious, sometimes antagonistic, but always stimulating. But the more pertinent gloss for expected romantic behavior is found in *Anna Karenina*, where Tolstoy describes Levin's awakening love for Kitty on the approach to their home: "He rode home thinking only of her, of her love, of his own happiness, and the nearer he came to the house the warmer grew his tenderness for her." Later, his excitation reaches its height in Kitty's presence, where Levin feels that his consciousness has blended with hers: "he was not simply close to her, . . . he could not tell where he ended and she began."[18]

We have considered Alfoxden fragments and sections of *Tintern Abbey* that allude to a similar but heightened psychological intimacy between Dorothy and William. Thus, we may conclude that William was clearly aware of the contrast he was making between a trance-state of unity and this condition of separation. Indeed, the lover's welcoming of the state of sleep can be interpreted as a mode of separation, because sleep requires a withdrawal of concern from the external world.[19] As the narrator nears Lucy's cottage, his interest in her and the world is receding with every beat of his horse's hoofs. Textual evidence supports this insight as well. In the 1798 text, the narrator comments, "My horse trudg'd on": in the final text, the poet corrects his belabored movement to read, "With quickening pace my horse drew nigh."[20] But while this emendation may have effaced the semantic indication of the lover's lack of eagerness, the almost preternatural slowing of time effected by the rhythm of "My horse moved on; hoof after hoof / He raised and never stopped," strongly suggests the subconscious message: the lover is reluctant to reach his destination.[21]

In the lover's state of increasing torpor, he becomes increasingly vulnerable to the fantasies of the unconscious, and the quiescent withdrawal he seeks to reach through sleep ("Kind Nature's gentlest boon!") is disrupted by the eclipse of Lucy and her moon. As Freud once remarked, because we do not expect to wish our loved ones out of existence, the censorship faculty of the mind relaxes with respect to such fantasies, and, consequently, the desires of the unconscious are revealed.[22] With the wards of the mind's respectability, the ego and superego, at rest, the unconscious seizes the moment to reveal its wish, of course, much to the lover's shock:

> Strange are the fancies that will slide
> Into a lover's head,
> "O mercy!" to myself I cried,
> "If Lucy should be dead!"
> (ll. 21-24)

In the unconscious, where wishes are omnipotent, fate is decided by a suggestion. The final stanza of the 1798 text implies that Lucy has died and suggests that the lover's memory of the premonition occurs with some frequency to renew his sense of loss, perhaps to atone for his guilt ("And when I think upon that night / My eyes are dim with tears" [ll. 27-28]).

Mary Moorman suggests that "Strange Fits of Passion" is most likely based upon a memory of Racedown (Moorman, Vol. I, p. 423), which is probably why Dorothy favored the poem. It seems William experienced something similar to the poem's optical illusion and discussed its fantasy with Dorothy, who laughed it off, yet felt pleased with her brother's concern. We thus face an interesting parallel. Having noted the similar circumstances of Racedown and Goslar—the boredom, the frustration, the isolation, the comparable depressions, the absence of Coleridge—it seems that in both cases Wordsworth recognized his commitment to Dorothy rather than Dorothy herself as being responsible for his plight. Because the circumstances of Racedown and Goslar were painfully similar, an experience of Racedown is recalled at Goslar to effect the same psychic release, but through the emotional control, aesthetic distance, and potential for understatement offered by balladic economy and restraint.[23]

If the expression of hostility towards Dorothy in "Strange Fits" afforded Wordsworth respite or imaginative escape, Wordsworth dwelt upon the fantasy of Lucy/Dorothy's death in succeeding Lucy poems to give full vent to that impulse. But as the abhorrent wish is being gratified, guilt for permitting the fantasy rises to be relieved. The role of the mourning lover becomes functional in this emotional economy: his grief atones for the poet's guilt. In fact, the lover persona goes through an entire process of mourning parallel to the intensity of the poet's desire to be rid of his beloved sister. The lover mourns most when feelings of ambivalence are strongest; his grief dissipates as the poet moves further from his fantasy, until, finally, both grief and ambivalence are spent in the last poem of the cycle, "I Travelled among Unknown Men," written several years later, under a cloud of another

separation from Coleridge.[24] Allied to this mixed expression of grief and
underlying hostility is an important strategy of denial that the poet employs
to efface Lucy's relationship to Dorothy. Lucy is virtually absent, physically
and mentally, from the poems devoted to her memory.

Guilt, with attendant grief and denial, is strongest in the Lucy poems
of the first phase—in other words, immediately after the fantasy's emergence. "She Dwelt Among the Untrodden Ways," which was also transcribed in the mid-December letter to Coleridge, seeks to rid the poet of
responsibility for the fantasy of Lucy's death by accounting for her death
metaphorically, as a bloom smitten by disease. Conspicuous in the following
text is Wordsworth's exaggerated attempt to establish Lucy's equivalence to
a flower. The rose, the woodbine, the violet, the broom—all compose the
bouquet that is Lucy:

1
My hope was one, from cities far,
Nursed on a lonesome heath;
Her lips were red as roses are,
Her hair a woodbine wreath.

2
She lived among the untrodden ways
Beside the springs of Dove,
A maid whom there were none to praise,
And very few to love;

3
A violet by a mossy stone
Half-hidden from the eye!
Fair as a star when only one
Is shining in the sky!

4
And she was graceful as the broom
That flowers by Carron's side;
But slow distemper checked her bloom,
And on the Heath she died.

5
Long time before her head lay low

> Dead to the world was she:
> But now she's in her grave, and Oh!
> The difference to me!
> (*EY*, pp. 236-37)

This plethora of imagery creates a presence without identity; in fact, without even a name. She is "She," a "maid," "My hope," and a kin to all the flowers of the heath, where she was nursed, lived, and wilted. When Wordsworth revised the poem for *Lyrical Ballads* (1800), Lucy's name was added:

> She *liv'd* unknown, and few could know
> When Lucy ceas'd to be;
> But she is in her Grave, and oh!
> The difference to me.
> (*LB*, p. 163, ll. 9-12)

But for now, identity is left vague. If "Strange Fits" is based upon a memory of Racedown, then the poet's consciousness of Lucy as surrogate for Dorothy is certain. But "Strange Fits" is a poem of anticipation. Developing a series of responses to the death foreseen required a denial of Lucy's relationship to Dorothy, and even a denial that the poems were very serious anyway. We noted earlier Wordsworth's comment to Coleridge that Dorothy would transcribe for him "two or three little Rhyme poems" which he hopes will "amuse" Coleridge (*EY*, p. 236). He also dispassionately criticizes the last stanza of "She Dwelt Among the Untrodden Ways" for containing the words "'Long time' as put in merely to fill up the measure but as injurious to the sense" (*EY*, p. 236).

The next Lucy lyric to be written, "A Slumber Did My Spirit Seal," remained permanently vague on the identity of the referent lest Wordsworth have to confront inevitable questions in this most ambivalent of his Lucy poems: Why am I again writing of my sister's (or her surrogate's) death? and, Why am I responding so strangely?

> A Slumber did my spirit seal,
> I had no human fears:
> She seem'd a Thing, that could not feel
> The touch of earthly years.
>
> No motion has she now, no force;
> She neither hears nor sees,

> Mov'd round in Earth's diurnal course
> With rocks, & stones, and trees!
> (STCL, Vol. I, p. 480)

This, the first text of "A Slumber," was included in the letter from Coleridge
to Poole (STCL, Vol. I, p. 480) on the death of his infant son. Berkeley's
recent death sent Coleridge into an extended meditation. He claims not to
have grieved for his child and gathers together ruminations on consciousness, being, and emotion suggested by "A Slumber," as if to justify his
comparable restraint against openly grieving. The letter is worth quoting at
length as a powerful and disapproving gloss on Wordsworth's "sublime
Epitaph" as well as on his growing autobiographical narrative composed out
of "recollective consciousness":

> My Baby has not lived in vain—this life has been to him what it is to
> all of us, education & developement! Fling yourself forward into your
> immortality only a few thousand years, & how small will not the
> difference between one year old & sixty years appear!—Conscious-
> ness—! it is no otherwise necessary to our conceptions of future
> Continuance than as connecting the *present link* of our Being with the
> one *immediately* preceding it; & *that* degree of Consciousness, *that* small
> portion of *memory*, it would not only be arrogant, but in the highest
> degree absurd, to deny even to a much younger Infant.—'Tis a strange
> assertion, that the Essence of Identity lies in *recollective* Consciousness—
> 'twere scarcely less ridiculous to affirm, that the 8 miles from Stowey
> to Bridgewater consist in the 8 mile stones.
> (STCL, Vol. I, p. 479)

If the "Essence of Identity" does not lie in *"recollective* Consciousness," wherein
does it lie? Apparently, in some continuous spiritual condition that precedes
and follows our mortal lives. The image of stones then suggests an hypothesis of undying energy to counter the lifeless science of Lucy's motion in "A
Slumber":

> What if the vital force which I sent from my arm into the stone, as I
> flung it in the air & skimm'd it upon the water—what if even that did
> not perish!—It was *life*—! it was a particle of *Being*—! it was *Power*—! &
> *how could* it perish—? *Life*, Power, Being!—organization may & probably
> *is*, their *effect*; their *cause* it *cannot* be!—I have indulged very curious
> fancies concerning that force, that *swarm* of motive Powers which I sent

out of my body into that Stone; & which, one by one, left the untracta-
ble or already possessed Mass. . . .
(*STCL*, Vol. I, p. 479)

With such faith in the constancy of energy and being and spirit, Coleridge
concludes that grieving is inappropriate, because there is no real death,
although, in the humility characteristic of his despondencies, Coleridge
acknowledges that the mind's quest for the permanence he has found may
be errant:

> 'Grief' indeed,
> Doth love to dally with fantastic thoughts,
> And smiling, like a sickly Moralist,
> Finds some resemblance to her own Concerns
> In the Straws of Chance, & Things Inanimate!
> (*STCL*, Vol. I, p. 479)

If Wordsworth's "Things Inanimate," his "rocks and stones and trees," reflect
his "Concerns," he, like Coleridge, is not grieving, but for different reasons.
Coleridge goes on:

> I cannot truly say that I grieve—I am perplexed—I am sad—and a little
> thing, a very trifle would make me weep; but for the death of the Baby
> I have *not* wept!—Oh! this strange, strange, strange Scene-shifter,
> Death! that giddies one with insecurity, & so unsubstantiates the living
> Things that one has grasped and handled!
> (*STCL*, Vol. I, p. 479)

Coleridge then introduces "A Slumber," which can now be read with a
fuller sense of its perplexity and pain: "Some months ago Wordsworth
transmitted to me a most sublime Epitaph / whether it had any reality, I
cannot say,—Most probably, in some gloomier moment he had fancied
the moment in which his Sister might die." (*STCL*, Vol. I, p. 479). "A
Slumber" begins with the lover's candid admission of naivete, but we will
see that this is not entirely so:

> A Slumber did my spirit seal,
> I had no human fears:
> She seem'd a Thing, that could not feel
> The touch of earthly years.

The opening phrasing and the tone of the poem are curiously reminiscent of the biographical circumstances the poet reported in his Fenwick note to "Written in Germany," which was probably written at nearly the same time, most likely Christmas Day, Dorothy's birthday—but *after* the first three Lucy poems. The note and the poem reveal that William and Dorothy shared some very tender moments at Goslar. Musing on the fate of a solitary fly in their frigid apartment, William contrasts their circumstances favorably with those of the unfortunate insect. When compared to Dorothy's situation, the fly has "no Brother," when compared to William's situation, the fly has "no Friend":

> No Brother, no Friend has he near him, while I
> Can draw warmth from the cheek of my Love;
> As blest and as glad in this desolate gloom,
> As if green summer grass were the floor of my room,
> And woodbines were hanging above.
>   (*LB*, p. 226, ll. 31-35)

Wordsworth says in the Fenwick note to this specific poem that he

> slept in a room over a passage that was not ceiled. The people of the house used to say, rather unfeelingly, that they expected I should be frozen to death some night; . . .
>   (*LB*, p. 393)

The association of sleep with slumber, the homonym of "ceiled" and "seal," the "unfeeling" response of the landlord and the comparable tone of the poem, Wordsworth's naive bravado in continuing to sleep over a drafty passage, as if he "had no human fears," and the association of these circumstances with the most openly loving poem of William for Dorothy, in which he claims that his sister's physical presence will keep him warm (and thus he won't freeze to death), lead to the conclusion that "A Slumber" is very much a synecdoche of the real experiences and circumstances of the Goslar apartment of the Wordsworths. But with the chief displacement of Dorothy's death for William's. While Dorothy's warm love will help her brother to survive, his dispassionate association with the voice of his landlord will look forward to and backward upon her death, perhaps, for providing that seductive warmth.

Related to the earlier Lucy poems, the literal reverie of "Strange Fits" here becomes a metaphor for the lover's casualness towards mortality, his own in the Fenwick note, and Lucy's in the poem, but there is a disconnect between experience and symbol. If it were during his hypnagogic state in "Strange Fits" that the lover experienced his fantasy of Lucy's death, then his slumber offered the opportunity for releasing his spirit, and the opportunity was taken. In "A Slumber Did My Spirit Seal," the beloved is not a woman in a cottage awaiting her lover's return, but "a Thing." There is no questioning the appropriateness of the term within the context of the poem, as the deceased will join other inanimate objects—rocks, stones, trees—in conforming passively to the earth's physical laws. But would a lover ever compare his beloved to "a Thing," except in retrospect, and for a purpose? Here it is especially important to remind ourselves that the poem is responding to a "fancied" death, and, as I am arguing here, a fancied death with a purpose. If the purpose is the imaginative elimination of the loved one for a reason and, let's say, an uneasiness over why one is dwelling upon the fantasy, then the referent's pejorative "thingness" is an extreme instance of denying the poem's relationship to the referent. There is also the need to deny what "Strange Fits" makes the poet responsible for—the fantasy of Lucy's death, and much deeper, the desire for it. "A Slumber" claims that he was naive, that he was unconcerned and foolishly casual about mortality. But to admit these shortcomings is an evasion. He is guilty of wishing Lucy dead, and she dies by fiat of premonition.

It is the second stanza, however, that more intriguingly displays the complex nature of the poem's emotion:

> No motion has she now, no force;
> She neither hears nor sees,
> Mov'd round in Earth's diurnal course
> With rocks, & stones, and trees!
> (ll. 5-8)

This statement of bald naturalism—as Carl Woodring says, "Naturalism . . . compressed into sublimity"—is usually read to support the contention of "the unsentimental sources of the grief's extraordinary power."[25] But the poet really has it both ways. The text is shockingly void of natural sentiment. Lucy "seem'd a Thing" in the first stanza, and the second stanza perceives her as that thing now literally one with the gravitational round of "rocks, & stones, and trees!" Contrasted with Coleridge's stone, which carries the life force of his energy as he flings it into the water, Wordsworth's perspective would be insufferable, were it not that the reader grants the poet an undue measure of sorrow. In other words, emotion is presumed to be greater for being controlled, or textually absent. The poet does not lose; he can treat Lucy with guarded hostility and have it interpreted as magnificent management of grief. Through a complex interaction of text with emotion, Wordsworth's ambivalence is perfectly expressed and the strategy of grief is consummately managed. The tone of understatement becomes the vehicle of the poet's released hostility.

But, finally, something else has happened to bring the cycle to a temporary close. When the cycle reopens in a few months with "Three Years She Grew in Sun and Shower," Lucy's life and death will have been transformed through mythologizing—made sacred to memory after the sacrifice, as it were—which leads us to conclude that the problems of love have been resolved. When the prospect of rejoining Coleridge arose at the close of this dreadful winter, Wordsworth returned to the Lucy theme, with new insight after composing the drafts on his boyhood development and with altered feelings towards "Lucy."

"Three Years She Grew" probably was written on the road sometime between February 23 and 27, 1799, or immediately after the Wordsworths left Goslar on a walking tour through the Harz forest (*CEY*, p. 263). The timing of its composition suggests that Wordsworth still thinks of Dorothy as an obstacle to his freedom, but the grief and shock of the original Lucy poems are gone and Lucy's death has been transferred to the myth of Nature as rival lover first rearing Lucy and then taking her away at puberty.

If Lucy moves as lightly as the clouds, it is because the "floating clouds their state" have lent her; if she is as lithe as the willow, it is because the willows bend for her and she assimilates their grace. Nature continues describing the osmotic influence he maintains over Lucy's life and, concomitantly, developing the justification for his claim to her:

> ["]Nor shall she fail to see
> Even in the motions of the storm
> A beauty that shall mould her form
> By silent sympathy.

> "The stars of midnight shall be dear
> To her, and she shall lean her ear
> In many a secret place
> Where rivulets dance their wayward round,
> And beauty born of murmuring sound
> Shall pass into her face.

> "And vital feelings of delight
> Shall rear her form to stately height,
> Her virgin bosom swell,
> Such thoughts to Lucy I will give
> While she and I together live
> Here in this happy dell."
> > (*LB*, pp. 221-222, ll. 21-36)

It seems particularly appropriate that Wordsworth would have composed this lyrical apology for Lucy's death while touring a forest area. After enduring the bondage Dorothy had caused at Goslar, he now ascribes a desire of an obviously male Nature to take her in the woods. Yet, having imagined his own death in "The Boy of Winander" and "A Poet's Epitaph," Dorothy's death as Lucy was no longer a terrible thing, and his response is more nostalgic than sorrowful:

> Thus Nature spake—The work was done—
> How soon my Lucy's race was run!
> She died, and left to me
> This heath, this calm and quiet scene,
> The memory of what has been,
> And never more will be.—
> > (*LB*, p. 222, ll. 37-42)

Part of the passing of sorrow was undoubtedly the feeling of freedom that leaving Goslar provided and the look ahead to the meeting with Coleridge, but how do we account for the mythologizing of Lucy's death?[26]

It is here that I would like to draw upon the anthropological insights of Dudley Young in *Origins of the Sacred* to understand what may have happened. Young writes of the philosopher:

> if, through some mysterious combination of reverence, self-mastery, and luck, he finds a way into sensual intimacy that can thrive this side of the penetrative conclusion, he may be blest by the greatest of love's gifts, significant access to the divine light that pours from and through the beloved's body. The erotic ecstasy, which consummation abbreviates, concludes, and distorts in ordinary lovers, is at once magically satisfied, frustrated, and kept alive for the philosopher in a vision of how life should and might be—a vision he can then communicate to

the beloved, a gift for a gift. . . . The agonizing temptations of
sexuality [thus] cannot be avoided by the aspiring philosopher, lover
of wisdom, for it is only in renouncing the all-too-human desire to
possess and therefore devalue the beauty of the loved-one that the
gods allow the chosen few access to the central mystery—that human
fulfillment can be possessed only by those who sacrifice their desire
to possess it. And this, according to Plato, is the life truly worth living,
where the energies for love and war are reconciled at least in the
generative perception of beauty.[27]

Applied to the mythopoeic turn in the Lucy cycle, Wordsworth's "energies
for love and war," his passion and anger towards his sister, as well as the
aggression vented in composing Part One of the 1799 *Prelude*, were "reconciled . . . in the generative perception of beauty," which was the creation of
his Lucy poems.

3. "Was it for this. . . ?"[28]

It will be useful to recall the contemporary historical situation before
seeking to understand the political relevance of Wordsworth's philosophical and autobiographical blank verse composed at Goslar. He returned to
the mode of philosophical blank verse practiced at Alfoxden in deducing
the causes for the corruption of the French Revolution, but now he took
the further step of implicating himself for his own natural human aggression in a morality tale for his time. In universalizing his personal experience—seeing the world in a grain of sand, as William Blake would have
said—Wordsworth found the seed of terror in human nature and its
antidote in the grand forces of the natural world. The primary poetry we
will explore in this section is the First Part of the poetic drafts we now call
the *Two-Part Prelude* (1799), Wordsworth's autobiographical psychonarra-
tive on the relationship of his imagination to history, which from beginning to end means the French Revolution.

When I discussed in Part One the implications of Freud's *Totem and
Taboo* for understanding the politics of *The Borderers*, I delayed considering
the historical veracity of that revolutionary day when the adult males slew
the dominant male of their tribe. As Peter Gay has summarized the matter:

A majority among cultural anthropologists have rejected Freud's speculative reconstruction of the moment when the human animal became

human, though some have argued . . . that this reconstruction makes sense if one abandons his notion that he has described a single historical event in favor of the more modest proposition that the dramatic murder and incorporation of the father is, if rarely a reality, a recurrent and virtually universal fantasy.[29]

This sort of taming of Freud reminds one of the parallel phenomenon in Wordsworth studies that H. W. Garrod complained about in 1929: "The real difficulty . . . of understanding Wordsworth proceeds from our finding it so hard to believe that he means what he says."[30] Although it is impossible to rest an argument comfortably upon the prehistoric past, what I would like to put forward is this: Quite apart from the baboons and other social hominids that might have developed laws for exogamy and breeding following one bloody day at the dawn of human culture, might one not reasonably grant that a century of revolutions against monarchy and other forms of despotism is a modern type of that ancient day—or perhaps it was an ancient period—comparable to our modern centuries of revolution? And this century or more of revolutions, from 1776/1789 to the communist revolutions of the twentieth century, has stamped its mark upon contemporary culture and politics as indelibly as some period of prehistoric uprisings against tribal dominant males.

Conservative analysts of the French Revolution interpreted the event in familial terms. Indeed, Edmund Burke likened France to an ailing father being savaged by primitive sons:

> we have consecrated the state, that no man should approach to look into its defects or corruptions but with due caution; that he should never dream of beginning its reformation by its subversion; that he should approach to the faults of the state as to the wounds of a father, with pious awe and trembling sollicitude. By this wise prejudice we are taught to look with horror on those children of their country who are prompt rashly to hack that aged parent in pieces, and put him into the kettle of magicians, in hopes that by their poisonous weeds, and wild incantations, they may regenerate the paternal constitution, and renovate their father's life.[31]

Wordsworth did not know he shared Burke's sentiments until he felt the force of his own moral culpability in the "spots of time."

Interestingly, our renewed interest in Wordsworth's political thought and life largely has left the spots of time untouched. James K. Chandler states that "one must . . . be able to say what is ideologically significant about those arresting childhood memories recounted in Book I" if discussions of the political dimensions of Wordsworth's major poetry are to be more than "peripheral."[32] But Chandler moves far from the compositional moment of the spots of time in thematically aligning passages from throughout the 1805 *Prelude* and *The Excursion* with the boat-stealing scene to show that

> When we consider the spots of time in reference to the structure in which they are embedded, then, we discover that an implicit tradition-alism is implied even in what seem to be Wordsworth's most intensely lyric and "psychological" moments (Chandler, pp. 206-07).

Chandler's argument is brilliantly supported throughout his chapter on "The Discipline of an English Poet's Mind" (pp. 184-215), but he fails to show that spots of time were politically colored from their origin. The psychological readings that continue to accrue are not pursuing a red herring,[33] but they are incomplete for missing the political context of the compositional present. At Goslar, Wordsworth is developing the narrative of his early life to understand the origin of individual and group aggression against authority.

The French Revolution was now, by all British accounts, as Coleridge was soon to say, "a complete failure" (*STCL*, Vol. I, p. 527). The influence of Burke's passionate and brilliant exposition of a conservative ideology in *Reflections on the Revolution in France* (1790) had won over the hearts and minds of his countrymen, because his dire prophecies of the Revolution's progress proved accurate. When British idealists were still giddy over the millennial potential of the Revolution, Burke had warned that "When antient opinions and rules of life are taken away, the loss cannot possibly be estimated. From that moment we have no compass to govern us; nor can we know distinctly to what port we steer" (*Reflections*, p. 129). Mary Wollstonecraft, Thomas Paine, and others scoffed at Burke's championing of prejudice over reason,[34] but by 1798-99 a skein of events in France, on the Continent, and in Great Britain proved Burke correct in judging the French ship of state to be morally rudderless. The September Massacres of 1792 had been followed by: the arrest and execution of the royal family (1793); the declaration of war against England and the allied forces (1793); the Reign of Terror (1793-94); French aggression against the independent republics of Venice (1796) and Switzerland (1798); the planned and attempted invasions of England by the French (1797-98); the French support of the armed insurrection against the government in Ireland that led to the massacre of 25,000 peasants (1798); and, the steady rise of Napoleon Buonaparte from field general to First Consul (1799).

Thanks to the recent work of Chandler, Nicholas Roe, Kenneth R. Johnston, Marjorie Levinson, and others, we appreciate more fully Wordsworth's growth and intellectual development in the revolutionary political climate of the 1790s. Nevertheless, the politics of Revolution has seemed but a remote affair to most who have contemplated the Goslar winter of 1798-99. Germany was not France, and E. P. Thompson has speculated outright, that "The poets, when they went to Germany, were hopping the draft,"[35] to avoid the pressure of being conscripted to protect the southwestern coast of England from French invasion. In other words, Germany was to be a political retreat. Thompson pictures Wordsworth morosely "isolated in Goslar in the winter of 1799, . . . pitting himself against all inclination to thresh the grain of humanism from the chaff."[36] However, the manuscripts from Goslar recently reedited for the Cornell *Lyrical Ballads* reveal an obsessed poet probing his experience for viable first principles of justice.

In six ruminative passages identified editorially as "Blank Verse Fragments Written in Germany" in *Lyrical Ballads,* Wordsworth deals philosophically with issues relevant to *The Recluse* as a poem on Man, Nature, and Society. In the first of these, the poet discerns that poverty can impede the benign influence of nature on the developing child, thus stunting his political and moral growth for life:

> There is a law severe of penury
> Which bends the cottage boy to early thought,
> To thought whose premature necessity
> Blocks out the forms of nature, preconsumes
> The reason, famishes the heart, shuts up
> The Infant being in itself, and makes
> Its very spring a season of decay.
> . . . .
> Then liberty is not and cannot be;
> But wheresoe'er he turns his steps the boy
> Is still a prisoner, when the wind is up
> Among the clouds, and in the antient woods;
> Or when the sun is rising in the heavens
> Quietly calm.
> . . . .
> The limbs increase; but liberty of mind
> Is gone for ever, and the avenues

> Of sense are clogg'd, and this organic frame,
> So joyful in its motions, soon becomes
> Dull, to the joy of its own motions dead; . . .
>
> (*LB*, pp. 307-08, ll. 1-7, 21-26, 33-37)

In the second passage, Wordsworth identifies real liberty as a self-actualiza-
tion inspired by hope:

> The food of hope
> Is meditated action; robb'd of this,
> Her sole support, she languishes and dies.
> We perish also,—for we live by hope
> And by desire; they are the very blood
> By which we move; we see by the sweet light,
> And breathe the sweet air of futurity,
> And so we live, or else we have no life.
>
> (*LB*, p. 309; ll. 16-23)

and inspired by good works:

> There is one only liberty; 'tis his
> Who by beneficence is circumscribed;
> 'Tis his to whom the power of doing good
> Is law and statute, penalty, and bond,
> His prison, and his warder, his who finds
> His freedom in the joy of virtuous thoughts.
>
> (*LB*, p. 310, ll. 39-44)

The poet then reflects on the poor man's economic responsibilities to "clothe
and nourish" his dependents as harmful to liberty, for "there is no freedom
in his love," and the whole family thereby becomes afflicted with a "con-
striction of the heart": "What then can we hope / From one who is the worst
of slaves, the slave /Of his own house? (*LB*, p. 311; ll. 2-18 passim).

In the fourth passage, Wordsworth criticizes the tendencies of late
eighteenth-century educational philosophy:

> There are who tell us that in recent times
> We have been great discoverers, that by dint
> Of nice experience we have lately given
> To education principles as fixed

And plain as those of a mechanic trade;
Fair books and pure have been composed that act
Upon the infant mind as does the sun
Upon a flower:
. . . .
    when will they be taught that here
In the unreasoning progress of the world
A wiser spirit is at work for us,
A better eye than theirs; most prodigal
Of blessings, and most studious of our good,
Even in what seem our most unfruitful hours?
  (*LB*, pp. 314-15, ll. 1-8; 31-36)

Finally, in lines more closely related to the growing body of his autobiographical verse, Wordsworth muses upon the origin of his own moral state and nature's program for human improvement. The argument proceeds from the poet's self-consciousness of his own moral condition: "I would not strike a flower / As many a man will strike his horse" but, if he did, "I would stop / Self-question'd, asking wherefore that was done" (*LB*, p. 312, ll. 1-2, 11-12). If you think this is being precious, the poet says, do you not take care to protect the individual flowers of your garden? He also believes that we should not be too enamored of our own creations, for it seems that "each access of strength" our "love of order" "gains / From human labours, by a course direct / Or sinuous, is productive evermore / Of littleness and pride" (*LB*, p. 313, ll. 36-39). Turning to nature as an antidote can temper our "exclusive dotage" on our own works, by the "silent growth / Of tenderness and gratitude" that creeps into our hearts in the face of her beautiful forms. Educated by our "teacher in this outward frame of things," even "the meanest object" of nature will take on importance as "a part / Of this great whole" (*LB*, p. 313, ll. 48-55). Henceforth, the earth will become "A temple—made for reverence and love." He then who can "respect a mute insensate form" will be increasingly sensitive to "the pleadings of a human heart" (*LB*, pp. 313-14, ll. 61, 73, 77). Furthermore, he will cease to look for self-projections in the world and rise thereby to a higher level of morality:

    Need I add,
That while he fosters such regard for things
In which he finds no traces of himself,
By this pure intercourse those bastard loves,
Those low and fickle yearnings of the heart,

> The wayward brood of vanity, must die
> Within him and benevolence be spread
> Like the Sun's light upon the open sea?
>   (*LB*, p. 314, ll. 83-90)

Still wrestling with Coleridge's skepticism over the inevitability of self-projection, Wordsworth believes that certain objects permit a "pure intercourse," or an untainted psychological identification with the thing in itself, because they do not seduce the ego into enjoying a "bastard" creation of itself in the thing.

The sixth and final passage reads like a scene from Piranisi in its imagery of the poet being assaulted in his bed:

> When in my bed I lay
> Alone in darkness, I have seen the gloom
> Peopled with shapes arrayed in hues more bright
> Than flowers or gems or than the evening sky:
> Processions, multitudes in wake or fair
> Assembled, puppetshews with tru[m]pet, fife,
> Wild beasts, and standards waving in the [?field].
>   (*LB*, p. 316, ll. 1-7)

Then comes a chase with hounds and possibly horses "That galloped like the wind through standing corn," followed by a "throng of faces . . . / Unutterably horribly arranged," and finally "files of soldiery with dazzling arms, / Still mounting, mounting upwards, each to each / Of all these spectra, every band and class, / Succeeding with fantastic difference / And instant, unimaginable change" (*LB* p. 316, ll. 11-20). If these images represent his nights at Goslar, those nights were very much akin to those of the later books of *The Prelude*, or perhaps they were the same nights, when accrued guilt for radical sympathies prevented restful sleep:

> Most melancholy at that time, O friend,
> Were my day-thoughts, my dreams were miserable;
> Through months, *through years*, long after the last beat
> Of those atrocities . . .
> . . . .
> I scarcely had one night of quiet sleep,
> Such ghastly visions had I of despair,
> And tyrrany, and implements of death,
> And long orations which in dreams I pleaded

Before unjust tribunals, with a voice
Labouring, a brain confounded, and a sense
Of treachery and desertion in the place
The holiest that I knew of—my own soul.
　　　　　(*Prelude*, Book X, ll. 368-80; emphasis added).

Thus, because the poet at Goslar was still affected viscerally by his experience of the Revolution, the seepage of politics and revolution into the fabric of his spots of time should be expected.

The natural landscape of Wordsworth's youth becomes a shadowy world for a confrontation between father and son over identity and control. Figuring his boyhood self as a Child of Nature, the poet employs natural forms to oversee his early moral development, which means learning to suppress his aggression. He also says that he has been recollecting experiences of reproach to goad himself into continuing his composition, so as to sustain his writing by writing: "Meanwhile my hope has been that I might fetch / Reproaches from my former years, whose power / May spur me on, in manhood now mature, / To honorable toil" (*1799*, Part I, ll. 450-53). But while a reproach theme may sustain his work, it does not explain why he felt the need for self-reproach.

　　　　We might note here that each generation has its explanation for the Fall of Man. John Milton and Alexander Pope believed it to be pride. As the child of a revolution gone wild, Wordsworth finds the chief fault in man to be innate, sometimes delirious and frenzied, aggression. He had begun to suspect that man has a heart of darkness. If Nature is to be of real moral use, the poet will have to convince himself that Nature contains appropriate controls for her human kindred. As he begins his story just this side of the womb, the soothing sound of waters offers an early maternal attempt at controlling the boy's fallen birthright:

　　　　　　　For this didst thou
O Derwent, travelling over the green plains
Near my "sweet birth-place," didst thou beauteous Stream
Make ceaseless music through the night and day,
Which with its steady cadence tempering
Our human waywardness, composed my thoughts
To more than infant softness, giving me,
Among the fretful dwellings of mankind,
A knowledge, a dim earnest of the calm

> Which Nature breathes among the fields and groves?
> (*1799*, Part I, ll. 6-15)

Shortly, and for no discernible reason except a primitive impulse, the boy reveals the makings of a savage, and Nature responds with a stronger force than murmuring water. Within ten lines, "a four year's child, / A naked Boy," becomes a "naked Savage," and Nature counters by transforming his wading pool into an ominous "thunder shower":

> Was it for this that I, a four year's child,
> A naked Boy, among thy silent pools
> Made one long bathing of a summer's day?
> Basked in the sun, or plunged into thy streams,
> Alternate, all a summer's day, or coursed
> Over the sandy fields, and dashed the flowers
> Of yellow grunsel, or when crag and hill,
> The woods and distant Skiddaw's lofty height
> Were bronzed with a deep radiance, stood alone,
> A naked Savage in the thunder shower?
> (*1799*, Part I, ll. 17-26)

Incapable of sensitivity, the boy exceeds the boundaries of animal delights in "dash[ing] the flowers" and stands alone in defiance against the thunder shower. The corrective incursion into the boy's mind hereafter begins in progressive relationship to his capacity for internalizing fear.

Following his days of obliviousness to thunder, the boy-child's conscience develops, but without behavioral improvement. He is troubled by the pursuit of "Low breathings" and "sounds / Of undistinguishable motion" after his poaching escapades (*1799*, Part I, ll. 35-49). While hanging above the raven's nest in a perilous attempt to rob the nest of its eggs, he hears a message more articulate than breathing: "With what strange utterance did the loud dry wind / Blow through [his] ears" (*1799*, Part I, 50-66). But the progression from thunder, to breathing, to utterance is unavailing. The boy is offered one further advance in auditory warning before his mind is usurped.

After impulsively absconding with a shepherd's boat for a night of rowing, "an act of stealth / And troubled pleasure," as the poet admits, the boy hears but ignores the "voice / Of mountain echoes" (*1799*, Part I, ll. 90-92), which is his last warning. The peak that protruded from behind the cliff at the shore line intervened, and the boy "struck":

When from behind that rocky steep, till then
The bound of the horizon, a huge Cliff,
As if with voluntary power instinct,
Upreared its head: I struck, and struck again,
And, growing still in stature, the huge cliff
Rose up between me and the stars, and still
With measured motion, like a living thing,
Strode after me.

(*1799*, Part I, ll. 107-14)

The boy reverses his direction and flees towards his parentless home. The protruding cliff that was "like a living thing" enters his mind with the "unknown mode" of its being, though its masculine gender becomes clear:

in my thoughts
There was a darkness, call it solitude
Or blank desertion; no familiar shapes
Of hourly objects, images of trees,
Of sea or sky, no colours of green fields:
But huge and mighty forms, that do not live
Like living men, moved slowly through my mind
By day, and were the trouble of my dreams.

(*1799*, Part I, ll. 122-29)

Precursors, one now can see, of those "Still mounting, mounting" "files of soldiery," troubling him in the compositional present.

Other passages, large and small, were composed to expand upon the theme of reproach. The next passage Wordsworth composes makes the leap from personal to social worlds in transferring his apprehensions over personal aggression into a sociopolitical sphere through the figure of the cottage card game. Doubtless, as many commentators have noted, Wordsworth's card game owes at least a lesson in how to write about card games to Pope's Game of Ombre in *The Rape of the Lock*. But this is a perfunctory association for a passage attacking society's grave potential for self-destruction. It is also unlikely that this poet, who had been in Revolutionary France during some of its hottest moments and who is troubled in the compositional present by dreams of converging armies, would be recalling Belinda's vanities and courtly chicanery rather than the immediate plight of Continental monarchies when he writes:

> Oh with what echoes on the board they fell—
> Ironic diamonds, hearts of sable hue,
> Queens gleaming through their splendour's last decay,
> Knaves wrapt in one assimilating gloom,
> And Kings indignant at the shame incurred
> By royal visages.
> (1799, Part I, ll. 220-25)

The boys' aggressive game throws nature into a rage of warning:

> Meanwhile abroad
> The heavy rain was falling, or the frost
> Raged bitterly with keen and silent tooth,
> And interrupting the impassioned game
> Oft from the neighbouring lake the splitting ice
> While it sank down towards the water sent
> Among the meadows and the hills its long
> And frequent yellings, imitative some
> Of wolves that howl along the Bothnic main.
> (1799, Part I, ll. 225-33)

Looked at retrospectively, Nature moves beyond thunder, breathings, utterances, and baleful forms to howl in prophetic rage at the Terror incipient in the boys' then innocent, though aggressive game. In the same spirit, Wordsworth later imposes as radically on the image of a child at gleeful, careless play to suggest a comparison with the abandon of French atrocities:

> Domestic carnage now filled all the year
> With feast-days: the old man from the chimney-nook,
> The maiden from the bosom of her love,
> The mother from the cradle of her babe,
> The warrior from the field—all perished, all—
> Friends, enemies, of all parties, ages, ranks,
> Head after head, and never heads enough
> For those who bade them fall.
> (Prelude, Book X, ll. 329-36)

Truly, "with what echoes on the board they fell." The sound of the cards thumping on the cottage table echoed into the future, which was 1789-1792:

> They found their joy,
> They made it, ever thirsty, as a child—
> If light desires of innocent little ones
> May with such heinous appetites be matched—
> Having a toy, a windmill, though the air
> Do of itself blow fresh and makes the vane
> Spin in his eyesight, he is not content,
> But with the plaything at arm's length he sets
> His front against the blast, and runs amain
> To make it whirl the faster.
>   (*Prelude*, Book X, ll. 336-45)

To this point in the narrative, Wordsworth claims to be fully in control of his reproach theme and "the unity / Of [his] argument," which might be protracted, he says, if there were a point to it. It may be, however, that he became unsettled over Coleridge's skepticism that *"recollective* consciousness" could lead to the "Essence of Identity." Those "8 miles from Stowey to Bridgewater consist[ing] in the 8 mile stones" could be a devastating analogy to Wordsworth's stringing together of incidents—regardless of the quality of the poetry—to represent the mystery of his life. Such criticism would have driven Wordsworth to inquire more deeply of himself, to be more speculative about being. Though he had covered much, he admits at this point that "much is overlooked," and realizes that "we should ill / Attain our object" if "delicate fears" about violating unity should abridge his enterprise. The narrative reaches a structural climax of three parts or episodes: the drowned man, the gibbet scene, and the death of his father, John Wordsworth. From our point of view, the text has been working fatally towards the father's death from the start, and yet it seems to have ambushed Wordsworth at the point of transition between figurative and literal representations of the human.

Returning briefly to Wordsworth's early life for a more complete sense of psychobiographical direction, we recall that following the death of his mother, almost everything relational was mismanaged by the father. Not only did the children lose "she who was the heart / And hinge of all [their] learnings and . . . loves" (*Prelude*, Book V, ll. 257-58), but their home life and relationship with their father were lost as well when the boys were sent to Hawkshead and Dorothy off to relatives. On the face of it, Dorothy suffered the worst fate of the siblings, but for William too the change was momentous. He recalls later in *The Prelude* the vivid restlessness of his early Hawkshead days:

Well do I call to mind the very week
When I was first entrusted to the care
Of that sweet Valley—when its paths, its shores,
And brooks, were like a dream of novelty
To my half-infant thoughts—that very week
While I was roving up and down alone,
Seeking I knew not what. . . .
                              (*Prelude*, Book V, ll. 450-56)

Richard Onorato argues that at this time in his life Wordsworth became "fixated to a trauma, obsessed by a vital relationship with Nature which has come to stand unconsciously for the lost mother."[37] Immediately following her death, Wordsworth most likely did unconsciously project what he most desired to find. Mother, father, brothers, sister, home, the entire web of family life had dissembled, and his listlessness and uncertainty were working themselves out in motility, a common reaction of children in mourning.[38] Indeed, much of Wordsworth's youthful behavior—his rebellion, his mischief, the briefly contemplated suicide at his grandfather's house, his sometimes hovering at the "abyss of idealism"—all could be attributed to a difficult mourning process caused by anger towards his father.

After he was sent to Hawkshead, as he now recollects, nature seemed to be preparing him for another loss. The three episodes of separation and death—the drowned man, the scene at the murderer's gibbet, and the death of John Wordsworth—conclude Wordsworth's poetic reconstruction of his boyhood with enigmatic force. Their meaning is difficult to state thematically because Wordsworth is faithful to the meaningful obscurity of a child's understanding. We see, with the poet, through the eyes of the five-year-old, the eight-year-old, the young adolescent on the crag, with the limitations of their respective understandings. The poet now faces directly the results of aggressive wishes against the father that Burke found acted out on a grand scale in the upheaval of 1789.

The spots of time frame the life the poet has been reconstructing emotionally and chronologically. The scene at the murderer's gibbet is the earliest episode of the boy's life; he is five. The father's death is the last incident of Part I, when the boy is fourteen. The recollection of either can nourish and repair the depressed mind (*1799*, Part I, ll. 290-94), apparently in a way different from the episodes recounted earlier, and thus have a distinct psychological status. The first spot of time, the scene at the murderer's gibbet, contains a range of hopes and fears that recreate the disturbing Oedipal world of the four- or five-year-old boy: the aspiration to manhood that riding the horse represents; the dashing of the pretense as the child dismounts after discovering he is lost; the fear that he may have been abandoned, rather than lost, by his father's servant; and then the revelation that intrudes upon the poet's compositional experience in transforming without comment the "girl who bore a pitcher on her head" into the "woman and her garments vexed and tossed / By the strong wind":

> through fear
> Dismounting, down the rough and stony moor
> I led my horse and, stumbling on, at length
> Came to a bottom where in former times
> A man, the murderer of his wife, was hung
> In irons; mouldered was the gibbet-mast,
> The bones were gone, the iron and wood,
> Only a long green ridge of turf remained
> Whose shape was like a grave. I left the spot,
> And reascending the bare slope, I saw
> A naked pool that lay beneath the hills,
> The beacon on the summit, and more near
> A girl who bore a pitcher on her head
> And seemed with difficult steps to force her way
> Against the blowing wind. It was in truth
> An ordinary sight, but I should need
> Colours and words that are unknown to man
> To paint the visionary dreariness
> Which, while I looked all round for my lost guide,
> Did, at that time, invest the naked pool,
> The beacon on the lonely eminence,
> The woman and her garments vexed and tossed
> By the strong wind.
>   (*1799*, Part I, ll. 305-27)

Two most meaningful details of this passage have yet to be fully explained in print. The site in Penrith to which Wordsworth here refers was not the execution site of a wife-murderer, and in later versions of the incident, Wordsworth "corrects" his text in simply referring to a "murderer."[39] As de Selincourt and Jonathan Wordsworth both agree, the gibbet Wordsworth most likely saw as a child marked the spot where a Thomas Parker had been murdered by Thomas Nicholson in 1766 or 1767. In explaining the 1799 detail of wife-murder, Jonathan Wordsworth suggests that Wordsworth is conflating Nicholson's execution site with the crime of one Thomas Lancaster, who had been hanged on a gibbet near Hawkshead in 1672 for poisoning his wife.[40]

I think, however, that the conflation goes another way. It is more likely that Wordsworth would have been thinking about the collier John Walford's wife-murder, a story which he had heard from Thomas Poole in 1797. Although the Walford story belongs to the Quantocks, rather than the Lake District, it is a more credible referent for several reasons; there is no evidence—and it seems extremely unlikely—that Wordsworth as a child of four would know of a murder committed one hundred years earlier and even more unlikely that he would have conflated anything as the biographical child during the experience. But the child created for the poem is another matter. Of greater relevance, Wordsworth was composing passages for his *Somersetshire Tragedy* at Goslar, which was based upon Walford's tale.[41] As far as the specific crime goes, the poet's imposition of a family murder on a memory from the child's past indicates that detail was being selected as an objective correlative of the child's anxiety and fear for himself, for a girl (his sister?), and for a woman (his mother?). Although one would not ascribe to the child's awareness anything this specific, he would be fearful that he had caused the father's retribution against him by having him abandoned. Having gotten rid of the boy as a rival for the love of the family women, the father might also be punishing the sister and mother for their transgressions with his son. The mother's later death, the sister's banishment from the family, and the boy's removal to Hawkshead parallel the emotional fears of this experience so closely that this first and most intense experience of separation-anxiety comes to function psychologically as a screen memory for the traumatic losses of mother, sister, and home overseen by the phallic beacon on the summit.

If the crime of John Walford is the referent for the wife-murder, there is an historical point that dovetails with the personal. Wordsworth heard of Walford's unfortunate personal life from Thomas Poole,[42] who certainly had a reputation as a neighborhood radical because of his sympathy for the French Revolution. Thus the tale may have begun with political coloring, and indeed, the narrative of Walford's execution reads like the execution of Sidney Carton in Charles Dickens's *A Tale of Two Cities*. Also, Walford was executed in 1789, a date of obvious historical and personal importance to a poet troubled by revolutionary nightmares and reveries at Goslar. On the face of it, this has the feel of an interpretive stretch, for not everything that happened, and certainly not much that happened in rustic England in 1789, is relatable—or ought to be related without good cause and even better sense—to the Fall of the Bastille and the French Revolution. Nevertheless, the associations we have been tracking between country and father/king (Burke), impassioned card games with the Reign of Terror, Wordsworth's sympathy for Louis as King and Father,[43] his death wishes against his own father for the harm he had done to the family following the death of his wife, and now his meaningful imposition of a fictitious crime upon his earliest memory, all combine to make for at least psychological credibility in finding an historical relevance to 1789 as the year of a wife-murder covering for a father/king receiving a deserved sentence of execution. In this context, the "visionary dreariness" the poet experiences in the recreated child's consciousness is a discovery of his prescient power now to foresee the future in this earliest memory: the mother's death, his sister's abandonment, the day of the father's death/ execution, the French regicide, and the overwhelmingly consequential political relevance of this tragic family romance.

If the first spot of time represents the fear of the Oedipal child that he has "seen" the future, the second spot of time represents the future arrived. Again Wordsworth describes with consummate literal detail the event as experienced, or as it has to be described to represent the emotion he recollects about the experience. "Feverish, and tired, and restless," impatiently awaiting the horses that will carry him and his brothers home for a Christmas break, the young man peers intensely through the foggy landscape to catch a first glimpse of the horses. The association is somewhat fugitive, but obtains in the narrative, that the first spot of time found the boy dismounting his horse in fear and this spot finds him still awaiting the horse that will take him to the life he had foreseen slipping away in his "visionary dreariness." The scene changes to the retrospect of the signal moment of the "dreary time" that came to be:

> Ere I to school returned
> That dreary time, ere I had been ten days
> A dweller in my Father's house, he died,
> And I and my two Brothers, orphans then,
> Followed his body to the grave. The event,
> With all the sorrow which it brought appeared
> A chastisement, and when I called to mind
> That day so lately passed when from the crag
> I looked in such anxiety of hope,
> With trite reflections of morality
> Yet with the deepest passion I bowed low

> To God, who thus corrected my desires; . . .
>   (*1799*, Part I, ll. 349-60)

The unstated desires can be read too easily to conform to an Oedipal interpretation which hardly requires further confirmation. The more significant information to be gained from this passage is the poet's vast egocentricity in believing his father's death to be God's retribution for his desires, regardless of what he may have desired. This is the mental omnipotence of the Lucy poems, where the mind controls the perception of reality with or without intention, to show that "the mind / Is lord and master, and . . . outward sense / Is but the obedient servant of her will" (*Prelude*, Book XI, ll. 270-72). At Goslar, when separation from Coleridge evokes the anxiety of future loss and abandonment, Wordsworth recalls the funereal mental landscape of:

>   wind, and sleety rain,
>   And all the business of the elements,
>   The single sheep, and the one blasted tree,
>   And the bleak music of that old stone wall,
>   The noise of wood and water, and the mist
>   Which on the line of each of those two roads
>   Advanced in such indisputable shapes, . . .
>   (*1799*, Part I, ll. 361-67)

Looking at the boy looking into the mist, the poet returns to this memory because it becomes one of hope for the father's mysterious return to relieve him of guilt. The allusion of "indisputable shapes" recalls the return of Hamlet's father "in such a questionable shape" to speak to his son about avenging his death and caring for his mother. In other words, Wordsworth could hope that his power of mind might control and shape the reality he wished for, but, of course, he was only seeing things.

4. "Alas that cannot be"

The return of father-figures becomes as obsessive a theme as abandonment during this dreadful winter, when the frigid weather of the coldest winter in the century must have brought back memories of John Wordsworth's death from exposure and caused Wordsworth himself to feel vulnerable to death. We recall the comments quoted earlier about the severity of the winter and the prediction of his landlords: "the people of the house used to say, rather unfeelingly, that they expected I should be frozen to death some night," because he slept "in a room over a passage which was not ceiled." The father figure(s) that Wordsworth recalls in a series of Goslar elegies are known together as Mathew, men from Wordsworth's past who came and went with regular unpredictability. The initial impulse for these poems was commemoration:

> —Thou soul of God's best earthly mould,
> Thou happy soul, and can it be
> That these two words of glittering gold
> Are all that must remain of thee?
> (*LB*, p. 212, ll. 29-32)

But the finest of the elegies, "The Fountain" and "The Two April Mornings," exceed a concern for Mathew's memory in the boy-narrator's attempt at filial relationship and the poet's awareness of its hopelessness. Although the two Mathew poems we are about to consider have not been associated with the April 1799 reunion with Coleridge in Germany, there is no evidence against the association and, because of the title of the second poem, "The Two April Mornings," there is at least some literal sense to it, which must count heavily in a discussion of Wordsworth.

"The Fountain" and "The Two April Mornings" explore the motivation of Mathew in rejecting a parent-child relationship with the narrator, even though both long for one. In "The Two April Mornings" (*LB*, pp. 212-14), Mathew associates an April morning of thirty years back, when he met a "blooming Girl" (l. 43) near his daughter's grave, with the April morning of the present, when he and the narrator are out for a day "among the hills" (l. 12). John Harrison, whom T. W. Thompson has identified as the Mathew of this poem, did have an eight-year-old daughter who died in April, shortly after Harrison became the schoolmaster at Hawkshead;[45] thus, in the month of her death, he would have been susceptible to associate many things with his loss. Mathew reveals a heightened sensitivity to association when he says that a "purple cleft" in the clouds and the hue of the sky "'Brings fresh into my mind / A day like this which I have left / Full thirty years behind'" (ll. 21-24). Mathew's reversal of mood from merriment to sobriety discloses the association that has been forming between the young narrator of the present and the dewy girl of the past. Both represent temptation to accept a surrogate for his departed daughter; or, better stated, both remind him that he cannot

love another child. "A day like this" is another day of painful awareness that
he has never finished mourning his daughter and, thus, he has not the love
to offer another child. The girl as fresh and bright as the dew glistening in
her hair must be rejected by a man whose love remains sickly invested in the
dead. The result is inevitable, as Mathew makes clear to the narrator: "There
came from me a sigh of pain / Which I could ill confine; / I look'd at her,
and look'd again; / And did not wish her mine" (ll. 53-56). Why does he tell
the narrator this, if not to warn him of the limits of their relationship? The
narrator, a motherless boy with an absent father, and Mathew, a melancholy,
childless man, only seem to be a perfect pair. Wordsworth fixes the enduring
relevance of Mathew's rejection in an image:

> Mathew is in his grave, yet now,
> Methinks I see him stand,
> As at that moment, with his bough
> Of wilding in his hand.—
>   (ll. 57-60)

"The Fountain" (*LB*, pp. 215-17) explicitly reveals the same emotional
paradox. After bemoaning his kindred "laid in earth" (l. 50), a loss which
has left him not "enough belov'd" (l. 56), this second Mathew figure
confronts a defensive narrator defensively. Using a bit of indirection
himself, the narrator says to Mathew, "Now both himself and me he
wrongs, / The man who thus complains," because not only does the
narrator "live and sing . . . / Upon these happy plains" (ll. 57-60) in spite
of his filial needs, but he is also with Mathew and expects, at the very
least, to have his affection for the old man recognized and appreciated.
To be sure he is not misunderstood, the narrator says directly: "And,
Mathew, for thy Children dead / I'll be a son to thee!" (ll. 61-62). But this
Mathew is as emotionally constricted as the other, and the narrator is
again firmly rejected: "At this he grasp'd his hands, and said, / 'Alas! that
cannot be'" (ll. 63-64). Their immediate departure becomes a hurried
flight from intimacy; they return to the village as if in a dream, stunned
by the limits of human love: "We rose up from the fountain-side, / And
down the smooth descent / Of the green sheep-track did we glide, / And
through the wood we went" (ll. 65-68). Shortly, their relationship resumes
its familiar pattern, though now the narrator feels the perplexity of
Mathew's humor on the passing of time: "And, ere we came to Leonard's
Rock, / He sang those witty rhymes / About the crazy old Church-clock,
/ And the bewilder'd chimes" (ll. 69-72).

When the Wordsworths visited Coleridge at Göttingen the inevitable topic arose: Would he join them in the north of England after his return? His answer was no. While separated from both Wordsworth and Poole, Coleridge reconfirmed that Poole was more essential to his emotional stability and certainly more committed to their relationship. Returning to the insight he had expressed earlier in his "Hexameters," Coleridge emphasized again in writing to Poole that "Wordsworth & his Sister . . . are all to each other" (*STCL*, Vol. I, p. 484). Coleridge describes his newly felt love for Poole and then his painful encounter with the Wordsworths:

> My *whole Being* so yearns after you, that when I think of the moment of our meeting, I catch the fashion of German Joy, rush into your arms, and embrace you—methinks, my *Hand* would swell, if the whole force of my feeling were crowded there.—Now the Spring comes, the vital sap of my affections rises, as in a tree! . . . Wordsworth & his Sister passed thro' here. . . . I walked on with them 5 english miles, & spent a day with them. They were melancholy & hypp'd—W. was affected to tears at the thought of not being near me, wished me, of course, to live in the North of England. . . . I told him plainly, that *you* had been the man in whom *first* and in whom alone, I had felt an *anchor*! With all my other Connections I felt a dim sense of insecurity & uncertainty, terribly uncomfortable/—W. was affected to tears, very much affected; . . .
>
> (*STCL*, Vol. I, pp. 490-91)

We might imagine Wordsworth's emotions towards Coleridge turning "round / As with the might of waters." The whole winter Wordsworth had been anticipating this moment with the hope of success, though with obvious apprehensions. Now hopes for their future residence and for the benefits of poetic collaboration were ended.

And yet, Coleridge mentions without comment an important statement that Wordsworth made about his own residential inflexibility. Wordsworth, he says, felt it imperative to return to the Lake District to be near "Sir Frederic Vane's great Library," for he "deemed the vicinity of a Library absolutely *necessary* to his health, nay to his existence" (*STCL*, Vol. I, pp. 490-91). Stephen Gill believes this was "a flimsy excuse for moving north,"[46] but Wordsworth must have recalled the earlier importance of Darwin's *Zoonomia* for his creativity, which was a kind of lesson on the reliability of books over friends in pursuing great intellectual goals. Certainly, Wordsworth would have preferred both the company of Coleridge *and* the library, but the poet in him knew what choice had to be made.

5. "To what end?"[47]

The Wordsworths returned to England thoroughly disheartened and nothing upon arrival served to improve their spirits. Penniless and homeless, they took up residence with the Hutchinsons at Sockburn-on-Tees in April 1799. Richard Wordsworth had been left in charge of financial matters, which Wordsworth had hoped would include repayment of a loan he had made to Basil Montagu, but Basil was as poor as ever. Joseph Cottle had ignored Wordsworth's request to transfer his copyright to *Lyrical Ballads* to Wordsworth's former publisher Joseph Johnson, so that the edition could have an access to the London market. A blow to finances and reputation was struck by Robert Southey, who gave *Lyrical Ballads* a mixed review in the *Critical Review*. Worst of all, however, was Coleridge's subsequent silence. Perhaps he was getting even for the Wordsworths' protracted silence in Germany, for during a period from early May until his return to England in July 1799, Coleridge wrote eight lengthy letters, but not one to Wordsworth. In fact, the Wordsworths heard nothing from him until the middle of September and did not see him again until the end of October.

A letter Coleridge sent to Wordsworth on or about September 10, 1799, provoked an interesting reaction from Wordsworth that indicates how intent he still was on winning Coleridge back from Poole. The topic was *The Recluse*:

> I am anxiously eager to have you steadily employed on "The Recluse."
> . . . My dear friend, I do entreat you go on with "The Recluse"; and I
> wish you would write a poem, in blank verse, addressed to those, who,
> in consequence of the complete failure of the French Revolution, have
> thrown up all hopes of the amelioration of mankind, and are sinking
> into an almost epicurean selfishness, disguising the same under the soft
> titles of domestic attachment and contempt for visionary *philosophes*. It
> would do great good, and might form a part of "The Recluse," for in my
> present mood I am wholly against the publication of any small poems.
>
> (*STCL*, Vol. I, p. 527)

In response to Coleridge's wishes, Wordsworth translated the gist and even the words of Coleridge's injunction into the text of this poem not addressed to political apostates, but to Coleridge:

> if in these times of fear,
> This melancholy waste of hopes o'erthrown,

If, 'mid indifference and apathy
And wicked exultation, when good men
On every side fall off we know not how
To selfishness disguised in gentle names
Of peace, and quiet, and domestic love,
Yet mingled, not unwillingly, with sneers
On visionary minds, if in this time
Of dereliction and dismay I yet
Despair not of our nature, but retain
A more than Roman confidence, a faith
That fails not, in all sorrow my support,
The blessing of my life, the gift is yours,
Ye Mountains! thine, O Nature!
                    (*1799*, Part II, ll. 478-92)

Upon being informed that the poem was addressed to him, Coleridge responded enthusiastically to the compliment, but reservedly to the enterprise:

I long to see what you have been doing. O let it be the tail-piece of "The Recluse!" for of nothing but "The Recluse" can I hear patiently. That it is to be addressed to me makes me more desirous that it should not be a poem of itself. To be addressed, as a beloved man, by a thinker, at the close of such a poem as "The Recluse," . . . is the only event, . . . capable of inciting in me an hour's vanity—vanity, nay, it is too good a feeling to be so called; it would indeed by a self-elevation *ab extra.*
                    (*STCL*, Vol. I, p. 538)

Wordsworth's strategy for drawing Coleridge back seemed appropriate, but despite this offering Coleridge made no move to visit Wordsworth. In the meantime, Wordsworth's frustration was rising, and his health was growing proportionately worse. Dorothy wrote of his being "sadly troubled with a pain in his side" (*EY*, p. 270), the Goslar ailments apparently returning with depression. At last, in October, Coleridge was sufficiently alarmed by reports of Wordsworth's health to make the trip to Sockburn (*STCL*, Vol. I, p. 545), though without informing his wife or Poole, who thought he went to Bristol to pick up a shipment of books from Germany. He traveled to the Lake District with Cottle, who had been meaning to visit. They reached Sockburn on October 26, and the very next day a revealing event occurred. Wordsworth was suddenly well enough to set out on a walking tour of the

Lakes! It would have been impossible for Cottle not to feel his intrusion on
the renewed intimacy of Wordsworth and Coleridge, and within a short
while he dropped out of the tour. As Mary Moorman says, "It was a tactful
departure. Wordsworth and Coleridge wanted to be by themselves" (Moorman, Vol. I, p. 447). Dorothy's absence was more significant, seeming a
concession to alleviate the present trial of their friendship.

After spending four extraordinarily busy months in London with his
family, deriving journalistic fervor from the political excitement of the
metropolis during Napoleon's rise to power, Coleridge felt a great desire
and, undoubtedly, some pressure, to finally begin his *Life of Lessing*. Wordsworth himself had comparably withdrawn from the political life of London
for vocational reasons in 1795. Although Coleridge had been promising
Poole that he would move to Stowey, at last he decided on the north of
England because, he claimed, too many inconveniences at Stowey would
interfere with his work. Poole was certain that Coleridge's motives were not
so practical or wise. In March 1800, we find Coleridge defending his opinion
of Wordsworth as a latter-day Milton, which Poole read ominously:

> You charge me with prostration in regard to Wordsworth. . . . Is it
> impossible that a greater poet than any since Milton may appear in our
> days? . . . Future greatness! Is it not an awful thing, . . ? What if you had
> known Milton at the age of thirty, and believed all you now know of
> him? . . . Would it not be an assurance to you that your admiration of
> the *Paradise Lost* was no superstition, no shadow of flesh and bloodless
> abstraction, but that the *Man* was even so, that the greatness was
> incarnate and personal?
>
> (*STCL*, Vol. I, p. 584)

It could have been no surprise to Poole when Coleridge finally opted for the
Lake District, though the argument was housed in domestic terms. The only
residences Poole could find were too small; Mrs. Coleridge's relatives at
Bristol would be too close; lately, Poole had turned his head when his
brother's widow insulted Mrs. Coleridge; and Poole himself might be leaving
Stowey for a year or two to travel about the Continent. The picturesque lake
village of Keswick, on the other hand, offered space, retirement, and beauty
that Coleridge never tired of extolling to his correspondents:

> The room in which I sit, commands from one window the Basenthwaite
> Lake, Woods, & Mountains, from the opposite the Derwentwater &
> fantastic mountains of Borrowdale—straight before me is a wilderness

of mountains, catching & streaming lights or shadows at all times. . . .

(*STCL*, Vol. I, p. 610)

Doubtless, however, Coleridge's greatest motivation was to revive the inspiration of the annus mirabilis. He had put up with inadequate housing in Nether Stowey when he needed Poole's economic stability; he had dreamt of Poole's love when feeling ignored by Wordsworth in Germany. But it was beyond time to produce, and vocational pressure was fearfully oppressive. Coleridge sought to find the creative magic that once had produced "Kubla Khan," *Ancyent Marinere*, and the first part of *Christabel*. In fact, the final poetic piece of this pattern of biographical repetition was Coleridge's returning to work on *Christabel* for a new edition of *Lyrical Ballads*.

Wordsworth too had renewed his life in moving to Grasmere, but his return is better represented as a rising spiral rather than a dubious recycling. Writing of his youth at Goslar and then at Sockburn provoked strong heart-stirrings for home. He and Dorothy needed to end the expension of energy on mistakenly motivated wanderings. He sought domestic stability for future work, with or without Coleridge. It is significant that the Wordsworths reached their Grasmere cottage in December, a year removed from their long winter in Goslar and the anniversary month of those important personal and family events we have noted several times earlier—their father's death, Dorothy's birth, Caroline's birth, etc.—and the season of as many: William's departure from France to be with Dorothy, his bold return to France to part from Annette without marrying, and their mother's death.

Returning to their native lakes had seemed a struggle. The winter storm that greeted them was allegorical of the forces they had suffered against successfully, it was now apparent, for sixteen homeless winters:

> Long is it since we met to part no more,
> Since I and Emma heard each other's call
> And were Companions once again, like Birds
> Which by the intruding Fowler had been scared,
> Two of a scattered brood that could not bear
> To live in loneliness; 'tis long since we,
> Remembering much and hoping more, found means
> To walk abreast, though in a narrow path,
> With undivided steps.[48]

Called Lucy while abroad, Dorothy has become Emma upon return to England. The biographical referent for the allegory of the "intruding Fowler"

194 THE POETRY OF RELATIONSHIP

scattering the brood would be the breaking up of family by their father. We
recall from Part One Dorothy's lament that she and her brothers had been
"scattered abroad." Nevertheless, this brother and his sister persisted
through time, and now challenged family fate upon their winter journey
home:

> Bleak season was it, turbulent and bleak
> When hitherward we journeyed, and on foot,
> Through bursts of sunshine and through flying snows,
> Paced the long vales—how long they were, and yet
> How fast the length of way was left behind,
> Wensley's long Vale and Sedbergh's naked heights.
> The frosty wind, as if to make amends
> For its keen breath, was aiding to our course
> And drove us onward like two Ships at sea.
> Stern was the face of nature; we rejoiced
> In that stern countenance, for our souls had there
> A feeling of their strength.
>
> (*H at G,* p. 50, ll. 218-29)

Like vessels successfully blown to safe harbor, the Wordsworths found a
deeper love in the reclusive peace of an emotional covert: "to a home /
Within a home, what was to be, and soon, / Our love within a love" (*H at G,*
p. 52, ll. 261-63).

What is this "home / Within a home" and "love within a love"? Perhaps
it means that Grasmere is their home, and this cottage is in Grasmere and
thus it is "a home / Within a home." Likewise for their love. Grasmere
provides a context of love for all of its animal and human inhabitants and
thus their own love is "within" that place of love. Yet the adverbial modifiers
unsettle a straightforward reading. Both the home within and the love within
seem to have been forthcoming at the time of their settlement at Grasmere,
but now they seem to have been achieved against some odds.

It happens that Grasmere is a place of danger for birds, and that the
Fowler who scatters broods may yet be abroad. There is an uncertain concern
for the "Quires of love" (*H at G,* p. 56, l. 319), because "two are missing—
two, a lonely pair / Of milk-white Swans" (*H at G,* p. 58, ll. 322-23) with
whom the poet and Emma had identified:

> From afar
> They came, like Emma and myself, to live

> Together here in peace and solitude,
> Choosing this Valley, they who had the choice
> Of the whole world. We saw them day by day,
> Through those two months of unrelenting storm,
> Conspicuous in the centre of the Lake,
> Their safe retreat. . . .
> . . . their state so much resembled ours;
> They also having chosen this abode;
> They strangers, and we strangers; they a pair,
> And we a solitary pair like them.
> They should not have departed; . . .
>   (*H at G*, p. 58, ll. 325-342)

His best speculation and worst fear is that they had been killed by a local Shepherd for some gain:

> The Shepherd may have seized the deadly tube
> And parted them, incited by a prize
> Which, for the sake of those he loves at home
> And for the Lamb upon the mountain tops,
> He should have spared; . . .
>   (*H at G*, pp. 58, 60, ll. 352-56)

As Pamela Woof notes in her edition of Dorothy's *Grasmere Journals*, hunting swans was permissible, although poaching their eggs was not.[49] William most likely had written of their identification with the swans in their first spring at Grasmere (*H at G*, p. 9). Dorothy's journal entry for October 17, 1800, causally reports: "A very fine grey morning. The swan hunt. Sally working in the Garden" (Woof, p. 27), as if there were no more significance to this event than there were to the skyscapes of Alfoxden. But what does the possibility of the swans having been slain mean to the poet? What is the danger he foresees for himself and his sister? And how are they to be protected?

These questions do not answer themselves. We had just been told that the brother and sister returned to Grasmere to reverse the expulsion of our original parents, the original siblings, from Paradise and thereby to boldly revise *Paradise Lost*:

> What Being, therefore, since the birth of Man
> Had ever more abundant cause to speak

Thanks, and if music and the power of song
Make him more thankful, then to call on these
To aid him and with these resound his joy?
The boon is absolute; surpassing grace
To me hath been vouchsafed; among the bowers
Of blissful Eden this was neither given
Nor could be given—possession of the good
Which had been sighed for, ancient thought fulfilled,
And dear Imaginations realized
Up to their highest measure, yea, and more.
                    (*H at G*, p. 44, ll. 117-28)

This is not the recovery of innocence defined by W. B. Yeats, when "all hatred driven hence, / The soul recovers radical innocence / And learns at last that it is self-delighting, / Self-appeasing, self-affrighting, / And that its own sweet will is Heaven's will".[50] It is rather the recovery of Paradise itself by a man who is now prepared to receive its blessings. Wordsworth's "good / Which had been sighed for, ancient thought fulfilled / And dear Imaginations realized" is a state of higher innocence unavailable in Milton's Paradise, where Adam and Eve had to fall to understand the value of what they had been given and had lost for evermore.

Wordsworth had caused his sister suffering in successfully wishing his father dead. The guilt borne since the fateful summer reunion of 1787, when the adolescent boy began to feel the debt he owed his sister for their father's death, and which was lately exacerbated by the self-exploration and aggression against her in Germany, was now conquered in their return home. Guilt now having passed, "The unappropriated bliss hath found / An owner, and that owner I am he. . ." (*H at G*, p. 42, ll. 85-86).

Grasmere, as a recovered Eden, however, contains an element of danger for natural lovers. The brother and sister may deserve to re-enter Paradise, but the absence of the swans arouses suppressed anxiety over how welcome they really are or can be in their father's region. The swans may have been heedlessly killed by a thoughtless, aggressive man; but, if one is intent on taking such things personally, their absence may be a sign to heed. The poet would prefer to believe his eyes and say with Miranda-like innocence that "There's nothing ill can dwell in such a temple."[51] The wishful heart must even be lauded for the temporary solace one receives in believing that those who dwell "in this holy place / Must needs themselves be hallowed" for "Thus do we soothe ourselves, and when the thought / Is passed we blame it not for having come (*H at G*, p. 60, ll. 366-67, 379-80).

Complementary mental experiences are also welcome, because they lead to
the same gentle fiction of natural human goodness:

> the stream
> Is flowing and will never cease to flow,
> And I shall float upon that stream again,
> By such forgetfulness the soul becomes—
> Words cannot say how beautiful.
>   (*H at G*, pp. 60, 62, ll. 383-87)

Thanks is to be given for "whatever . . . of outward form":

> Can give us inward help, can purify
> And elevate and harmonize and soothe,
> And steal away and for a while deceive
> And lap in pleasing rest, and bear us on
> Without desire in full complacency,
> Contemplating perfection absolute
> And entertained as in a placid sleep.
>   (*H at G*, p. 62, ll. 390-97)

But is there a point to this knowing self-deception beyond temporary
respite? It seems not, and thus there is a problem for this poet in Grasmere.
    In *Paradise Lost*, after witnessing the vision of the future corruption of
mankind and the salvation of Christ's death, Adam says that he will find his
good "by small / Accomplishing great things, by things deemed weak /
Subverting worldly strong, and by worldly wise / By simply meek; . . . (*PL*,
Book XII, ll. 65-69). The Archangel Michael responds favorably:

> "This having learnt, thou hast attained the sum
> Of wisdom; . . .
> . . . .
>   . . . only add
> Deeds to thy knowledge answerable, add faith,
> Add virtue, patience, temperance, add love,
> By name to come called charity, the soul
> Of all the rest: then wilt thou not be loath
> To leave this Paradise, but shall possess
> A paradise within thee, happier far.
>   (*PL*, Book XII, ll. 575-87)

We can now understand that Wordsworth's "home / Within a home" and "love within a love" are comparable internalizations for Paradise, reachable through trance-like states of consciousness against the danger without.

But Wordsworth also genuflects in the direction of the Lake District's economic and political patriarchy in coming overtly to terms with their Power: "here there is / A Power and a protection for the mind, . . . / In this enclosure [where] many of the old / Substantial virtues have a firmer tone / Than in the base and ordinary world" (H at G, pp. 66, 68, ll. 457-68). In reestablishing a home site for the sibling-family in this region of "paternal sway," Wordsworth had transformed their family tragedy into a romance:

> beautiful and quiet home, enriched
> Already with a Stranger whom we love
> Deeply, A Stranger of our Father's house,
> A never-resting Pilgrim of the Sea,
> Who finds at last an hour to his content
> Beneath our roof; and others whom we love
> Will seek us also, Sisters of our hearts,
> And one, like them, a Brother of our hearts,
> Philosopher and Poet, in whose sight
> These mountains will rejoice with open joy.
> Such is our wealth: O Vale of Peace, we are
> And must be, with God's will, a happy band!
> (H at G, pp. 92, 94, ll. 863-74)

The revision of the past held temporarily. Their brother John, the never-resting Pilgrim of the Sea, did find temporary solace in the home of his brother and sister, until September 29, 1800, when he left Grasmere forever to take up the captaincy of the *Earl of Abergavenny*; Mary Hutchinson, Sister of their hearts, would permanently join the household through marriage with William; Coleridge returned, but without joy, and, much like Satan cursing the love of Adam and Eve in Paradise, found himself envious of the love Dorothy and Mary lavished upon William.[52]

Wordsworth too could not deceive himself for long over the vitality of the traditional moral and economic systems he accepted in returning to the Lake District, nor over the relational power and influence he had with his loved ones. It was not simply that the political and economic revolutions of the age were still raging abroad, like the frost, with keen and silent tooth. It was rather that, as before, the danger to home values was in the heart of the cottage itself, the home within a home. Wordsworth's next great poem, *Michael,* poignantly reveals that the corruptive subtleties of human relationship make futile any hope for the recovery of a golden age.

Coda

Second Selves

The first edition of *Lyrical Ballads* concluded with *Lines Written A Few Miles Above Tintern Abbey*, a poem of great strength in facing historical and personal doubts. But as a young poet assured of his imaginative power and of his emotional resources in his friend and sister, Dorothy, William was confident of their combined power to withstand the assault of the world. The signature poem of the second edition of *Lyrical Ballads* is *Michael*, also composed last, and also a kind of developmental climax to both Wordsworth's art and his life since *Tintern Abbey*. Now enacting the role of father in the guise of a resolute shepherd, Wordsworth peers more deeply into the fault lines of domestic love in Michael's cottage. The composition of *Michael* also bore adversely on Wordsworth's relationship with Coleridge.

Michael was undertaken because, for reasons left unstated, Wordsworth decided that *Christabel*, now including Part II, would not do as the concluding poem of the new edition of *Lyrical Ballads*. It was a late decision. On October 4, 1800, Coleridge visited with the Wordsworths after completing *Christabel*. Dorothy records: "Exceedingly delighted with the 2nd part of Christabel" (Woof, p. 24). The next entry for "Sunday Morning 5th October" indicates that Coleridge again read the poem and Dorothy records, "we had increasing pleasure" (Woof, p. 24). The following day, however, without explanation, Dorothy tersely states: "Determined not to print Christabel with the LB" (Woof, p. 24). This ended the matter for the Wordsworths, but not for Coleridge. On October 17, Dorothy records that "Coleridge had done nothing for the LB" (Woof, p. 25); on October 22, we read: "Coleridge came in to dinner. He had done nothing" (Woof, p. 28). On October 30, 1800, nine days after his twenty-eighth birthday, Coleridge wrote:

> He knew not what to do—something, he felt, must be done——he rose, drew his writing-desk suddenly before him—sate down, took the pen—& found that he knew not what to do.
>
> (*STCNB*, Vol. I, entry 834)

Kathleen Coburn reminds us that October was Coleridge's cruelest month: his birthday was a constant reminder of how much he had not accomplished, which sharpened his yearning for achievement, as his October 1797 composition of "Kubla Khan" attests; recalling that he wed in October always depressed him; Wordsworth's rejection of *Christabel* this October hurt him very badly and, in fact, disabled him, as his notebook entry, and the hypochondriacal ailments that immediately followed, reveal (*STCNB*, Vol. II, note to 834). Coleridge wrote to his friend, the brilliant young scientist Humphrey Davy, that Wordsworth decided on excluding *Christabel* because of its length and because

> the poem was in direct opposition to the very purpose for which the Lyrical Ballads were published—viz—an experiment to see how far those passions, which alone give any value to extraordinary Incidents, were capable of interesting, in & for themselves, in the incidents of common Life.
>
> (*STCL*, Vol. I, p. 631)

It was a good rationalization, especially since Wordsworth was hard at work on the Preface that justified his experimental verse, but Coleridge himself hardly believed it. Reflecting back upon this period in 1818, he said that both Wordsworths displayed "cold praise and effective discouragement of every attempt of mine to roll onward in a distinct current of my own—who *admitted* that the Ancient Mariner [and] the Christabel . . . were not without merit, but were abundantly anxious to acquit their judgements of any blindness to the very numerous defects."[1] Coleridge's poetic production languished with his confidence.

Wordsworth also strained for copy after ordering that the printer destroy the proofs of *Christabel.* The poem was to have taken up 1,300 lines, which were needed to make the second volume of *Lyrical Ballads* equal in length to the first. Faced with the necessity of quickly producing a long poem, Wordsworth planned a pastoral whose subject would be a shepherd's tale he had learned of from Ann Tyson, with whom he had boarded while attending the Hawkshead Grammar School.

On October 11, the Wordsworths set out for Greenhead Gill in search of a sheepfold, it seems for inspiration, somewhere near a spot they had selected for a new home:

> It was a delightful day & the views looked excessively chearful & beautiful chiefly that from Mr Oliff's field where our house is to be built.

The Colours of the mountains soft & rich, with orange fern—the Cattle
pasturing upon the hilltops Kites sailing as in the sky above our heads—
Sheep bleating & in lines & chains & patterns scattered over the
mountains. They come down & feed on the little green islands in the
beds of the torrents & so may be swept away. The Sheepfold is falling
away it is built nearly in the form of a heart unequally divided.

(Woof, p. 26)

As Stephen Maxfield Parrish first observed, the first drafts of *Michael* were
"crudely comic" as Wordsworth experimented with the new form of
pastoral ballad.[2] Always referred to as "the sheep-fold," Dorothy records
eight times in the next two weeks the difficulty her brother was having
with the poem (October 15, 18, 20, 21, 22, 23, 24, 25). And then Dorothy
mentions that William walked and composed in "the Firgrove" near the
end of October (Woof, p. 29). In the month of November, William "burnt
the sheep fold" (Woof, p. 31), began anew, and by November 26, he had
become "very well & highly poetical" (Woof, p. 33). *Michael* was completed
by December 9, 1800. What are we to make of this false start, poetical
reversal, and completion of the major poem of *Lyrical Ballads* (1800) in the
short space of a month?

The mention of the fir grove is intriguing, because the grove of poetic
consequence to Wordsworth belongs to the Matron's tale in *Home at Grasmere*:

The Dame
Who dwells below, she told me that this grove,
Just six weeks younger than her eldest Boy,
Was planted by her Husband and herself
For a convenient shelter, which in storm
Their sheep might draw to. "And they know it well,"
Said she, "for thither do we bear them food
In time of heavy snow." She then began
In fond obedience to her private thoughts
To speak of her dead Husband.

(*H at G*, pp. 74, 76, ll. 611-20)

One would then expect to hear where the Matron's "private thoughts" take
her. However, just as he would later silence his Leech Gatherer in order
to explore his reaction to the Leech Gatherer's woeful tale, so here the
poet salvages the spirit of the Matron's words and discovers a new
inspiration in pathos:

Is there not
An art, a music, and a stream of words
That shall be life, the acknowledged voice of life?
Shall speak of what is done among the fields,
Done truly there, or felt, of solid good
And real evil, yet be sweet withal,
More grateful, more harmonious than the breath,
The idle breath of sweetest pipe attuned
To pastoral fancies? Is there such a stream,
Pure and unsullied, flowing from the heart
With motions of true dignity and grace,
Or must we seek these things where man is not?
Methinks I could repeat in tuneful verse
Delicious as the gentlest breeze that sounds
Through that aerial fir-grove, could preserve
Some portion of its human history
As gathered from that Matron's lips and tell
Of tears that have been shed at sight of it
And moving dialogues between this Pair,
Who in the prime of wedlock with joint hands
Did plant this grove, now flourishing while they
No longer flourish; he entirely gone,
She withering in her loneliness. Be this
A task above my skill; the silent mind
Has its own treasures, and I think of these,
Love what I see, and honour humankind.
(*H at G*, pp. 76, 78, ll. 620-45)

The stream Wordsworth found flowing from his poet's heart was driven by the pure example of the Matron's unsullied pathos, which *Michael* shares.

At an extraordinary moment of domestic drama in *Michael* when the old shepherd comes to his wife, Isabel, with a plan for saving their patrimonial fields by relying upon their eighteen-year-old son, Luke, the poet opens the veil on the fundamental difference in values secretly coexisting in the Shepherd's cottage:

["]Our Luke shall leave us, Isabel; the land
Shall not go from us, and it shall be free,
He shall possess it free as is the wind

> That passes over it. We have, thou knowest,
> Another kinsman, he will be our friend
> In this distress. He is a prosperous man,
> Thriving in trade, and Luke to him shall go
> And with his Kinsman's help and his own thrift
> He quickly will repair this loss, and then
> May come again to us. If here he stay
> What can be done? Where every one is poor
> What can be gain'd?"
>   (*LB*, p. 261, ll. 254-65)

Isabel muses inwardly upon Michael's words, but not exactly as Michael (or we) might have expected:

> At this the old man paus'd,
> And Isabel sate silent, for her mind
> Was busy, looking back into past times.
> There's Richard Bateman, thought she to herself,
> He was a parish Boy—At the church door
> They made a gathering for him, shillings, pence,
> And halfpennies, wherewith the Neighbours bought
> A Basket which they fill'd with Pedlar's wares,
> And with this Basket on his arm the Lad
> Went up to London, found a Master there
> Who out of many chose the trusty Boy
> To go and overlook his merchandise
> Beyond the seas, where he grew wondrous rich,
> And left estates and monies to the poor,
> And at his birth-place built a Chapel, floor'd
> With marble which he sent from foreign Lands.
> These thoughts and many others of like sort
> Pass'd quickly through the mind of Isabel
> And her face brighten'd. The Old Man was glad
> And thus resumed.
>   (*LB*, pp. 261-62, ll. 265-84)

We should find a great deal in Isabel's fantasy of Richard Bateman to trouble Michael, but chiefly that the parish Boy went far abroad to grow rich; to do good works for others, it is true, and to grace his parish with a better chapel; but it seems never to return, or at least his return is irrelevant to Isabel's daydream. Not a thought of Isabel's spontaneous musing is devoted to Luke as Luke. It matters to her that he escape; Luke's return would ruin her story.[3]

Michael cannot read his wife's mind or heart. In a moment of powerful irony, when he sees her face brighten, we assume that he believes Isabel has been imagining the success of *his* plan for their son—Luke will leave for a while, save enough money to cover the debt that will save their patrimonial fields, and return posthaste to pick up his shepherd's staff—and Michael could only suppose that she would be pleased with her boy's return. The poet knows that if Isabel spoke what she thinks aloud, he could not write that Michael would "be glad . . . and resume."

Luke has assimilated the values of his mother, or to put it more critically, one sees that the minor characters of the narrative—the woman, and the son through whom she wishes to live vicariously—represent a silent collusion against Michael's values. Somehow in this quiet and remote setting, far from the cutting edge of modernity in London, the world was changing. The cultural revolution, like the political revolution Wordsworth describes in *The Prelude,* was like springtime which leaves no corner of the land untouched.

Michael senses that something is amiss. Although he knows Luke's excitement at leaving home is natural, Michael senses a deeper malady and stages, haltingly, the powerful scene at the sheepfold to assure Luke's family commitment with a covenant. The many dashes in the following section of Michael's monologue are typographic emblems of the silent confusion in the old man's mind as he faces the visible evidence that Luke desires more deeply to leave than he can understand or admit:

> Heaven bless thee, Boy,
> Thy heart these two weeks has been beating fast
> With many hopes—it should be so—yes—yes—
> I knew that thou could'st never have a wish
> To leave me, Luke,—thou hast been bound to me
> Only by links of love, when thou art gone
> What will be left to us!
> (*LB,* p. 265-66, ll. 407-13)

Peter J. Manning makes an important association between Michael's address to Luke and the poet's address to his sister in *Tintern Abbey:*

> *Michael,* the concluding poem of the second volume of *Lyrical Ballads,* seems most like the concluding poem of the first volume: *Tintern Abbey.*

In both, the assertions of continuity are ringed with doubt: in Michael's
exhortations to Luke we seem to encounter again Wordsworth's address
to Dorothy, a conscious intent to pass on values to, and be remembered
by, the next generation, mingling with a more urgent need to recapture
through it the speaker's own former self.[4]

I agree with all of this, except for the "urgent need" being personal to the
poet. Rather, the poet's faith in his sister has been supplanted in *Michael* by
the faith he now places in future poets to record the inexorable dissolution
of traditional England, while Michael as father and shepherd is left with no
place to turn at all. The division over values between Michael, Isabel, and
Luke represents the hard-won insights into human relationship of an experienced brother, lover, friend, and poet.

Wordsworth makes a pointed distinction now between loving domestic relationships and poetic relationships, between friendship and vocation,
in transferring hope from his sister to a brotherhood of poets who would
hold his values and aspirations:

> Therefore, although it be a history
> Homely and rude, I will relate the same
> For the delight of a few natural hearts,
> And with yet fonder feeling, for the sake
> Of youthful Poets, who among these Hills
> Will be my second Self when I am gone.
> (*LB*, p. 253, ll. 34-39)

Wordsworth has had many second selves who have explored the breach that
Michael and Isabel remain oblivious to, despite the fact that it ruins their
lives. Indeed, troubled relationships, especially between men and women,
rather than transcendent nature, may be seen as the chief object of poetic
misprision among the strong poets who have paid particular attention to
Wordsworth in specific works. For example, and to mention only a few—
Percy Shelley (*Adonais* and *Julian and Maddalo*), Mary Shelley (*Frankenstein*),
Lord Byron (at least in *Manfred*), Matthew Arnold ("The Buried Life"),
Thomas Hardy ("The Broken Appointment"), W. H. Auden ("As I Walked
Out One Evening"), and especially Robert Frost ("Home Burial" and "Death
of the Hired Man"). These make for a poignant theme for literary influence,
whether the relationship considered is the failed ideal of perfect similarity
that Wordsworth establishes in *Tintern Abbey* or the subtle break in the marital
relationship of *Michael*.

The issue is poignant for at least two reasons. When Wordsworth's Second Selves consider nature in their poems, they either ironize his natural supernaturalism, or write with something of the passionately disinterested eye of Dorothy Wordsworth. Compare, for example, one of the Alfoxden journal entries that Hyman Eigerman has represented as the third poem of Dorothy's "free verse" in his edition of *The Poetry of Dorothy Wordsworth* (1940):

> Young lambs
> In a green pasture in the Coombe—
> Thick legs,
> Large heads,
> Black staring eyes.

Robert Frost's "The Pasture" is hardly indebted to Dorothy Wordsworth, but his perception of young animal life is comparably disinterested in empathizing with its mute existence:

> I'm going to fetch the little calf
> That's standing by the mother. It's so young
> It totters when she licks it with her
> tongue.[5]

On the other hand, when Frost writes of his country couples, they are more likely to share the now explicitly gendered differences of Isabel and Michael. As Richard Poirier says, "Frost is often at his best when 'home' is at its worst,"[6] and home is worst at times of crisis, which means a time of discovered conflict between heretofore unstated perceptions and values. Often underlying the conflict, as in *Michael,* is the repression that women experience in the cottage. At other times, it is the natural order of difference. The wife in "Home Burial" accuses her husband of indifference to the death of their child, because he is able to dig the little boy's grave, as she perceives, unfeelingly: "'You can't [speak of our child with love] because you don't know how to speak. / If you had any feelings, you that dug / With your own hand—how could you?—his little grave; / I saw you from the window there, / Making the gravel leap and leap in air, / . . . / I thought, Who is that man? I didn't know you.'"[7] Although the conflict is now open, rather than suggestively suppressed, it is Wordsworth's *Michael* that first draws the veil on the window of relationships in the rustic cottage. And how could he have done so, even unwittingly, without experiencing for himself the real tensions of the poetry of relationship?

Appendix

Effusion XXXV
(Eolian Harp)

Composed August 20th, 1795, at Clevedon, Somersetshire

My pensive Sara! thy soft cheek reclin'd
Thus on mine arm, most soothing sweet it is
To sit beside our cot, our cot o'er grown
With white-flower'd Jasmin, and the broad-leav'd Myrtle,
(Meet emblems they of Innocence and Love!)
And watch the clouds, that late were rich with light,
Slow-sad'ning round, and mark the star of eve
Serenely brilliant (such should Widsom be)
Shine opposite! How exquisite the scents
Snatch'd from yon bean-field! and the world *so* hush'd!
The stilly murmur of the distant Sea
Tells us of Silence. And that simplest Lute
Plac'd length-ways in the clasping casement, hark!
How by the desultory breeze caress'd,
Like some coy Maid half-yielding to her Lover,
It pours such sweet upbraidings, as must needs
Tempt to repeat the wrong! And now its strings
Boldlier swept, the long sequacious notes
Over delicious surges sink and rise,
Such a soft floating witchery of sound
As twilight Elfins make, when they at eve
Voyage on gentle gales from Faery Land,
Where *Melodies* round honey-dropping flowers
Footless and wild, like birds of Paradise,
Nor pause nor perch, hov'ring on untam'd wing.

And thus, my Love! as on the midway slope
Of yonder hill I stretch my limbs at noon

Whilst thro' my half-clos'd eyelids I behold
The sunbeams dance, like diamonds, on the main,
And tranquil muse upon tranquillity;
Full many a thought uncall'd and undetain'd,
And many idle flitting phantasies,
Traverse my indolent and passive brain
As wild and various, as the random gales
That swell or flutter on this subject Lute!
And what if all of animated nature
Be but organic Harps diversly fram'd,
That tremble into thought, as o'er them sweeps,
Plastic and vast, one intellectual Breeze,
At once the Soul of each, and God of all?
But thy more serious eye a mild reproof
Darts, O beloved Woman! nor such thoughts
Dim and unhallow'd dost thou not reject,
And biddest me walk humbly with my God.
Meek Daughter in the Family of Christ,
Well hast thou said and holily disprais'd
These shapings of the unregenerate mind,
Bubbles that glitter as they rise and break
On vain Philosophy's aye-babbling spring.
For never guiltless may I speak of Him,
Th' INCOMPREHENSIBLE! save when with awe
I praise him, and with Faith that inly *feels*;
Who with his saving mercies healed me,
A sinful and most miserable man
Wilder'd and dark, and gave me to possess
PEACE, and this COT, and THEE, heart-honor'd Maid!

Notes

Introduction

1. McFarland's "The Symbiosis of Coleridge and Wordsworth" appeared originally in *Studies in Romanticism* 11 (Fall 1972), pp. 263-303, and is reprinted in *Romanticism and the Forms of Ruin: Wordsworth, Coleridge and the Modalities of Fragmentation* (Princeton, NJ: Princeton University Press, 1981), pp. 56-103; Paul Magnuson, *Coleridge and Wordsworth: A Lyrical Dialogue* (Princeton, NJ: Princeton University Press, 1988); Lucy Newlyn, *Coleridge, Wordsworth, and the Language of Allusion* (Oxford: Clarendon, 1986); Gene W. Ruoff, *Wordsworth and Coleridge: The Making of the Major Lyrics, 1802-1804* (New Brunswick, NJ: Rutgers University Press, 1989).

2. The identification and title of the new genre, greater Romantic lyric, appears in M. H. Abrams's influential essay, "Structure and Style in the Greater Romantic Lyric," in *From Sensibility to Romanticism: Essays Presented to Frederick A. Pottle*, eds. Frederick W. Hilles and Harold Bloom (New York: Oxford University Press, 1965), esp. pp. 552-57.

3. *The Collected Works of Samuel Taylor Coleridge*, gen. ed. Kathleen Coburn, Bollingen Series 75 (Princeton, NJ: Princeton University Press, 1969- . *The Cornell Wordsworth*, gen. ed. Stephen M. Parrish (Ithaca, NY: Cornell University Press, 1975-).

4. *Lyrical Dialogue*, pp. 18-19.

5. Mikhail Bakhtin, *Problems of Dostoevsky's Poetics*, ed. and trans. Caryl Emerson (Minneapolis, MN: University of Minnesota Press, 1984), p. 197.

6. See Anne K. Mellor, *Romanticism and Gender* (New York: Routledge, 1993), pp. 144-69.

7. Elizabeth A. Fay, *Becoming Wordsworthian: A Performative Aesthetics* (Amherst, MA: University of Massachusetts Press, 1995), pp. 2-3, 113.

8. Coleridge writes that the power of imagination "reveals itself in the balance or reconciliation of opposite or discordant qualities: of sameness, with difference; of the general, with the concrete; the idea, with the image; . . . and while it blends and harmonizes the natural and

the artificial, still subordinates art to nature; ..." (*BL* Vol. II, pp. 16-17)

9.   Abrams says, "It seems to me that Hazlitt and his contemporary viewers of the literary scene were, in their general claim, manifestly right: the Romantic period was eminently an age obsessed with the fact of violent and inclusive change, and Romantic poetry cannot be understood historically, without awareness of the degree to which this preoccupation affected its substance and form." From "English Romanticism: The Spirit of the Age," in *Romanticism Reconsidered: Selected Papers from the English Institute,* ed. Northrop Frye (New York: Columbia University Press, 1963), pp. 28-29.

10.   *The Writings and Speeches of Edmund Burke,* gen ed. Paul Langford, Vol. VIII, *The French Revolution 1790-1794,* ed. L. G. Mitchell (Oxford: Clarendon, 1989), p. 60.

11.   *Breathes* is an appropriate metaphor for a poem described as structurally systolic and diastolic in Albert S. Gerard's *English Romantic Poetry: Ethos, Structure, and Symbol in Coleridge, Wordsworth, Shelley, and Keats* (Berkeley: University of California Press, 1968), pp. 24-29.

12.   Coleridge's famous poem was published in several significantly different forms with titles altered by wording and spelling. Throughout this text, when the 1798, or original, text of the poem is under consideration, the poem's title will be *Rime of the Ancyent Marinere.* When the later version, principally the text of 1817, is intended, the title will reflect the later, modernized spelling, *Rime of the Ancient Mariner.*

13.   *Michael,* ll. 38-39 in *LB,* p. 253.

Part One

1.   *Donne: Poetical Works,* ed. Herbert J. C. Grierson (1929; Oxford: Oxford University Press, 1933), p. 45, ll. 21, 24. *The Traveller, or a Prospect of Society. A Poem. Collected Works of Oliver Goldsmith. Vol. IV. The Vicar of Wakefield, Poems, The Mystery Revealed,* ed. Arthur Friedman (Oxford: Clarendon, 1966), p. 249, l. 10: "And drags at each remove a lengthening chain."

2.   *Aristotle's Poetics: A Translation and Commentary for Students of Literature,* trans. Leon Golden and commentary by O. B. Hardison, Jr. (Englewood Cliffs, NJ: Prentice Hall, 1968), p. 13.

3. *The Borderers*, Act I, Scene i, l. 68, in *The Borderers*, ed. Robert Osborn (Ithaca, NY: Cornell University Press, 1982). Section headings and quotations in the text are all from the early or 1797-99 version of the play.
4. "The Blessing of my later years / Was with me when a Boy; / She gave me eyes, she gave me ears; / And humble cares, and delicate fears; / A heart, the fountain of sweet tears; / And love, and thought, and joy." (Gill, p. 239, ll. 15-20)
5. Stephen Gill, *William Wordsworth: A Life* (Oxford: Clarendon, 1989), p. 18.
6. Richard, the eldest brother, was working for a relative at Branthwaite (*CEY*, p. 66.) and thus was excluded from this newfound intimacy of his siblings; he will figure prominently afterwards as a parent figure in discharging financial affairs for his brothers and sister.
7. Dorothy's recent biographers, Robert Gittings and Jo Manton, are particularly insensitive on the point of Dorothy's paternal rejection. Though they acknowledge that the severe separation John Words-worth imposed on Dorothy may have been problematic—"the failure of her father to have her home for even the briefest visit remained an obscurely hurtful mystery, even in adult life"—their surprising, even contradictory, conclusion is: "During the happy years at Halifax Dorothy had almost forgotten her father, since she never went home, even for Christmas, which was her own Birthday. 'The day,' she wrote rather sadly, 'was always kept by my Brothers with rejoicing in my Father's house, but for six years (the interval between my Mother's death and his) I was never home.'" *Dorothy Wordsworth* (Oxford: Clarendon, 1985), pp. 15, 6.
8. Hayden, Vol. I, p. 62, ll. 427-449.
9. *1799*, Part One, pp. 51-52, ll. 353-360.
10. Duncan Wu, "Wordsworth and Helvellyn's Womb," *Essays in Criticism*, 44 (January 1994), p. 15.
11. The fury with relatives that caused Wordsworth at age nine to consider suicide (Moorman, Vol. I, p. 13) is a pertinent gloss.
12. The desire to reach for something palpable when feeling psychologically unstable seems related to the experience Wordsworth describes in his comments to Isabella Fenwick on *Ode: Intimations of Immortality*: "Many times while going to school have I grasped at a wall or tree to recall myself from this abyss of idealism to the reality. At that time I was afraid of such processes" (Hayden, Vol. I, p. 978). Richard J. Onorato has defined such experience as a passive "fall into oblivion"

in contrast with the active approach to inwardness Wordsworth would later cultivate. *The Character of the Poet: Wordsworth in* The Prelude (Princeton, NJ: Princeton University Press, 1971), p. 119.

13. Dorothy's letters indicate that her sexual confidence and self-esteem increased after an extended visit with William in the winter of 1790-91. Prior to this period, Jane's curiosity about Dorothy's romantic feelings aroused either defensiveness and self-effacement or testiness: "I can only say that no man I have seen has appeared to regard me with any degree of partiality; nor has any one gained my affections, . . . Mr. W[ilberforce] would, were he ever to marry, look for a Lady possessed of many more accomplishments that I can boast, . . ." (*EY*, p. 28). In irritation with Jane's response to a letter in which Dorothy had mentioned "a very pleasant young man" and had imagined Jane "look[ing] significant" (*EY*, p. 30), Dorothy retorts: "I shall not answer your foolish raillery any more. . . . I shall think you unkind if you say any thing more to me upon the subject" (*EY*, p. 42). After William's visit, however, we find this postscript in a letter to Jane in reference to a marriage at Halifax: "Pray make my congratulatory Compts to Mr. *Edward Swain.* Ought *I* to *rejoice* at his marriage, for do I know what might have been my chance for him?" (*EY*, p. 47).

14. *The Borderers*, Act III, Scene v, l. 23.

15. As Mark Reed notes, ll. 423-28 of *Evening Walk* appear in Dove Cottage Manuscript 7, below drafts of *Descriptive Sketches* (*CEY*, p. 310). Use of distinctive black ink makes it likely that several passages from *Evening Walk*, including Wordsworth's dream for a future home with Dorothy, were composed concurrently with *Descriptive Sketches*. James Averill concurs with Reed's assessment in his editorial Introduction to the Cornell edition (*EW*, p. 8), but neither associate passages based upon ink color. The other inks of Dove Cottage Manuscript 7 are brown and black-brown (*EW*, p. 97).

16. George McLean Harper states: "The nobility of his character, and his subsequent behaviour towards Annette, as well as her continued affection for him, make it impossible to suppose that he abandoned her voluntarily." On the issue of marriage, Harper adds: "It may be that the objection to an immediate marriage between a royalist and Catholic young woman of little or no fortune and a foreign lad who was a republican, a free-thinker . . . came as much from the side of her relations as of his" (*William Wordsworth: His Life, Works, and Influence*, 3d ed. [London: Murray, 1929], p. 97). Herbert Read also finds "lack of money" a sufficient motivation for Wordsworth's departure and be-

lieves that since Wordsworth planned such an immediate return to France, there is no reason to question his intention to marry Annette (*Wordsworth* [1930; London: Faber and Faber, 1949], pp. 77, 85). George Wilbur Meyer also maintains that "Wordsworth's intentions toward Annette Vallon were wholly honorable when he returned to England. In 1793 his purpose was to make her his wife. So far as we know, events—not Wordsworth's change of heart—made this impossible" (*Wordsworth's Formative Years* [Ann Arbor: University of Michigan Press, 1943]: pp. 131-32). Mary Moorman emphasizes the practical problems the young couple faced on the issue of marriage, leaving it vague whether she believes Wordsworth intended to return. Her Wordsworth is more a republican than a lover and she finds him anxiously waiting to leave Annette in the final weeks of her pregnancy to enjoy the political excitement in Paris (Moorman, Vol. I, pp. 201-02). Being niggardly with the empathy required of this biographical situation, Stephen Gill dismisses the matter: "there is simply no evidence on which to conjecture either way that Wordsworth was deeply in love with Annette, or, conversely, that his union with her was a short-lived passion which he was forced to take seriously only because she became pregnant" (*William Wordsworth: A Life* [Oxford: Clarendon, 1989], p. 65). Emile Legouis rightly observes, "Another man might have . . . married Annette straightway, then placed before his guardians the accomplished fact." He believes Wordsworth's "native wariness inclined to procrastination" (*William Wordsworth and Annette Vallon* [New York: E.P. Dutton, 1922], p. 27).

17. 1850 *Prelude*, Book X, ll. 222-25, 229-31. The 1805 text is essentially the same, but fails to include the chain metaphor which is consequential for my argument.
18. *BL*, Vol. I, p. 77.
19. Christopher Wordsworth, *Social Life at the English Universities in the Eighteenth Century* (Cambridge, England, 1874), p. 589. Noted in *EW*, p. 10.
20. *Borderers*, Act V, scene iii, l. 185.
21. Margaret Homans, *Women Writers and Poetic Identity* (Princeton: Princeton University Press, 1980), pp. 12, 29-40.
22. Susan M. Levin, *Dorothy Wordsworth and Romanticism* (New Brunswick, NJ: Rutgers University Press, 1987), p. 109. Nevertheless, some have experimented with shaping Dorothy's artful prose into free verse, the most notable experiment being that of Hyman Eigerman, ed. *The Poetry of Dorothy Wordsworth* (New York: Columbia University Press, 1940). He says in his Preface: "I have tried to fulfill by lifting out of the context

those passages of her journals which have seemed to me to rise into poetry, preserving the words and the word order of the original, only marshaling them within the free-verse form which was unknown to the author" (unnumbered page in his Preface).

23.   Susan J. Wolfson, "Dorothy Wordsworth in Conversation with William" in *Romanticism and Feminism*, ed. Anne K. Mellor (Bloomington: Indiana University Press, 1988), p. 142.

24.   "Irregular Verses," ll. 15-16, 60-77, in "Appendix One: The Collected Poems of Dorothy Wordsworth" (*Dorothy Wordsworth & Romanticism*) pp. 201-03.

25.   Elizabeth A. Fay, *Becoming Wordsworthian: A Performative Aesthetics*, pp. 133-37.

26.   Annette Vallon's letters to William and Dorothy are included as Appendix II to Emile Legouis's *William Wordsworth and Annette Vallon* (1922; New Haven: Archon Books, 1967), pp. 124-133. The quoted lines are from p. 127 and read in the French: "Votre dernière me fait une sensation si vive; à chaque ligne je voyais la sensibilité de votre âme et cet intérêt si touchant que vous prenez à mes peines. Elle[s] sont grand[es], ma chère soeur, . . ."

27.   David V. Erdman, "Wordsworth as Heartsworth; or, Was Regicide the Prophetic Ground of Those 'Moral Questions'?" in *The Evidence of Imagination: Studies of Interactions Between Life and Art in English Romantic Literature*, eds. Donald H. Reiman, Michael C. Jaye, and Betty T. Bennett (New York: New York University Press, 1978), p. 30.

28.   *Reminiscenses by Thomas Carlyle*, ed. James Anthony Froude (New York: Harper & Bros., 1881), p. 334. In his important historical study, *Wordsworth and Coleridge: The Radical Years* (Oxford: Clarendon, 1988), Nicholas Roe provides an interesting though stinted speculation on Carlyle's testimony: "Carlyle's account of a further encounter in October 1793 remains unsubstantiated as historical fact, despite his emphasis that Wordsworth had witnessed the death of Gorsas 'in particular.' Given that lack, perhaps Carlyle's recollection should be taken as an imaginative truth, in which case Wordsworth's shadowy presence at the scaffold was not only as appalled spectator but simultaneously as victim and as executioner too" (p. 41). In *The Politics of Nature: Wordsworth and Some Contemporaries* (New York: St Martin's Press, 1992), however, Roe comes out strongly on the side of Wordsworth's second visit (pp. 101-16). On the death of Gorsas, in particular, one wonders how much Wordsworth knew of the Deputy. In Robert Darnton's brilliant social history, *The Literary Underground of the Old*

Regime (Cambridge, MA: Harvard University Press, 1982), Antoine-Joseph Gorsas is described as the "excrement of literature" (p. 10) haunting Grub Street. Police archives describe him thusly: "Gorsas: proper for all kinds of vile jobs. Run out of Versailles and put in [a jail for disreputable criminals] by personal order of the king for having corrupted children whom he had taken in as lodgers, he has withdrawn to a fifth floor on the rue Tictone. Gorsas produces *libelles*. . . . He is suspected of having printed obscene works. . . . He peddles prohibited books" (p. 26).

29. George McLean Harper, *William Wordsworth, His Life, Work, and Influence*, rev. ed. (New York, 1929), p. 241.

30. Stephen Gill, *Wordsworth: A Life*, p. 78.

31. Moorman, Vol. I, p. 242.

32. See Erdman, "Wordsworth as Heartsworth," p. 37, n. 11, for meteorological evidence of an unusual snowfall in October 1793 that supports the argument that Wordsworth visited with Annette, because snowfall is also mentioned in *The Prelude*'s thinly veiled tale of their romance, the tale of Vaudracour and Julia.

33. Annette felt very strongly the need to marry for emotional as well as practical reasons. Her respectability as well as the right to raise her child was at stake. Because Annette had not married, Anne Caroline initially was entrusted to the care of another by Annette's family. (Moorman, Vol. I, p. 180, n. 2)

34. See Brenda Banks, "'Vaudracour and Julia': Wordsworth's Melodrama of Protest," *Nineteenth-century Literature* 47 (December 1992), pp. 275-302, for an excellent historical analysis of "the Tale's grappling with the Revolution as historical phenomenon" (p. 278) intended by Wordsworth as a parable to revive political dialogue over its failed ideals.

35. See William Godwin's description of Mary Wollstonecraft's life in *Memoirs of the Author of* The Rights of Woman, ed. Richard Holmes (New York: Penguin, 1987), especially pp. 238-55 for her affair with Gilbert Imlay.

36. Erdman argues: "The parallels in the 'Vaudracour and Julia' story are clear if we posit that Julia's father's house equals France, that her lover's father's house equals England. 'Vaucracour . . . hie[d] / Back to his father's house . . . to obtain a sum of gold' [*Prelude*, Book IX, ll. 646-48) means Wordsworth went back to England . . . to raise money. Violence (compare the outbreak of hostilities between England and France in January) for which Vaudracour shares the guilt of a 'Murderer' (killing a man to be with Julia, but landing in jail instead) then forces him to

stay 'Quietly in his Father's house' (l. 698) 'nor take / One step to reunite himself with her'—i.e., Wordsworth is compelled to stay in England, away from Annette, before the birth of Caroline. Yet, Vaudracour sneaks back to his love's house for a happy but precarious and hazardous meeting with mother and child, which I take as confirmative evidence for the inference that Wordsworth paid a clandestine trip to France in October 1793, after the war was in motion." (Erdman, "Wordsworth as Heartsworth," pp. 15-16)

37. The text of the du Fosse story is taken from the photo-reprint of the 5th edition (1796) of Helen Maria Williams's *Letters Written in France*, ed. Janet M. Todd, (Delmar, New York: Scholars' Facsimiles & Reprints, 1975), pp. 123-94. Hereafter cited as Williams in the text. The relevance of this source was first pointed out by F. M. Todd (*Politics and the Poet: A Study of Wordsworth* [London: Methuen, 1958]). Kenneth R. Johnston has shown in his comparison of texts that Wordsworth made two significant changes from Williams's tale: Wordsworth's Vaudracour is ambiguously heroic in contrast with the romantically brave du Fosse, and Wordsworth's tale is tragic in conclusion, while Williams's tale ends joyfully after far more incredible miseries suffered by the du Fosses. (*Wordsworth and* The Recluse [New Haven: Yale University Press, 1984]), pp. 179-80.

38. Williams, *Letters Written in France*, pp. 129, 133.

39. Legouis, *William Wordsworth and Annette Vallon*, p. 132. The French reads: "Je vouderois bien pouvoir vous dire pour les arrêttez que je suis heureuse, mais je vous tromperois; vous ne pouriez le croire; mais au moin je peu vous assuré avec vérité que si il est possible que mon ami puisent venire me donner le titre glorieux de son épouse, malgret la cruelle nécessité qui l'obligera de quitter aussi tôt sa femme et son enfant, je suporterai plus aisément une absence pénible à la vérité, mais je serai à même de trouver dans sa fille un dedomagement qui m'est interdi jusqu'à cette époque." I would like to thank my colleague, Maurice Geracht, for assistance in translating several passages from the French.

40. There is no murder in Williams's tale of du Fosse, which causes one to believe that either Wordsworth is conflating several tales to create a factor that will complicate the possibility of marriage or he is venting aggression against the relations who thwarted his probable expressed intention to marry Annette.

41. Erdman, "Wordsworth as Heartsworth," p. 31.

42. See de Selincourt's edition of *The Prelude*, p. 359, app. crit. to ll. 817-18.

43. Taking on responsibility is an essential correlate to reducing guilt feelings. Cf. Carroll E. Izard, *Human Emotions* (New York: Plenum, 1977), p. 422.

44. The phrase comes from Johnston's article title, "The Triumphs of Failure: Wordsworth's *Lyrical Ballads* of 1798," in *The Age of William Wordsworth: Critical Essays on the Romantic Tradition*, eds. Kenneth R. Johnston and Gene W. Ruoff (New Brunswick, NJ: Rutgers University Press, 1987), pp. 133-59.

45. *WPW*, Vol. III, p. 4, note to ll. 9-14. The note Wordsworth dictated to Isabella Fenwick on the published version of the poem reads in part: "The sonnet was written some years after in recollection of that happy ramble, that most happy day and hour."

46. *Borderers*, Act IV, Scene ii, l. 78.

47. Moorman noted such advances (Moorman, Vol. I, pp. 247-48) and Paul D. Sheats emphasized their significance as "a distinct, prophetic, and largely unrecognized phase of [Wordsworth's] poetic apprenticeship," with particular focus on "their ardent naturalism" (*The Making of Wordsworth's Poetry, 1785-1798,* [Cambridge, MA: Harvard University Press, 1973], pp. 95-96).

48. Marjorie Levinson, *Wordsworth's Great Period Poems* (Cambridge: Cambridge University Press, 1986), p. 21.

49. As we considered earlier, Wordsworth believed that God caused his father's death for his moral instruction: "The event / . . . appeared / A chastisement; . . . / . . . I bowed low / To God, who thus corrected my desires" (*Prelude*, Book XIII, ll. 368-75). All quotations from *The Prelude*, unless otherwise noted, will be taken from the 1805 version.

50. Kenneth R. Johnston, "Philanthropy or Treason? Wordsworth as 'Active Partisan'", *Studies in Romanticism* 25 (Fall 1986), pp. 371-409.

51. *CEY* indicates that Wordsworth and Godwin met nine times between February and August 1795.

52. This is partly suggested by Paul D. Sheats, who says, "Godwin's more extreme suspicions of 'gratitude, conjugal fidelity, filial affection, and the belief of God'—to cite the grievance of Coleridge (*STCL*, Vol. I, p. 199) may have offered ways of rationalizing a break with Annette," however, he discounts "the philosopher's role [as] instrumental only": "if [Godwin] forged the knife of an analytical and dissecting reason, it was Wordsworth who took this knife 'in hand' for his own ends" (*The Making of Wordsworth's Poetry*, p. 107).

53. William Wordsworth, *An Essay on Morals* (1798), (*Prose*, Vol. I, pp. 103-04).

54. Godwin, *Enquiry Concerning Political Justice: And Its Influence on Modern Morals and Happiness* (Harmondsworth, England: Penguin, 1976), p. 762. Hereafter cited as *Enquiry* in the text.

55. One might think that Wordsworth would have to consider his relationship with his sister as irrational if judged by Godwinian standards, except that Wordsworth considered Dorothy a friend first and a sister second. In *Tintern Abbey* Dorothy is "my dearest Friend, / My dear, dear Friend" (ll. 115-16) before she is "My dear, dear Sister!" (l. 121).

56. Johnston, "Philanthropy or Treason," p. 399.

57. Nicholas Roe, *The Politics of Nature*, p. 115.

58. Jane soon married and eventually had eleven children.

59. Quoted and translated in Moorman, Vol. I, p. 181.

60. Emile Legouis, *The Early Life of William Wordsworth: 1770-1798* (New York: Dutton, 1918), pp. 266-67; Ernest de Selincourt, *Prelude*, p. 605; Reed, *CEY*, p. 174; Sheats, *The Making of Wordsworth's Poetry*, p. 105; George Wilbur Meyer, *Wordsworth's Formative Years* (Ann Arbor: University of Michigan Press, 1943), pp. 153-170. Mary Moorman (Moorman, Vol. I, p. 286) and George McLean Harper (*William Wordsworth*, p. 215) doubt that there was a severe crisis, though they agree that William was depressed at Racedown.

61. Herbert Read, *Wordsworth* (1930; rev. ed. London: Faber and Faber, 1949), Chapter Four, "The Deeper Malady," 77-97.

62. *Borderers*, Act III, Scene v, l. 43.

63. In his important review article of the Cornell editions, James K. Chandler argues for a view supportive of political radicalism in the Salisbury Plain poems, in other words, for a Godwinian view that finds deplorable social conditions causing the murder out of necessity: "Wordsworth stresses that the soldier's proper human impulses—for sexual fulfillment, for fair treatment, and for the material well-being of his family—are turned against themselves by a social system, and the murder is clearly portrayed as an eventual consequence of this perversion." In "Wordsworth Rejuvenated," *Modern Philology*, 84 (November 1986), p. 200.

64. Besides feeling like a homeless wanderer, living here and there with not always sympathetic relatives, Dorothy found at Windy Brow that she could enjoy the literal experience of wandering about with her brother. She wrote of their peripatetic experience to one of her former female repressors: "I cannot pass unnoticed that part of your letter in which you speak of my 'rambling about the country on foot.' So far from considering this as a matter of condemnation, I rather thought

it would have given my friends pleasure to hear that I had courage to make use of the strength with which nature has endowed me, when it not only procured me infinitely more pleasure than I should have received from sitting in a post-chaise—but was also the means of saving me at least thirty shillings." (*EY*, p. 117)

65. Alan Liu, *Wordsworth: The Sense of History* (Stanford: Stanford University Press, 1989), p. 226. Hereafter cited as Liu in the text.
66. *Borderers*, Act III, Scene v, l. 64.
67. *Borderers*, Act II, Scene i, ll. 51-54. The text of *The Borderers* that will be analyzed is the early version of 1797-99.
68. Oscar James Campbell and Paul Meuschke, "*The Borderers* as a Document in the History of Wordsworth's Aesthetic Development," *Modern Philology*, 23 (1926), p. 466.
69. R. F. Storch, "Wordsworth's *The Borderers*: The Poet as Anthropologist," *English Literary History*, 36 (June 1969), pp. 340-41, 360.
70. David V. Erdman, "Wordsworth as Heartsworth," p. 33.
71. Thomas McFarland, "The Play of Absence: *The Borderers* and the Winds of Culture" in *Wordsworth: Intensity and Achievement* (Oxford: Clarendon, 1992), p. 45.
72. David Perkins, *Is Literary History Possible?* (Baltimore: Johns Hopkins University Press, 1992), p. 146.
73. Michael H. Friedman, *The Making of a Tory Humanist: William Wordsworth and the Idea of Community* (New York: Columbia University Press, 1979), pp. 42-43. For "The Last of the Flock" see *LB*, p. 87, ll. 81-90.
74. See *The Borderers*, 1842 Text, Act I, Scene i, ll. 182-87.
75. Alan Liu is the only scholar to make something of the son's absence from the play, but he assumes the boy died in Antioch (Liu, p. 269).
76. William Shakespeare, *The Tragedy of Macbeth*, in *The Riverside Shakespeare*, 2nd. ed., gen. ed. G. Blakemore Evans (Boston: Houghton Mifflin, 1997), p. 1367, Act II, Scene ii, ll. 12-13. Hereafter cited as *Riverside Shakespeare*. Unless otherwise indicated, all quotes from Shakespeare's plays are from this edition.
77. Shakespeare's influence on Wordsworth's *Borderers* is well-documented. Echoes and character types from the great tragedies, *Hamlet*, *King Lear*, *Macbeth*, and *Othello*, are especially plentiful. See, for example, Jonathan Bate's discussion of Shakespeare and *The Borderers* in *Shakespeare and the English Romantic Imagination* (Oxford: Clarendon, 1989), pp. 91-93. The issue of a blind father not recognizing his son occurs in *King Lear*, when Edgar leads his father Gloucester to Dover where Gloucester wishes to commit suicide (See especially Act IV, Scene i,

Riverside Shakespeare, pp. 1329-30). However, a son's chiding his blind
father for failing to recognize him, with the sort of implied consequences I am suggesting in the text, derives rather from the comedy,
The Merchant of Venice. Shylock's servant Launcelot Gobbo says to his
father: "indeed if you had your eyes you might fail of knowing me; it
is a wise father that knows his own child. Well, old man, I will tell you
the news of your son. Give me your blessing; truth will come to light;
murder cannot be hid long; a man's son may, but in the end truth will
out" (*Merchant of Venice,* Act II, Scene ii, lines 75-80, *Riverside Shakespeare,*
p. 295).

78. Jonathan Wordsworth developed the concept of Wordsworth's bor-
der figures as those figures in his poetry who "approach, or seem to
approach, a border-line which is the entrance to another world." See
Jonathan Wordsworth, "Wordsworth's 'Borderers'" in *English Romantic
Poets: Modern Essays in Criticism,* 2nd ed, ed. M. H. Abrams (New York:
Norton, 1975), p. 171.

79. Wordsworth used travel literature of the Cumberland region of his
early youth and family life to represent the landscape of the play's
action: William Gilpin's *Observations . . . on Cumberland, and Westmoreland*
(1786); William Hutchinson's *An Excursion to the Lakes in Westmoreland and
Cumberland* (1776); Thomas West's *Guide of the Lakes in Cumberland, Westmoreland, and Lancashire* (1778); and James Clarke's *Survey of the Lakes of
Cumberland, Westmoreland, and Lancashire* (1787), as noted in Robert
Osborn's introduction to *The Borderers,* pp. 18-19. Wordsworth's phrase
for the powerful moments in his early life, his "spots of time," have
been lucidly described by Jonathan Wordsworth as passages "showing
the expected progression from an opening, detailed and quite ordinary
description, through the poet's heightened and heightening response,
to a new, odder, and more general vision. . . ." See "Wordsworth's
'Borderers'", p. 171.

80. Even the most cautious of Wordsworthians find it impossible to ignore
the poet's richly suggestive implications of a fatherly presence in the
landscape. Ernest de Selincourt calls attention to the allusion from
Hamlet, for example, in Wordsworth's peering into the mist for the
horses that were to carry him home the Christmas season of his father's
death. The mist, he says, "advanced in such indisputable shapes";
Hamlet's father returns in "a questionable shape." Cf. De Selincourt's
edition of *The Prelude,* p. 615, note to l. 382.

81. Friedman, *The Making of a Tory Humanist,* p. 126.

82. I am aware that I am using the play to reconstruct or "postdict" the

child's understanding that William Wordsworth would have ascribed to his father's breaking up of household; that is, that John Wordsworth was punishing the brother and sister for their love. I am not alleging anything more, but even this may seem to some to be too much to conclude without historically grounded evidence. The range of normal behavior in the relationship between children of different sexes provides many examples of what used to be called "naughtiness," such as genital exposure. So while no single behavior need be identified, any one will do to support the hypothesis that a child might interpret an unfortunate event as a punishment for inappropriate behavior. On the issue of "retrodiction" in psychobiography see "Reconstruction" in William McKinley Runyan's *Life Histories and Psychobiography: Explorations in Theory and Method* (New York: Oxford University Press, 1984), pp. 206-08.

83.   Mary Robinson, "To the Poet Coleridge" in *Poetical Works of the Late Mrs. Mary Robinson*, ed. Maria Robinson, 3 vols. (London: Richard Phillips, 1806), Vol. I, pp. 228-29, ll. 58-71.

84.   Robert Osborne's presentation and analysis of the manuscripts reveals that the scene in question was not included in the first form of the play found in the "Rough Notebook," Dove Cottage Manuscript 12, which relates to Wordsworth's claim to have a "first draught" completed in a letter of February 27, 1797. Nor does Act III, Scene ii, ll. 39-56 seem to belong to the next stage of composition, which Osborne identifies as "Drafts for the Deception," which includes 38 verso - 42 verso of "MS. 2: The Early Version." The passage in question is on 38 recto, and thus probably belongs to a later stage of composition.

85.   Essays of the special issue of *Studies in Romanticism*, 27 (Fall 1988), *"The Borderers: A Forum,"* find the biographical perspective so common that they avoid it entirely. Not a single essay out of six mentions biography, except to complain of its faults and overuse (see esp. William Jewett, "Action in *The Borderers*," p. 399).

86.   In a clever, deconstructive turn on this argument, Reeve Parker suggests that Rivers may have been the creator of "Wordsworth": "If we think of the figure of Rivers who emerges in the play and in the psychobiographical prefatory essay as the result of a heuristic ventriloquism that leads Wordsworth on to imagine the Pedlar in the various stages of the *Ruined Cottage* complex, we can then think of Rivers' tales about himself and others as fathering not only 'Mortimer' but the Wordsworth who grew out of the Pedlar. . . ." "'Oh Could You Hear His Voice': Wordsworth, Coleridge, and Ventriloquism," in *Romanti-*

cism and Language, ed. Arden Reed (Ithaca: Cornell University Press, 1984), p. 131.

87. In opposition to this biographical perspective, Robert Osborne believes that the character Falkland from Godwin's *Caleb Williams* is the appropriate source for Rivers (*The Borderers,* p. 62, n. 1).

88. W. J. B. Owen, ed. *Wordsworth and Coleridge:* Lyrical Ballads *1798,* 2d ed. (New York: Oxford University Press, 1969), pp. 148-49, note to p. 109. "The Convict" also was published as the penultimate poem of *Lyrical Ballads* (1798).

89. "*The Borderers* and the Drama of Recognition," chapter 2 in Alan Richardson, *A Mental Theater: Poetic Drama and Consciousness in the Romantic Age* (University Park: Pennsylvania State University Press, 1988), pp. 20-42.

90. Dudley Young has a fascinating updating of Freud's text in *Origins of the Sacred: The Ecstasies of Love and War* (New York: St. Martin's Press, 1991), pp. 93-123.

91. *Totem and Taboo* and *Other Works* in *The Standard Edition of the Complete Psychological Works of Sigmund Freud,* trans. and ed. by James Strachey, Vol. XIII (London: Hogarth Press, 1953), pp. 143-44.

92. It is surprising how many astute readers ignore the improbability of the starvation and thus miss the significance of the act's insignificance. Thus, Geoffrey H. Hartman· Mortimer "unintentionally causes his [Herbert's] death by forgetting to leave him his scrip of food" (*Wordsworth's Poetry: 1787-1814,* [1964; New Haven, Yale University Press, 1971], p. 127) and more recently Alan Richardson: "For Oswald, who in his own promising youth abandoned his ship's captain to starve on a barren island, will lead Marmaduke to abandon an old man to starve on a barren heath" (*A Mental Theater,* p. 22).

93. See for example, Jonathan Bate, *Shakespeare and the Romantic Imagination,* p. 91.

94. Hartman, *Wordsworth's Poetry,* p. 129.

95. See John Milton, *Paradise Lost,* Book II, ll. 871ff, in *John Milton: Complete Poems and Major Prose,* ed. Merritt Y. Hughes (New York: Odyssey Press, 1957), pp. 252-53. All future references to *Paradise Lost* will be taken from this edition.

96. "Dramatic Essay No. IV" from *London Magazine,* April 1820, in *The Complete Works of William Hazlitt,* ed. P. P. Howe, (London: J. M. Dent and Sons, 1933), Vol. 18, p. 305.

Part Two

1. *Donne: Poetical Works*, p. 48, l. 74. The version of "The Exstasie" that Wordsworth would have used is in Robert Anderson, ed. *The Works of the British Poets. With Prefaces, Biographical and Critical* (13 vols., London, 1792-95), Vol. 4, pp. 34-35. This text was unavailable; however, I would like to thank Duncan Wu for providing me with the bibliographical information.

2. Paul Magnuson argues for the intertextuality of *Ruined Cottage* with *Christabel* in *Coleridge and Wordsworth: A Lyrical Dialogue* (Princeton, NJ: Princeton University Press, 1988), pp. 96-138. While I will acknowledge that there is no way to decide definitively on the texts of intertextual interplay—thus making the inference one of persuasiveness and judgement—nevertheless, a shared line between *Ruined Cottage* and *Ancient Mariner* that refers to the auditors of both poems becoming sadder but wiser is strongly suggestive of two poets actively and mutually considering how to achieve transformation of their auditors through these parallel narratives. The shared line will be discussed below.

3. *CPW*, pp. 173-75.

4. W. J. B. Owen, "The Poetry of Nature," *The Wordsworth Circle*, 18 (Winter 1987), p. 3.

5. Cf. *Paradise Lost*, Book VIII, ll. 398 ff.

6. Paul D. Sheats, *The Making of Wordsworth's Poetry, 1785-93* (Cambridge, MA: Harvard University Press, 1973), p. 165.

7. Brett and Jones, 40-44.

8. Paul Magnuson, *Coleridge and Wordsworth: A Lyrical Dialogue*, pp. 4-32 *passim*.

9. Norman Fruman, *Coleridge: The Damaged Archangel* (New York: George Braziller, 1971): Chapter 21, "Miracles and Rare Devices," passim.

10. George Whalley associates the Mariner with Coleridge and the Albatross with his imagination, which was thoughtlessly destroyed by opium addiction. ("The Mariner and the Albatross" in *Coleridge: A Collection of Critical Essays*, ed. Kathleen Coburn [Englewood Cliffs: Prentice-Hall, 1967], pp. 32-50. Rpt. from *University of Toronto Quarterly*, XVI (1946-47). Robert Penn Warren's classic essay "A Poem of Pure Imagination: An Experiment in Reading" first identified the Albatross with the secondary, or creative, imagination. *Selected Essays* (1946; New York: Random House, 1958), pp. 198-305.

11. *BL*, Vol. I, pp. 27-29.

12. Cf. the note to "Sonnets Attempted in the Manner of Contemporary Writers" in *CPW*, p. 209.

13. Charles Lloyd, *Edmund Oliver*, 2 vols, (Bristol: Bulgin and Rosser, 1798), Vol. II, pp. 92-93.

14. For evidence of William Wordsworth's nickname being Edmund see the first published version of Coleridge's *Dejection: An Ode*, where he addresses Wordsworth repeatedly as Edmund, as in the lines: "O EDMUND! in this wan and heartless mood . . . " (*Dejection. An Ode*, in *Coleridge's* Dejection: The Earliest Manuscripts, ed. Stephen Maxfield Parrish [Ithaca, NY: Cornell University Press, 1988], pp. 50-63, ll. 25, 48, 67, 76, 114, 129).

15. *A Tale of a Tub To Which is Added The Battle of the Books and the Mechanical Operation of the Spirit by Jonathan Swift*, eds. A. C. Guthkelch and D. Nichol Smith. 2d ed. (Oxford: Clarendon, 1958), p. 215.

16. Robert Penn Warren reminds us in quoting from Poe's "The Black Cat" that "the spirit of Perverseness" is always to be suspected, although it is not Coleridge's motivation. Warren argues that Poe's perversity is the equivalent of Coleridge's Original Sin. See "A Poem of Pure Imagination," pp. 230-31.

17. To take an obvious, though wonderful, example from "Lord Randall," which uses the "wild wood" as a metonymy for the dangers of love: "I hae been to the wild wood; mother, make my bed soon, / For I'm weary wi' hunting, and fain wald lie down."

18. Keats wrote in his letter of December 27 (?), 1817: "Coleridge [was] . . . incapable of remaining content with half knowledge." (*The Letters of John Keats, 1814-1821*, Vol I, ed. Hyder Edward Rollins [Cambridge, MA: Harvard University Press, 1958], p. 194)

19. The version of *Ancyent Marinere* used here is from *Lyrical Ballads* (1798) in Brett and Jones, pp. 9-35. It will be cited in the text as *AM*.

20. Stanley Cavell also concludes that the Mariner kills the Albatross not in defiance of the bird's love, but in order to deny the claim of love upon him. ("In Quest of the Ordinary: Texts of Recovery," in *Romanticism and Contemporary Criticism*, eds. Morris Eaves and Michael Fischer [Ithaca: Cornell University Press, 1986], pp. 193ff.)

21. In *The Critical Review* Southey referred to it "as a Dutch attempt at German sublimity"; a reviewer for *The Atlantic Review* described it as having "more of the extravagance of a mad German poet, than of the simplicity of our ancient ballad writers"; Dr. Burney referred to it as "the strangest story of a cock and a bull that we ever saw on paper," as well as a "rhapsody of unintelligible wildness and incoherence" in *The*

Monthly Review. Even Coleridge's friend Francis Wrangham said of *Ancyent Marinere* in *British Critic* that "the beginning and the end are striking and well-conducted; but the intermediate part is too long, and has, in some places, a kind of confusion of images, which loses all effect, from not being quite intelligible." See Appendix C, "Some Contemporary Criticisms of *Lyrical Ballads*" in Brett and Jones, pp. 276-77; 319-24.

22. See Brett and Jones, pp. 276-77, for the complete text of Wordsworth's note to *Ancient Mariner* in *Lyrical Ballads* (1800).

23. In the analysis that follows, Manuscript B of *Ruined Cottage* will be used because it is the version of the poem developed contemporaneously with *Ancyent Marinere*, mainly between January-March 1798. Nevertheless, although composed prior to the end of March 1798, several of the passages that will be quoted in the textual analysis are printed in *RC* as a part of Manuscript D, composed between February-December 1799. I will indicate in the notes where the evidence in *RC* can be found for the dating of such passages, but to simplify the reading of the analysis I will cite pages from *RC* rather than identifying Reader Versions of manuscripts or specific photo-facsimile transcriptions. The scholarly reader familiar with the Cornell Wordsworth project will understand the diverse nature and value of the evidence and the often difficult scholarly arguments for the dating of passages; the scholarly reader or general reader unfamiliar with the Cornell project will more likely become confused and weary with such matters.

24. Scholarly consideration of the epistemological issue of projection and perception in the work of Coleridge and Wordsworth remains at an impasse. David Simpson, for example, finds Wordsworth threatened by the literal; Paul Magnuson develops an intertextual canon generated by Wordsworth's ambition to read nature literally. Simpson argues in *Wordsworth and the Figurings of the Real* (Atlantic Highlands, NJ: Humanities Press, 1982) "that the emphasis on the predetermined nature of our seeing, which thus operates in terms of unconsciously chosen or imposed figures, was an urgent concern for Wordsworth" (p. xii), but that Wordsworth believed literal seeing to be misguided for "'suppos[ing] all the higher qualities of the mind to be passive, and in a state of subjection to external objects'" (pp. 22-23; the internal quote is from Wordsworth, *Prose,* Vol. III, p. 26). Simpson continues that rather than uncovering or perceiving the thing-in-itself, Wordsworth sees that "there is no privileged figuring of the real, which becomes an objective standard of normalcy; there is only a series of

figurings, wherein a whole set of positions will be taken up from time to time, rising to vanish like clouds in the sky, and living on in the modified figures of the imaginative memory" (p. 66). The pursuit of common meaning then is not to be fulfilled in sharing the same figurings, but by holding in common the cycle of active and passive relations with environment (p. 67). In *Coleridge and Wordsworth: A Lyrical Dialogue*, Magnuson discusses the vicissitudes of figuration as Wordsworth's central dilemma in defining himself as a natural poet. He identifies figuration as the chief issue of an evolving intertextual debate in Coleridge's conversation poems, which Wordsworth purposefully misreads:

> Wordsworth avoids the troubling aspects of Coleridge's poems by reading them as though they were a set of isolated fragments and by reading them with the same inattention to their figurative language as he tried to read nature itself. . . . One result of this borrowing is that the incorporation of Coleridge's within Wordsworth's poetry, has, ironically, placed a Wordsworthian stamp on Coleridge's poems that succeeding generations have continued to read with Wordsworth's interpretive stamp. (p. 142)

Magnuson refuses to acknowledge the importance of mood in Coleridge's thought and thus simplifies the psychological issue while making his formalist argument of intertextual exchange more complex than necessary. The position that will evolve here brings emotion back to the epistemological equation as a preeminent perceptual force. Coleridge argues that we can find and thus know only what we have projected of ourselves into the object, while Wordsworth takes the lighter side in exploring and mimetically representing altered states of consciousness that permit a union and an experience of unity with the world of nature outside the self. *Ruined Cottage* and *Ancyent Marinere* provide the first dialogue on an issue that divided the poets at least until Wordsworth composes "Elegiac Stanzas" (1805).

25. These lines are included in Manuscript D, although they were an addition to Manuscript B composed by March 1798. See *RC*, p. 277, for a photocopy of the manuscript evidence.

26. Although not included in Manuscript B, the note to the photoreproduction of the manuscript in *RC*, p. 241, indicates that the passage quoted here was composed before March 5, 1798.

27. Jonathan Barron and Kenneth R. Johnston, "'A Power to Virtue Friendly': The Pedlar's Guilt in Wordsworth's 'Ruined Cottage'" in *Romantic Revisions*, eds. Robert Brinkley and Keith Hanley (Cambridge: Cambridge University Press, 1992), pp. 74-75.

28. See the draft transcriptions of Manuscript B on pp. 203 [21v] and 277 [53r] and the editor's explanation on p. 131 for evidence that this passage was composed by March 1798.

29. See *RC*, p. 241, for the photocopy and transcription of the draft passage as well as the editor's note on its being completed by March 1798.

30. See the transcription of Manuscript B2 draft and note, *RC* p. 241, which indicates this passage was also composed before March 6, 1798.

31. This passage was also completed by March 1798. See *RC*, pp. 131, 257.

32. See *RC*, p. 277, for evidence of this passage belonging to the January-March 1798 time frame.

33. See also *RC*, p. 195, ll. 16-25, for the transcription of the original manuscript.

34. In "'The Meaning of 'The Ancient Mariner,'" Jerome J. McGann identifies such a reading as revealing an Enlightenment mentality, which sees "(a) that all phenomena are mind mediated and (b) that these mediations are culturally and historically determined." Agreed. In *Critical Inquiry*, 8 (1981), p. 59.

35. The 1817 text can be found in *Coleridge's* Ancient Mariner: *An Experimental Edition of Texts and Revisions, 1798-1828*, ed. and commentary by Martin Wallen (Barrytown, NY: Station Hill Literary Editions, 1993), pp. 5-92.

36. Wallen, p. 28.

37. See Wallen, 1817 text, p. 27, gloss to ll. 158-62; p. 29, gloss to ll. 177-80.

38. Interestingly, *De Denorum Rebus Gestis Seculis III et IV*, or the *Beowulf* manuscript, was discovered among the Cottonian Manuscripts in the British Library, transcribed in 1787, and first published in 1815. But of course the Medieval revival had been ongoing since the 1770s; in 1790, the editors Joseph Ritson published *Ancient Songs* and George Ellis published *Specimens of the Early English Poets*; and in 1794, Thomas Percy's *Reliques of Ancient English Poetry* came out in a 4th edition.

39. See Frederic Klaeber, "The Christian Coloring," from *Beowulf*, 3rd ed. (Lexington, MA.: D.C. Heath, 1950), pp. xlviii-li. Rpt. in *Beowulf: The Donaldson Translation, Backgrounds and Sources, Criticism*, ed. Joseph F. Tuso (New York: Norton, 1975), pp. 102-05.

40. Hayden, Vol. I, p. 269.
41. See Kenneth R. Johnston, "The Idiom of Vision" in *New Perspectives on Wordsworth and Coleridge*, ed. Geoffrey H. Hartman (New York: Columbia University Press, 1972), pp. 1-39; Michael C. Jaye, "William Wordsworth's Alfoxden Notebook: 1798," in *The Evidence of Imagination: Studies of Interactions Between Life and Art in English Romantic Literature*, eds. Donald H. Reiman, Michael C. Jaye, and Betty T. Bennett (New York: New York University Press, 1978), pp. 42-85.
42. This is the early text of the poem from Beth Darlington, "Two Early Texts: A Night-piece and The Discharged Soldier," in *Bicentenary Wordsworth Studies*, ed. Jonathan Wordsworth (Ithaca: Cornell University Press, 1970), p. 431. The 1815 text, or the first published text of the poem, is found in *WPW*, Vol. II, pp. 208-09.
43. Jonathan Wordsworth, *The Music of Humanity: A Critical Study of Wordsworth's* Ruined Cottage (New York: Harper & Row, 1969), pp. 184-201.
44. Also see the photocopy and transcription of the manuscript passage in *RC*, pp. 120-23.
45. H. W. Piper, *The Active Universe: Pantheism and the Concept of Imagination in the English Romantic Poets* (London: Athlone, 1962), p. 79.
46. Wordsworth was proudest of just that endeavor when looking over his life's work in 1845. Stephen Maxfield Parrish, *The Art of the Lyrical Ballads* (Cambridge, MA: Harvard University Press, 1973), pp. 45-46.
47. Thomas McFarland, *Coleridge and the Pantheist Tradition* (Oxford: Clarendon, 1969), Chapter 3, "Coleridge and the Dilemmas of Pantheism," pp. 107-90.
48. *WPW*, Vol. V, App. A, pp. 343-44, no. vi.
49. Molly Lefebure reaches the same conclusion following a different line of argument. Interpreting Dorothy's uncharacteristic meanness towards Sara Coleridge, Lefebure writes: "It is difficult to escape the conclusion that, in Dorothy Wordsworth, we have a young woman who has fallen in love with a married man and is voicing her jealousy of that man's wife: a jealousy made keener for Dorothy because, although she was able to provide S.T.C. with a certain kind of company and stimulation not in Sara's capacity, Coleridge was still in love with his wife and drew 'transcendental joy' from his conjugal and domestic bliss.'" (*The Bondage of Love: A life of Mrs. Samuel Taylor Coleridge* [New York: Norton, 1987], p. 94.)
50. John Lempriere, *A Classical Dictionary Containing a Copious Account of All the Proper Names Mentioned in Ancient Authors with the Value of Coins, Weights,*

and Measures Used Among the Greeks and Romans and A Chronological Table (1788; New York: E. P. Dutton, undated reprint), p. 201, entry on "Diana." Hereafter cited as Lempriere.

51. In her edition of the journals, Mary Moorman fails to print Mr, as other editions had done, calling it a clear "misreading" by G. W. Knight, the only editor to have derived a text directly from the manuscript of the Alfoxden Notebook. Moorman's reasoning is simple: Coleridge was out of town, so how could Dorothy mean she had stayed with him? (Cf. n. 2 to the entry of April 13, 1798, *DWJ*, p. 13). I would think, however, that because Dorothy *never* referred to Coleridge as Mr., Knight's special attention would have been drawn to the uniqueness of this entry and, thus, he would not have erred in reading so simple an abbreviation used not once but twice in Dorothy's relatively good hand.

52. Anne K. Mellor, *Romanticism and Gender* (New York: Routledge, 1993), p. 157. See also the entire brilliant chapter on William and Dorothy Wordsworth, "Writing the Self/Self Writing: William Wordsworth's *Prelude*/Dorothy Wordsworth's *Journals*," pp. 144-69.

53. See Nicholas Roe, *Wordsworth and Coleridge: The Radical Years* (Oxford: Clarendon, 1988), pp. 234-62, for a lucid historical analysis of the rampant paranoia over French invasion in the Bristol area.

54. Brett and Jones, pp. 58-60.

55. James H. Averill, *Wordsworth and the Poetry of Human Suffering* (Ithaca: Cornell University Press, 1980), pp. 153-58. Kenneth R. Johnston makes only passing mention of Darwin's influence in his important study *Wordsworth and* The Recluse, p. 20.

56. Erasmus Darwin, *Zoonomia; or the Laws of Organic Life*, Vol. I (London: J. Johnson, 1794), p. 1. Hereafter cited in the text as *Zoonomia*.

57. This fine phrase is Carl Woodring's from *Wordsworth* (Cambridge, MA: Harvard University Press, 1968), p. 39.

58. Kathleen Coburn writes: "For Darwin [Coleridge] developed considerable dislike, probably not for his poetry or his ideas, though he never thought highly of either, but because of Darwin's contempt for philosophy and his irresponsible proposal to demolish without reading them all his predecessors . . . and his arrogance as 'an Atheist by intuition' towards Christianity" (*STCNB*, Vol. II, note to entry 188). Nevertheless, Darwin's many references to divinity in *Zoonomia* make it difficult to understand Coleridge's charge that Darwin was "an Atheist by intuition," unless this sort of intellectual arrogance came out only in Darwin's conversation.

59. Wordsworth's "spots of time" share this philosophical-rhetorical pattern, but are, as I here argue, inspired by Darwin. See Herbert Lindenberger, *On Wordsworth's* Prelude (Princeton, NJ: Princeton University Press, 1963), pp. 143-47, for what is still the best rhetorical analysis of this important Wordsworthian innovation.

60. *William Wordsworth: Selected Prose*, ed. John O. Hayden (New York: Penguin, 1988), p. 105.

61. "My First Acquaintance with Poets," in *The Complete Works of William Hazlitt*, ed. P. P. Howe, (London: J. M. Dent and Sons, 1933), Vol. 17, p. 117.

62. One recalls Wordsworth's Darwinian insight from "The Tables Turned" on the necessity of good physical and emotional health for poetry: "Spontaneous wisdom breathed by health, / Truth breathed by chearfulness" (ll. 19-20).

63. Harold Bloom's reading of *Tintern Abbey* has been the most influential in emphasizing the nervous poet: the "urgency in the tone . . . which deepens almost to a desperation," the "waning faith, or faith affirmed more vehemently even as it ebbs," constitute the Wordsworth of Bloom (*The Visionary Company: A Reading of English Romantic Poetry* [1961; Ithaca, NY: Cornell University Press, 1971], pp. 138-39). See also Paul Sheats, who argues that Wordsworth is becoming tentative in his relationship with nature, because, in Wordsworth's words, "'Death the skeleton and time the shadow'" are breathing down his back (*The Making of Wordsworth's Poetry*, p. 244) and Richard J. Onorato, who argues that Wordsworth's relationship with nature is strained because, as surrogate mother, she may betray the poet as he unconsciously feels his mother had done at her death (*The Character of the Poet: Wordsworth in* The Prelude [Princeton, NJ: Princeton University Press, 1971], pp. 51-64).

64. Thomas McFarland, "Wordsworth's Best Philosopher," in *The Wordsworth Circle* 13 (Spring 1982), p. 62.

65. Marjorie Levinson, *Wordsworth's Great Period Poems: Four Essays* (Cambridge: Cambridge University Press, 1986), pp. 15-16, 39. Although Levinson has been given the credit for the details of her argument so that she might receive the discredit her New Historical argument attracts, the substance of her argument and the details were established by Kenneth R. Johnston's very sane essay, "The Politics of Tintern Abbey,'" in *The Wordsworth Circle* 14 (Winter 1983), pp. 6-14.

66. From Nicholas Roe in *The Politics of Nature*; from M. H. Abrams in "On

Political Readings of 'Tintern Abbey,' in *Romantic Revolutions*, ed. Kenneth R. Johnston et al. (Bloomington, IN: Indiana University Press), and especially from Thomas McFarland in *William Wordsworth: Intensity and Achievement* (Oxford: Clarendon, 1992).

67. This felicitous term was suggested by the editors of *Romantic Poetry: Recent Revisionary Criticism*, eds. Karl Kroeber and Gene W. Ruoff (New Brunswick: Rutgers University Press, 1993), p. 123.
68. McFarland, *William Wordsworth: Intensity and Achievement*, p. 29.
69. See Kenneth R. Johnston's essay of volume criticism that discusses the antiphony between the natural and moral worlds that the placement of the poems in the volume represents. In "The Triumphs of Failure: Wordsworth's *Lyrical Ballads* of 1798," in *The Age of William Wordsworth: Critical Essays on the Romantic Tradition*, pp. 133-59. Johnston says that the "Lines" or nature poems, are "placed at roughly equal intervals throughout the volume, every three to five poems, thus forming a pattern of hopeful, optimistic belief in the natural beneficence of this world, counterpointing the intervening tales of unrelieved human suffering" (p. 148).
70. Don H. Bialostosky, *Wordsworth, Dialogics, and the Practice of Criticism* (Cambridge: Cambridge University Press, 1992), pp. 76-77.
71. Alexander Pope, *An Essay on Man*, Epistle I, ll. 217-18. *The Poems of Alexander Pope*, ed. John Butt (New Haven: Yale University Press, 1966), p. 512.
72. See Appendix for the 1795 text of Coleridge's poem.
73. These are the Ciceronian divisions of an oration, popularized by Hugh Blair, whose *Lectures on Rhetoric and Belles Lettres* went through 130 editions in the eighteenth and nineteenth centuries.
74. See my "Classical Argument and Romantic Persuasion in 'Tintern Abbey,'" *Studies in Romanticism* 25 (Spring 1986), pp. 97-129, for a fuller exposition of Coleridge's use of the form in his conversation poems. Also see Don H. Bialostosky's description of its wider influence on Wordsworth's early autobiographical experiments in *The Prelude*, "The Invention/Disposition of *The Prelude*, Book I," in *Rhetorical Traditions and British Romantic Literature*, eds. Don H. Bialostosky and Lawrence D. Needham (Bloomington, IN: Indiana University Press, 1995), pp. 139-48.
75. This quote is from Moorman, Vol. I, p. 402, n. 1.
76. Johnston, "The Politics of 'Tintern Abbey,'" p. 127.
77. Quoted from *British Literature: 1780-1830*, eds. Anne K. Mellor and Richard E. Matlak (Fort Worth, TX: Harcourt Brace, 1996), p. 140.

78. From Prefatory Memoir to *Poems Chiefly Written in Retirement* (1801);
     (Oxford: Woodstock Books, 1989), p. xxxvi.

79. See Duncan Wu, *Wordsworth's Reading: 1770-1799* (Cambridge: Cam-
     bridge University Press, 1993), p. 4, note 7, which informs us that
     Wordsworth would have had access to Coleridge's thirteen- volume
     set of Robert Anderson's *The Works of the British Poets* from July 1797,
     on. Coleridge acquired his set in April 1796. In 1798, Wu says,
     Wordsworth copied lines from Donne's sonnet, "Death be not
     proud," in the Notebook containing *Ruined Cottage* (*Wordsworth's
     Reading*, p. 48, note 80).

80. *Donne: Poetical Works*, pp. 46-48.

81. Johnston, "The Politics of 'Tintern Abbey,'" (p. 133) and Mark Jones,
     "Spiritual Capitalism: Wordsworth and Usury," *Journal of English and
     Germanic Philology* 92 (January 1993), p. 54.

82. *The Poems of John Keats*, ed. Jack Stillinger (Cambridge, MA: Harvard
     University Press), pp. 369-370.

83. The father of William (1771-1829) and Raisley (1773-1795) Calvert
     had been the steward to the Duke of Norfolk. He died in 1791, leaving
     his eldest son the estate of Bowness on the east shore of Bassenthwaite,
     near Keswick, as well as other properties. William Calvert was a
     schoolmate of William Wordsworth's at Hawkshead.

84. Carl Woodring, "The New Sublimity in 'Tintern Abbey.'" In *The
     Evidence of Imagination*, 86-100, reprinted in *Critical Essays on William
     Wordsworth*, ed. George H. Gilpin (Boston: G. K. Hall, 1990), pp.
     11-23.

85. This echoes Lionel Trilling's argument in "The Intimations Ode," rpt.
     English Romantic Poets: Modern Essays in Criticism, ed. M. H. Abrams, 2d
     ed. (New York: Cornell University Press, 1975), p. 151.

86. See Richard Onorato's reading of the intensive *did* as Wordsworth's
     attempt to deny what he most feared, that his mother abandoned him
     intentionally through her death. *The Character of the Poet*: "'Never did
     betray' seems to be recalling a past betrayal, rigidly denied, that
     resembles the present sense of betrayal because of an unconsciously
     held resemblance between the mother and Nature. . . . [T]here is no
     clearer model of betrayal than the mother who leaves her children
     orphaned early in life" (p. 38).

87. Appendix One, "The Collected Poems of Dorothy Wordsworth," in
     Susan M. Levin, *Dorothy Wordsworth and Romanticism* (New Brunswick,
     NJ: Rutgers University Press, 1987), pp. 219-20, ll. 33-52.

Part Three

1. Mark Jones, *The 'Lucy Poems': A Case Study in Literary Knowledge* (Toronto: University of Toronto Press, 1995), p. 215.
2. Thus Brian Caraher: "It is curious that Matlack [sic] offers no readings of the so-called 'Lucy' poems until he has fully stated the context in which they are to be read. The evidence for this psychobiographical context comes solely from sources and authorities other than the poems and the experience of reading them. . . . This privileging of one set of texts (letters) and evidence (psychobiographical deductions) over another set (the poems) and the evidence that they might have to offer (the particularities of the activity of reading) betrays an 'important assumption' about Matlack's [sic] critical procedure: The activity of reading a poem cannot itself begin to specify the context in which the poem can be understood, its particularities drawn out and accounted for" (*Wordsworth's Slumber and the Problematics of Reading*, [University Park, PA: Pennsylvania State University Press, 1991], p. 71). And Mark Jones: "The search for Lucy's bones is an illuminating, because both extreme and graphic version of the 'referential fallacy,' and it was, with the rise of formalist analysis, castigated as such. As befits a 'fallacy,' one is inclined to regard it simply as a critical naivete, and to locate its essential failure not in the inability to prove a specific objective referent, but in the more basic failure to consider what *that* could prove. . . . " (*The 'Lucy Poems'*, p. 81). My comment that these are not disabling criticisms of the psychobiographical approach is based upon, first, Caraher's confusion of critical reading with the rhetoric of exposition. Obviously, I didn't first forge a container with substance from the Wordsworth-Coleridge letters and Freud's *Collected Works* in which to pour the poems without having attended carefully to their complexities, although the exposition of the argument in my "Wordsworth's Lucy Poems in Psychobiographical Context" (*PMLA* 93 [January 1978], pp. 46-65) presents the case as context followed by readings. Nevertheless, if the psychobiographical approach is fundamentally flawed, one would hope to see its readings convincingly critiqued. Caraher's criticisms, however, are theoretical, rather than practical. On the other hand, Jones leaves the matter of an approach's usefulness open: "though assumptions of the identification-readings have been in disgrace in recent years, I think it would be mistaken to dismiss them altogether" (p. 81).
3. Coleridge's letter of March 12, 1795, to the Rev. John Edwards

mentions the last of Coleridge's fears: "Since I last wrote you, I have been tottering on the edge of madness. . . . Mrs Coleridge dangerously ill, and expected hourly to miscarry" (*STCL*, Vol. I, p. 188). A week later he wrote to the same correspondent that "Yesterday Mrs Coleridge miscarried—but without danger and with little pain" (*STCL*, Vol. I, p. 192). Hartley Coleridge was born on September 19, 1796.

4. This is the line of argumentation taken by the deconstructive reading of Susan Eilenberg in *Strange Power of Speech: Wordsworth, Coleridge, and Literary Possession* (New York: Oxford University Press, 1992), pp. 108-35.

5. This is not the place for a discussion of when Coleridge developed his specific ideas (borrowed from the German) on fancy and imagination. I mean the more general sense of the terms' connotations, as described by William K. Wimsatt, Jr. and Cleanth Brooks in their *Literary Criticism: A Short History* (New York: Random House, 1957): "The relative dignity of the two *terms* 'imagination' and 'fancy' was so well established in English usage by the end of the 18th century that no matter what revised *meanings* Wordsworth and Coleridge and others might assign to them, it was almost inevitable that the superior *term* should be imagination" (p. 386).

6. I borrow the phrase "aesthetic emotion" from Paul Magnuson's fine essay "Wordsworth and Spontaneity" in *The Evidence of Imagination: Studies of Interactions Between Life and Art in English Romantic Literature*, eds. Donald H. Reiman, Michael C. Jaye, and Betty T. Bennett (New York: New York University Press, 1978), pp. 101-18.

7. From the final line of Coleridge's poem, "Hexameters," the relevant version of which is dated December 1798 in *STCL*, Vol. I, pp. 451-52.

8. "Journal of A Visit to Hamburgh and of A Journey from Hamburgh to Goslar (1798)" in *Journals of Dorothy Wordsworth* Vol. I, ed. E. de Selincourt (New York: Macmillan, 1941), p. 19.

9. See my *"Licentia Biographia: or, Biographical Sketches of Coleridge's Literary Life and Plagiarisms,"* *European Romantic Review* 4 (Summer 1993), pp. 57-70.

10. From the Lucy poem eventually revised and entitled "Strange Fits of Passion," but, in the context of Part Three, better derived from the letter to Coleridge dated December 14 or 21, 1798 (*EY*, pp. 238, l. 24). See also *LB*, pp. 293-94, l. 24.

11. The remainder of the works composed in Germany are "Ellen Irwin, or the Braes of Kirtle," "Lucy Gray," "To A Sexton," "Song for the Wandering Jew," "Ruth," "Three Years She Grew in Sun and Shower,"

"Between Two Sister Moorland Rills" ("The Danish Boy"), a series of Matthew elegies ("Could I the priest's consent have gained," "Just as the blowing thorn began," "Carved, Mathew, with a master's skill," "I bring, ye little noisy crew"), various introductions to "Nutting," "Travelling," "There is a law severe of penury," "There is an active principle in all things," "For let the impediment be what it may," "There are who tell us that in recent times," "When in my bed I lay," and finally more passages associated with the 1799 *Prelude* Part I. The editors of the Cornell *Lyrical Ballads* also indicate that "The Two April Mornings" and "The Fountain" were probably composed by December 28, 1798, but for reasons that will be discussed later, I will argue for an April 1799 compositional period.

12. The phrase is Percy Shelley's from *Hymn to Intellectual Beauty*, l. 45. In *Shelley's Poetry and Prose: Authoritative Texts and Criticism*, eds. Donald H. Reiman and Sharon B. Powers (New York: Norton, 1977), p. 94.

13. The phrase is from John Milton's *Paradise Lost*, Book IX, l. 734 p. 395 and comments on the success of Satan's temptation of Eve: "He ended, and his words replete with guile / Into her heart too easy entrance won" (ll. 733-34). The temptation was successfully prepared for by Eve's dream of her fall in Book V, ll. 28-94, which suggests that the dreams of imaginative narratives lead to results, as the Lucy poems likewise show.

14. Our commonly available and contemporary classical dictionaries leave out several of the important points Lempriere offers. For example, there is no mention of Diana as Lucina, or her fearful celibacy, or her anxieties over childbearing in the Diana entries of either Brewer's *Dictionary of Phrase and Fable* (1870), the *Oxford Classical Dictionary* (1970), or the *Oxford Guide to Classical Mythology in the Arts* (1993).

15. Mary Wollstonecraft, of course, would have approved: "I will go further, and affirm, as an indisputable fact, that most of the women, in the circle of my observation, who have acted like rational creatures, or shewn any vigour of intellect, have accidentally been allowed to run wild—as some of the elegant formers [Rousseau, Milton, etc.] of the fair sex would insinuate." (*A Vindication of the Rights of Woman*, ed. Carol H. Poston [New York: Norton, 1975], p. 43)

16. William McKinley Runyan, *Life Histories and Psychobiography: Explorations in Theory and Method* (New York: Oxford University Press, 1984), p. 42, but see as well the whole chapter, "Why Did Van Gogh Cut Off His Ear? The Problem of Alternative Explanations in Psychobiography," pp. 38-50.

17. *Shelley's Poetry and Prose,* p, 114, l. 33.

18. Tolstoy, *Anna Karenina,* trans. Rosemary Edmonds (Harmondsworth, England: Penguin, 1954), p. 508.

19. *Collected Psychological Works of Sigmund Freud,* Vol. XVI, p. 417.

20. *LB,* p. 162, n. to line 11.

21. William H. Galperin suggests that the reader may also be left behind "as another version of the 'horse,' whose path habitually leads to Lucy," but who learns in short order that s/he is to be left out of the narrator's singularly personal lamentation. In *Revision and Authority in Wordsworth: The Interpretation of a Career* (Philadelphia: University of Pennsylvania Press, 1989), p. 98.

22. Cf. "Dreams of the Death of Persons of Whom the Dreamer is Fond," *Collected Psychological Works of Sigmund Freud,* Vol. IV, pp. 248-71, esp. 250-55, where Freud considers dreams of the death of brothers and sisters.

23. Wordsworth purchased Thomas Percy's *Reliques of Ancient English Poetry* in Hamburg, which certainly offers a primer on obscurely representing romantic feelings about the death of lovers and family members in poems such as "Edward" and "Lord Randall."

24. The full tale of the Lucy cycle can be found in my "Wordsworth's Lucy Poems in Psychobiographical Context," cited earlier and also reprinted in *Critical Essays on William Wordsworth,* ed. George H. Gilpin (Boston: G. K. Hall, 1990), pp. 267-99.

25. Carl Woodring, *Wordsworth* (Cambridge, MA: Harvard University Press, 1968), p. 47; David Ferry, *The Limits of Mortality* (Middletown, CT: Wesleyan University Press, 1959), p. 22.

26. The exit from Goslar, which became a literal metaphor for locations that inhibit poetry and freedom, is recalled in the opening of *The Prelude* (1805/1850). In addressing a spring breeze of inspiration upon leaving the town, Wordsworth says: "A captive greets thee, coming from a house / Of bondage, from yon city's walls set free, / A prison where he hath been long immured (*Prelude,* Book I, ll. 6-8).

27. Dudley Young, *Origins of the Sacred: The Ecstasies of Love and War* (New York: St. Martin's Press, 1991), pp. 158-59.

28. 1799 *Prelude,* Part One, l. 1.

29. Editor's introduction to selections from *Totem and Taboo* in *The Freud Reader,* ed. Peter Gay (New York: Norton, 1989), p. 482.

30. H. W. Garrod, "Wordsworth's Lucy" in *The Profession of Poetry and Other Lectures* (Oxford: Clarendon, 1929), p. 83. Quoted in Jones, p. 191.

31. In *The Writings and Speeches of Edmund Burke*, gen ed. Paul Langford, Vol. VIII, *The French Revolution 1790-1794*, ed. L. G. Mitchell (Oxford: Clarendon, 1989), p. 146.

32. James K. Chandler, *Wordsworth's Second Nature: A Study of the Poetry and Politics* (Chicago: University of Chicago Press, 1984), p. 185.

33. Douglas Wilson, for example, recently has published an excellent psychological study *The Romantic Dream: Wordsworth and the Poetics of the Unconscious* (Lincoln: University of Nebraska Press, 1993) that treats the spots of time as "the uncanny" (pp. 42-54).

34. In all there were some 70 published responses to Burke's *Reflections* in the four years following its publication. Thus Wollstonecraft in the first of the responses to Burke in *A Vindication of the Rights of Men, in a Letter to the Right Honorable Edmund Burke* (1790): "I perceive, from the whole tenor of your Reflections, that you have a mortal antipathy to reason; but, if there is any thing like argument, or first principles, in your wild declamation, behold the result—that we are to reverence the rust of antiquity, and term the unnatural customs, which ignorance and mistaken self-interest have consolidated, the sage fruit of experience; nay, that, if we do discover some errors, our *feelings* should lead us to excuse, with blind love, or unprincipled filial affection, the venerable vestiges of ancient days." (*The Works of Mary Wollstonecraft*, eds. Janet Todd and Marilyn Butler, Vol. V [New York: New York University Press, 1989] p. 10) Thomas Paine's attack upon Burke in his *Rights of Man* (1791) was pointedly ad hominem: "It is painful to behold a man employing his talents to corrupt himself. . . . He is not affected by the reality of the distress touching his heart, but by the showy resemblage of it striking his imagination. He pities the plumage, but forgets the dying bird. Accustomed to kiss the aristocratical hand that hath purloined him from himself, he degenerates into a composition of art, and the genuine soul of nature forsakes him. His hero or his heroine must be a tragedy-victim expiring in show, and not the real prisoner of mystery, sinking into death in the silence of a dungeon." (*The Rights of Man* in *Two Classics of the French Revolution: Reflections on the Revolution in France* and *The Rights of Man* [New York, Anchor, 1973], p. 288)

35. E. P. Thompson, "Disenchantment of Default? A Lay Sermon," in *Power and Consciousness*, eds. Conor Cruise O'Brien and William Dean Vanech (New York: New York University Press, 1969), p. 168.

36. Thompson, p. 180. In a still unpublished manuscript, *The Young Wordsworth*, Kenneth R. Johnston speculates that Wordsworth may have

been performing surreptitious service for the crown of England while in Germany.

37. Onorato, *The Character of the Poet:*, p. 64.

38. Erna Furman, *A Child's Parent Dies: Studies in Childhood Bereavement* (New Haven: Yale University Press, 1974), p. 196.

39. The 1805 and 1850 versions of *The Prelude* read identically: "where in former times / A murderer had been hung in iron chains" (1805, Book XI, ll. 288-89; 1850, Book XII, ll. 235-36).

40. *Prelude*, p. 9, n. 8. De Selincourt, p. 614, n. to lines 279-316.

41. See *LB*, p. 317.

42. There is a thorough recounting of the story in *LB*, pp. 460-63.

43. As Onorato comments, "The figure of the king attracts [Wordsworth's] attention, not as a hated historical symbol, but as a domestic figure, pathetically husband and father" in *Prelude*, Book X, ll. 42-44. (*The Character of the Poet*, p. 336).

44. This echo was first suggested by de Selincourt in his edition of *The Prelude*, p. 615, n. to line 382.

45. T. W. Thompson, *Wordsworth's Hawkshead*, ed. Robert Woof (Oxford: Oxford University Press, 1970), p. 161.

46. Stephen Gill, *William Wordsworth: A Life* (Oxford: Clarendon, 1989), p. 166.

47. *H at G*, p. 50, l. 231.

48. The text used for this analysis will be *Home at Grasmere*, manuscript B, pp. 38-106, in *H at G*. The passage quoted here is on p. 48, ll. 171-79.

49. Woof, p. 174, n. to entry for October 17, 1800.

50. "A Prayer for My Daughter," ll. 65-69, *W.B. Yeats: The Poems*, ed. Richard J. Finneran (New York: Macmillan, 1983), pp. 188-90.

51. *The Tempest*, Act I, Scene ii, l. 458 in *Riverside Shakespeare*, p. 1667.

52. Upon first seeing the human lovers in Eden, Satan says "O hell! what do mine eyes with grief behold" (*PL*, Book IV, l. 358). Coleridge said of the conditions in Wordsworth's household: "I saw him more & more benetted in hypochondriacal Fancies, living wholly among *Devotees*—having every the minutest Thing, almost his very Eating & Drinking, done for him by his Sister, or Wife—& I trembled, lest a Film should rise, and thicken on his moral Eye" (*STCL*, Vol. II, p. 1013).

Coda

1. Quoted in *STCL*, Vol. I, p. 631, note 2.

2. Parrish, "*Michael* and the Pastoral Ballad" in *Bicentenary Wordsworth Studies*, p. 53.
3. As the real story of Robert, not Richard, Bateman goes, he did indeed rebuild a chapel and "gave £1000 for purchasing an estate, and erected eight alms-houses for as many poor families, besides a donation of £12 per annum to the curate. This worthy benefactor . . . from a state of indigence succeeded in amassing considerable wealth by mercantile pursuits. He is stated to have been poisoned, in the straits of Gibraltar, on his voyage from Leghorn, with a valuable cargo, by the captain of the vessel." Quoted from *The Poetical Works of William Wordsworth*, ed. William Knight, Vol. 2 (Edinburgh: William Patterson, 1882), p. 143.
4. Peter Manning, *Reading Romantics: Texts and Contexts* (New York: Oxford University Press, 1990), p. 48.
5. *The Poetry of Robert Frost*, ed. Edward Connery Lathem (New York: Holt, Rinehart and Winston, 1975), p. 1, ll. 5-7.
6. Richard Poirier, *Robert Frost: The Work of Knowing* (New York: Oxford University Press, 1977), p. 111.
7. Frost, "Home Burial," p. 53, ll. 71-78.

Index